The Great Powers

MAX BELOFF

The Great Powers

ESSAYS IN
TWENTIETH CENTURY POLITICS

Ruskin House
GEORGE ALLEN & UNWIN LTD
MUSEUM STREET LONDON

327
B41g

PRINTED IN GREAT BRITAIN
in 10 point Pilgrim type
BY SIMSON SHAND LIMITED
LONDON, HERTFORD AND HARLOW

PREFACE

IT is always considered necessary to provide a justification for reprinting occasional essays: as explained in the Introduction, the papers in the present volume are closely linked by theme, but they have been published in rather a large number of different books or journals, and in different countries, and are here brought together for the first time. The lecture on Theodore Roosevelt has not previously been published. In the case of the others, the sources and dates are given in the table of contents.

For permission to reprint, I am grateful to the following: Messrs Bowes & Bowes, Chapter 2; the Editor of *Foreign Affairs* and the Council on Foreign Relations, Chapter 3; the Editor of *Confluence*, Chapter 4; the Manager of *The Times*, Chapter 5; the Editor of *The Twentieth Century*, Chapters 6 and 13; the Editor of *Political Studies* and the Clarendon Press for Chapter 7; the Editor of *The Year Book of World Affairs* and Messrs Stevens & Sons, Chapter 8; the Editors of *The European Year Book* and Messrs Martinus Nijhoff, Chapter 9; *The Contemporary Review*, Chapter 10; the Editor of *History* and Messrs George Philip & Son Ltd, Chapter 11; the Manchester Literary and Philosophical Society, Chapter 12; the Editor of *The University of Toronto Quarterly*, Chapter 14; the Editor of *Commentary*, Chapter 15.

I must also thank the Harvard University Press for permission to quote from *The Letters of Theodore Roosevelt*, and the Johns Hopkins University Press for permission to quote from Professor H. K. Beale's book *Theodore Roosevelt and the Rise of America to World Power*. I must thank my Research Assistant at Nuffield College, Miss Yoma Crosfield, for making the Index.

The text of the essays is in every case reprinted unchanged, but I have made a number of cuts in the footnotes where particular references now seem unnecessary.

All Souls College M.B.
   Oxford
May 1958

CONTENTS

CONTENTS

PART I

THE PROBLEM FOR
HISTORIANS

I

Introduction

THE essays collected in this volume represent three main themes which have occupied my own mind over the last decade, as they must have occupied the minds of many others whose concern it is to try to understand and interpret the political problems of our age. In the first place, there is the question of how far such interpretation is possible at all; how far does the training of an historian or a political scientist equip him to see any more clearly into his own times than the ordinary citizen who sees them by glimpses only in the course of his probably scanty leisure, or than the professional politician who is concerned with advocating or putting into effect particular solutions to particular problems, or than the administrator who is engaged in bringing order into some highly specialized field of activity? In the second place, there is the question of the appropriate scale for political activity and organization in the modern world, of the proper size of political units and of the forces which make for their integration or disintegration especially among free societies. Finally, there is the striking emergence on the world scene of the greatest single Power dedicated to political freedom, and the difficulty that it has found in applying its own democratic philosophy to the harsh world of international relations.

I have not included in the present collection any writings dealing directly with a theme of at least equal importance to these, namely the nature of the challenge presented to the whole of the rest of the world by the growth and spread of Soviet Communism. For this apparent omission three reasons will suffice. In the first place, although the principal writings of mine on the subject were written some time ago,[1] I do not feel that there has been any important reason for revising our views as to the essentials of Soviet policy; and although there have been tactical fluctuations in the way it has been

[1] *The Foreign Policy of Soviet Russia, 1929-1941* (OUP 2 Vols, 1947, 1949); *Soviet Policy in the Far East, 1944-1951* (OUP 1953).

conducted, especially since the death of Stalin, there is nothing that amounts to an abandonment of fundamentals either as regards objectives, or as regards the means to their attainment. I remain as convinced now as I was ten years ago that change, if it were to come, could only be the result of important shifts in the social basis and ideological content of the regime itself and for this reason it is Soviet internal development rather than Soviet foreign policy that we should study. In saying this I do not of course intend to suggest that Soviet policy may not in one respect be obliged to accept an important revision of method for the same reason as non-Communist countries, namely the existence of the new weapons of mass-destruction. But that is a point to which we shall have to return. My other reason for not dealing with Soviet affairs is that I have a considerable sympathy with the point of view put forward by Professor George Kennan in his Reith Lectures, namely that we in the West would do better to concentrate more upon the problems of our own societies, and cease to be hypnotized quite to the extent we are by the Communist challenge.[1] Like Professor Kennan, I do not underestimate the gravity of the challenge nor the depth of Soviet hostility to our way of life; it is simply that on problems like the extent of integration in the Western world or like that of our relationship to non-Communist countries in Asia and Africa, there are decisions of moment in which we can participate. On the other hand, we can do little to influence the development of the Soviet world—much of what we try to do in this direction may indeed be self-defeating—and many of our contacts with it, particularly diplomatic contacts, are little more than shadow-boxing. Finally, I must confess that when I look at the repetitive nature of so much of my own and other people's recent writing about the Soviet Union, I am inclined to think it not altogether our fault. The Soviet world does not at the present stage of its development present the historian or the political scientist with material for reflection as interesting as that which is provided not only by the Western world but also by those countries like India which are still endeavouring to combine advanced economic and social policies with a respect for individual rights and legal procedures largely inspired by Western models. I can see that for the students of economic growth, of the development of some of the natural sciences and of certain branches of technology, especially military technology, the spectacle of Soviet achievements is an all-absorbing one. But to those whose concern is with the elaboration of the institutions through

[1] George F. Kennan, *Russia, the Atom and the West* (OUP 1958).

14

which we in the West have learned to combine collective action with active consent, the spectacle of great societies still politically, in some respects, at the stage of primitive despotism can hardly be exhilarating. Just as Western lovers of literature and the arts find Soviet books and pictures excessively unsubtle, excessively unconcerned with those moral and philosophical problems, and aesthetic issues which they regard as all-important, so the student of law or politics, although he needs to know about these matters in their Soviet context is unlikely to find there anything exciting or stimulating to the creative imagination.

There is also nothing here that arises directly from my personal concern with the fate of the Jewish people in these tortured decades of their own and the world's history. I am fully convinced that in many respects the attempt by Nazi Germany to extirpate the Jewish race—itself a part of an even wider and more fantastic plan to reshape the whole world in the name of a mythology of race—is the key event of our own times; and not only because of the tragic magnitude of its consequences in the destruction of human life, for this has not been a century tender to life. It is also a key event because it exposed as nothing else has done so clearly the extraordinary fragility of modern civilization, the ease with which a seemingly civilized people can be captured and put to the service of the sadistic imaginings of madmen without even the rationale of national self-interest which has served in the past to justify the holocausts of war. Again, the fact that there has been something in the nature of a conspiracy of silence about these things is not due, I believe, wholly to considerations of political expediency, and still less to a philosophical aversion to the idea of retribution, but principally to a failing of the imagination. People forget 'war crimes' because they cannot properly apprehend them and therefore feel that they must have been exaggerated; just as the nature of totalitarianism itself—out of which these and similar repudiations of the ties of common humanity ultimately spring—is something which free people find it difficult to grasp for more than some of the time.

I have dealt elsewhere with the situation of the Jewish people during the years that have elapsed since Hitler's death and with the impact upon it of the 'cold war'.[1] But there are two particular reasons why the whole subject would deserve more extended treatment

[1] See my introductory chapter, 'Le Monde Après 1945', to the collective work: *Dix Ans Après la Chute de Hitler* edited by J. M. Machover and published by the Centre de Documentation Juive Contemporaine (Paris 1957).

than I feel qualified to give it. In the first place, the rise of the Jewish national movement and the partial fruition of its aspirations provides one of the most extraordinary examples of the force of the national idea itself. Almost none of the conventional attributes by which students have defined the idea of a nation existed in the case of the Jews of Europe. They have proved it possible to create a nation by an act of will; and at a time when all material factors seem to point to the obsolescence of the nation as a political unit; this is surely something worthy of attention. Secondly, the fact that the State of Israel has been created in Palestine though in a way inevitable if the history of Zionism be studied from the inside, is nevertheless from the wider viewpoint, a paradox in itself. One of the uncontested features of the history of the last two decades has been the retreat of the European Powers from the areas of control or influence successively occupied by them in Asia and Africa over the previous three and a half centuries. Nowhere has this process been more important and more dramatic than in the Mediterranean basin and the Middle East. The failure of many people in the West — and more particularly in the United States — to understand that this particular triumph of nationalism may also be a blow to the cause of ordered civilization and to the material welfare of the people concerned is the theme of some later essays in this volume. The lands to the South and East of the Mediterranean are perhaps those in which the negative aspect of the process is clearest. The assertion of control by the European Powers in the nineteenth and earlier twentieth centuries, however self-interested their motives, may be regarded as the check to a process of decay extending over many centuries — perhaps back to the decline of Rome and Byzantium. In the face of this general retreat the creation of an oasis of modern technical civilization and of modern concepts of social welfare and social responsibility in the shape of the State of Israel is all the more astounding an achievement. But this long-range view has understandably been obliterated for many students, both Jewish and non-Jewish, by the immediate urgencies of the critical political situation and the unresolved human problem that the achievement itself has helped to produce.

On a different level, there is less here than I should have liked about the effect of these vast changes in the world upon the domestic scene in our own country and its near European neighbours. In particular I should have wished to have found room for some consideration of the contemporary rôle of France. France has had a bad press in this country and still more so in the United States for most of the decade covered in these essays—a decade ended perhaps by the dramatic events of May 1958. With some of the charges most commonly made in that period, I found myself in little sympathy. It is true that the French have been less ready than many people in this country to make a virtue of the retreat from Empire, and less ready to accept the view that the surrender of European positions is bound in all cases to redound to the immediate benefit of those concerned. They have been sceptical of the sentimental view (so justly criticized by Professor Kennan) that the imperial record of the West has placed our countries in a position where we are bound to make moral as well as material restitution to the countries where we formerly exercised control. They do not so generally agree to the notion that the poverty of poor countries is not due to an inherent paucity of resources or to the lack of the human qualities and social patterns needed to make the best use of them, but rather to the legacy of imperial rule; they perhaps pay more attention to the fact that this legacy itself—whether by providing the basic needs of the economy, or a common language adapted to the requirements of modern science—is often the only thing that has made possible the independent existence of these countries within their present frontiers.

Again, the concern of the French for their own overseas settlers in North Africa, and for the cultural institutions they have maintained in many lands, seems to me to be not only proper but admirable. To moralize over France's difficulties and to intervene in the tragic convolutions of her own debate on these grave and often tragic issues has seemed to me even less justifiable in the case of Britain—which has had, and still has, not dissimilar problems of her own—than in the case of the United States where such experience is lacking.

What can fairly be said—and what has been said by many Frenchmen—is that France has been much hampered by an inability to adjust herself rapidly enough to the undoubted fact of her diminished power in world affairs, and that the retardation of such adjustments has made them more painful than they otherwise need have been. It can also be said—and this is why France continues to attract the attention of the student of politics—that this inability to act quickly which often means an inability to take the actual decisions and to achieve a national consensus in their favour, has arisen from certain identifiable weaknesses in her political institutions and political habits.[1] France has thus represented the paradox of a country enjoying internally a very considerable revival from the demographic and economic points of view, and still culturally creative, but continually thwarted in its search for social and political stability by institutional weaknesses that affect only a part, and in a sense only a superficial part, of the whole complex of her contemporary activities.

I have indicated elsewhere my hope to set on foot in the immediate future a fairly wide-ranging study of the impact of these changes in the scale of world politics, and of the consequent interdependence of previously sovereign States, upon the governmental and political structures of some of them, including, of course, both France and Britain.[2] But although my immediate concern will be with questions of government, with how governments, designed to function autonomously, can and do operate when their sovereignty is severely limited by the letter of international treaties, and still more by the actual facts of the economic and military situation, this approach is dictated very largely by practical considerations.

It is at the institutional level that the problem is easiest to identify, and it is there that solutions will ultimately have to be found. But the real source of it lies elsewhere, in the attitudes and expectations that the different peoples have formed as a result of their own history, and their interpretation of its lessons. The conclusion that I have formed as a result of the work done by the study-group of the Council of Europe of which I was rapporteur-general, and which was concerned with the whole nature and prospects of the movement for greater unity in Europe is in my view unassailable.[3] And it is confirmed by the experience of those who have been concerned to secure wider co-operation within the Commonwealth.[4] It is that on the one hand, the arguments for closer links between Britain and Europe on the one side and between Britain and the Commonwealth on the other are unanswerable and by no means mutually exclusive. Some of the arguments about the limitations on the possibilities of

[1] See for instance my essays: 'The Fourth Republic 1945-1955' in J. M. Wallace-Hadrill and J. McManners ed. *France: Government and Society* (Methuen, 1957), and 'Intellectual Classes and Ruling Classes in France', *Occidente*, 1954.

[2] *The Tasks of Government: an inaugural lecture* (Clarendon Press, 1958).

[3] See my report: *Europe and the Europeans* (Chatto & Windus 1957).

[4] On Commonwealth affairs, I must acknowledge my indebtedness to the remarkable book by Patrick Maitland, MP: *A Task for Giants* (Longmans 1957).

European integration where Britain is concerned that appear in the subsequent essays or elsewhere relate rather to the proposed methods by which integration is sought than to the objective itself.[1] But it is equally true on the other hand, that these arguments do not make a direct appeal to the masses of our people and that, without popular support, plans for integration cannot be effective.

It may partially be the case that the weakness of their appeal is due to public confusion over the very different kinds of international institution for which support is canvassed. Because of the preoccupation about relationships with the Soviet world to which I have already referred and because it has been felt necessary to find methods of co-operating with countries with which intimate association is at present politically impossible, many people, convinced of the inadequacy of national solutions for our problems, pin their faith to the United Nations Organization and its subsidiary organs. But although this institution has certain useful, perhaps essential, diplomatic functions to perform, it cannot, given a divided world, assist in the process of integrating into larger wholes units which are too small to stand alone, and may indeed through its very commitments to universalism, actually hamper such integration.

Whether or not this be the case, it has certainly been difficult to persuade large sections of our population that the Atlantic Community or United Europe, or for that matter the Commonwealth, provide much more immediate and promising fields for the creation of common institutions and the solution of genuinely common problems. Where such institutions have been created and worked, the responsibility has been taken by experts, civil and military. But this clearly limits what can be done, and creates a certain uneasiness in the public lest the effective control over government has slipped away.

Looked at from one point of view, this is merely an extreme case of the rather obvious fact that in international relations democratic States—States where governments ultimately depend upon broad currents of public opinion—are handicapped by comparison with those where opinion itself is a tool of government.[2] But since what one is trying to do is to get people to accept in theory and practice the virtual obliteration of the old distinction between foreign and

[1] See for example my article: 'Can Europe Unite?' (*Commentary*, New York, April 1958).

[2] See my Albert Shaw lectures: *Foreign Policy and the Diplomatic Process* (Baltimore: Johns Hopkins Press: London, OUP 1955).

domestic policy, the problem itself has taken on an entirely new dimension. What we are trying to do is then, once more, to achieve by consent what in the totalitarian world is done by a mixture of force and persuasion, the latter exercised through monopoly of the means of communication with a consequent relative immunity from the political penalties for telling lies.

We have to face the fact that the more democratic our society, the harder a revolution of this kind is to carry through. The instincts of large groups of people who now for the first time play a dominant role in the affairs of Western countries are almost wholly nationalist in their fundamental orientation, not of course in the sense that there is no genuine internationalist sentiment in the Labour movement for instance, but simply that its own real problems incline it to see things in terms of the national unit. It was impossible for the mercantile classes, so influential in British politics for so long, to overlook the dependence of the economy on events and conditions overseas. It is much harder for a trade union leader to take the same view at a time when Britain's position is in fact much more vulnerable. The trade union leader may well accept the fact that wages must depend to some extent on the prosperity of the industry concerned, and that a rise in the standard of living for those he represents must depend upon a rise in productivity in the industry, or even in the national economy at large. The employer may be prepared to accept the claim that such a rise should be taken up by wages rather than by profits or re-investment; but both the trade unionist and his employer may find it hard to assimilate the idea that external pressures may make it necessary for both of them to forego their share and for the whole increment to go in the form of cheaper goods or outright 'aid', to other countries. In other words, there is obviously a pressure arising out of the whole situation in the world today as a result of which the use to which progress in one country can be put with safety is something which that country itself cannot necessarily decide upon, still less some particular section of its productive force. The claims on advances in productivity have become internationalized, while the domestic bargaining structure is based on the premise that they are wholly national.

For this reason, among others, there is in most of the countries we are concerned with a sense of unreality where their own political processes are concerned. And for most of us in Western Europe there is the additional sense of being so much dependent upon a single political system, that of the United States. How the United States treats its problems, economic, strategic and political, is the thing of most immediate concern to us, and if so many of these essays appear to revolve round this question of American attitudes and American issues, this correctly reflects my own belief as to the relative importance of this theme.

We come now to the problem touched upon when dealing with Soviet attitudes and policies. The other major reason for our political disputes often seeming so unreal, and for our feeling that we have entered a new era in relations between States, is that we may have reached the point in history where the development of the art of war has ruled war out as a means of solving political conflicts between major Powers. If the power to inflict annihilation rests with more than one Power then only a failure of nerve, or a presumed failure of nerve can bring about war between such Powers. We may of course be presuming too much and it is always possible that some new scientific invention—a foolproof automatic anti-missile missile—might make defence possible again and so renew the danger of war though by means other than those of mass-annihilation. But at the present juncture, it does look as though we have arrived at a point where all the rules for the conduct of policy have ceased to operate, where the ultimate sanction of policy is a sanction no longer.

If this be so, it would however be an additional reason for refusing to waste too much of our energies on the hope of finding a 'solution' to the struggle between the Communist and non-Communist worlds, wrongly and very misleadingly called the struggle between East and West. Accepting, as we would have to, a stalemate of indefinite duration in this struggle, we could concentrate upon our own more manageable affairs, and in particular upon the problem presented by the gap between the nature of our institutions and the issues they are called upon to handle.

As to whether an academic analysis of such questions can be achieved and in what spirit it should be looked for, I have little to add at present to what is said in the first group of essays. I would only make two final points. I have become more and more convinced during these years of the relevance of historical experience to our own problems, provided we know where to look for this experience and how to apply it.[1] As it happens the work on which I have been engaged while getting these essays ready for reprinting has been con-

---

[1] This is my excuse, if excuse be needed, for including the essays on Franklin and Tocqueville under the heading of 'Twentieth Century Politics'.

cerned with the break-up of the first British Empire in the American Revolution and the creation of new common institutions for the American States. And I have been struck once again by the almost painful pertinence of so many discussions that took place under circumstances so seemingly different from our own. I would hazard the guess that familiarity and unfamiliarity with this story lies at the root of half the contemporary divergences over the problems of federalism. In the second place, and just because of the relevance of so much of our past political experience to our practical problems, I have become steadily more impatient of two attitudes dangerously prevalent today. There are those who hold that no history can be studied properly except that of the relatively distant past, and who treat the history of our own times as a seedy and disreputable hanger-on, thus obscuring the essential and inescapable connection between past and present, without which the present is meaningless and the past dead. And there are those who hold that the past is, as it were, given, so that all one need trouble about is a purely intellectual concern with the truth, whereas contemporary history raising living issues can be used to bolster up particular arguments or to provide ammunition for private armies and can therefore be treated quite differently. They apply sometimes perhaps unconsciously, often I fear, cynically, an essentially double standard of proof and relevance to a subject which is really one.

This temptation to exploit one's knowledge, or even one's presumed knowledge, for purely partisan purposes, is one that academic persons often find it hard to resist. It is partly the inevitable result of a proper desire to communicate the results of thinking or research to a wide, non-academic audience. But it is the measure of such a person's right to speak that he appreciates the nature of this temptation, and that he at least attemps to fight against it.

Such a requirement does not, and cannot, mean an impossible standard of detachment; since absolute detachment cannot be expected of anyone concerned with living realities; for as a citizen, if not as a student, he may be called upon to take sides. But what one must try to do is to see that the views one holds about the present and the past are in accordance with some general view of the historical process, and some consistent set of social and political values. One does not need, in order to achieve this, to accept one of the competing all-embracing philosophies of history or ideologies, or to become involved in a dogmatic determinism. But those who claim to be governed by a wholly empirical approach too often make this an excuse for a whole rag-bag of incompatible preferences and prejudices. And while this may not be so obvious when they are writing about the more distant past, it prevents them from using their knowledge of this past as a guide to judgment in the present. And historical knowledge about whatever period that does not contribute to one's understanding of one's own world is no more than harmless antiquarianism.

2

The Frontiers of Political Analysis[1]

THE histories of the sciences—including the social sciences—have rarely run on a straight course or at an even speed. It has more often been the case that periods of intense and fruitful activity have been followed by others in which the sense of direction seems to have been lost, and in which the work that is done, is done out of a sense of academic conformity and propriety rather than from conviction. The reasons for this may lie in either of two facts. It may simply be the case that a formula once used with success has now exhausted its possibilities and is incapable of giving further original results. Or it may be that developments in the outside world—from which, whether we like it or not, the social sciences derive their justification and their inspiration—present new problems that the existing structure of the particular science is not equipped to take into account.

Despite the fact that the political studies in this country give an outward appearance of health, it appears to me that none of us are really happy about our subject, and that as soon as we discuss the practical questions of what to study, and in particular of what to teach, we betray a degree of uncertainty which cannot well be concealed. We seem to have come to a point at which both the reasons suggested for such a situation are operating simultaneously. Where the external world is concerned, it is clear that a major change of the last fifteen years has been a shifting back of interest from the economic to the political plane. The notion, fashionable less than a generation ago, that the really important problems are those of production and distribution can no longer seriously be entertained, still less the corollary that if one looks after the economics of a situation the politics can be trusted to look after

[1] This paper gives the substance of a lecture delivered at the London School of Economics on October 27, 1950.

24

themselves. For as many examples remind us, the whole economic calculus, the whole apparatus of prediction upon which so much time and effort have been and are being spent, is liable to be set at nought at any moment, not merely by a major catastrophe such as a world war, but by any lesser change in the political atmosphere.

Nor, indeed, is economics the only social science that finds itself demoted by the current political situation. The assumptions upon which sociology rests are also ceasing to have validity over wide areas of human experience. For the idea that societies or communities possess individual patterns of behaviour which can be analysed scientifically rests upon the assumption that such groupings have some measure of continuity, and are at least in part, the product of acquired habit. The nature of the physical environment, the availability of resources, and the character and inherited attitudes of the populations combine to set life in certain channels which may be impeded or diverted by some external impact but which are durable enough to give the sociologist his opportunity.

Modern political decisions, however, make light of such things. When people from many different communities and walks of life find themselves herded together in concentration camps—the typical social institution of the twentieth century—when any individual may suddenly find himself far from friends and home digging a canal or mining uranium, a unit in a labour force, not a man, what light can the conventional sociological technique throw upon his life or that of his fellows? In the past, voluntary migrants have been influenced in their choice of destination by the openings available for their existing skills; but when Poles or Letts are dumped upon the semi-arid lands of Central Asia, the question of assimilation takes on a new aspect. Nor does forced migration with all the cruelties it entails, exhaust the possibilities of modern political planning. One may have—as in Germany's dealings with Jews and Gypsies—the simpler procedure of mass extermination. And there is no sociology of death, though the Germans with their habitual thoroughness and ingenuity managed to make a grim kind of economics out of it. Finally the resources available to modern tyrants for conditioning the mind raise altogether new problems of a type hitherto confined to imaginative literature. The political use of the lie has become a commonplace to any serious student of the Nazi or Soviet worlds.

The consequences of such facts for the academic study of politics are more far-reaching than some people are disposed to admit. And it is arguable that the present academic shape of political studies makes the handling of the most serious of contemporary issues needlessly difficult.

The study of politics both here and in the United States has tended to fall into three well-known categories: 'political theory', 'political institutions' and 'international relations'. And the normal practice has been to treat each of them as an independent specialism with no necessary relation to the others. But when one attempts to apply these categories to the world of experience, one finds that the questions it poses obstinately refuse to classify themselves accordingly.

In our time, the clash of ideologies and of institutions based upon these ideologies, or inspired by them, is the thing that provides the very stuff of which political life is made. It is not a case only of the existing conflict between the Russians as the vehicles of Soviet communism and the Americans as exponents of liberal capitalist democracy. There is also the fact, for instance, that in the Second World War, we and our allies specifically proclaimed our opposition to 'fascism' and 'national socialism' and Japanese 'militarism' and that when it was over, we set to work in our various ways to re-educate—as we put it—the erring nations and to teach them the spirit and practices of democracy.

This view of the purposes of the Western Allies was held not just by a few idealists, but by practical men of affairs. It has been the expressed conviction of General Douglas MacArthur that he has succeeded. General Clay in his recent book on his proconsulship in Germany is rather more modest about his achievements.[1] But he nowhere treats it as strange or novel that a conquering Power should make it is business to confer upon the conquered ideas and institutions that will be better for them and make them less dangerous neighbours. Yet if one thinks of the tacit assumptions that lie behind such objectives, the mind almost reels at their audacity. For they suggest that it is widely believed today that the analytical problems that have preoccupied political thinkers in the past have now been solved, that we know in what our democracy consists, can distinguish between its fundamentals and those incidentals that arise from national peculiarities, and can introduce the former into those societies from which they have been expelled, or where they have never existed at all.

It is perhaps natural that Americans should take this view. Their

[1] Lucius D. Clay: *Decision in Germany*.

26

own history has been one of the assimilation of new groups of immigrants into an institutional and ideological structure that was held to exist independently of them. But for us in this country, facing the balance sheet of our attempts to introduce our ideas on law and government into India where they have ended, and into Africa where we are accelerating them, scepticism would be more natural. Even the Englishmen of Lord Macaulay's generation who set out confidently to 'civilize' the ancient civilizations of the East, stopped short of endeavouring to transplant directly the institutions and habits of political action in which they had grown up at home. But if we do in fact indulge in such enterprises, then the investigation of their principles should surely become the core of our academic studies of politics.

Even if we abandon such attempts ourselves, they will be made by others. The Russians have certainly no inhibitions on this score. And the speed with which the sovietization of their satellites has been carried on suggests complete confidence on their own part that they know what must be done.[1] And quite apart from those cases where such a transplantation of ideas or institutions is the result of the application of force, there are enormous areas where the peoples are still free to adopt and adapt the ideas either of ourselves or of Soviet Communism. What the outcome of this will be in countries such as China or Burma or Indonesia, no one with sense will wish to prophesy. But the subject is hardly one that the serious student can avoid.

A more specific example of our inadequate theoretical preparation may be added. Within the last five years or so, there has been a new vogue of the idea, or perhaps merely of the word 'Federalism'. But for anyone who has followed the discussions on European matters at Strasbourg and elsewhere, and who is also familiar with the history of federal institutions in the United States, Canada or Australia, the most obvious feature of it all is its total unreality. Few people seem to have any clear idea what federalism means or implies. And one has only to get back to the Commonwealth and compare the vagueness with which European federation is handled with the hard-headed discussions of federation for the West Indies, for instance, to be struck by the difference.

Yet this state of affairs can hardly be met by claiming that federation is a secret, available only to those brought up within the Anglo-

[1] See on this point the emphatic opinions expressed by Hugh Seton-Watson in the introduction to his book: *The East European Revolution*.

Saxon tradition. What has not been done is to analyse the experience that the older federations have had, so as to make it available for those now facing similar problems, and to see how it is affected by the new problem that neither the United States nor Australia have had to face, the relation between different national institutions and institutional habits, and the international framework into which it is sought to fit them. The question of creating multi-national federations is merely the most obvious instance of how impossible it is to decide where 'political theory' or 'political institutions' leaves off, and where 'international relations' begin.

This threefold division of political studies, like many other examples of academic behaviour, owes its strength to the fact that it rests upon an unspoken major premise. The *Politics* of Aristotle for instance, presupposed 'a small Mediterranean world which was a world of "urbanity" or civic republics (the largest with an area of 1,000 square miles but many with 100 or less), and which stood, as such, in contrast with the world of "rurality" in which the nations or *ethne* lived'.[1] Yet, of course, at the very time Aristotle was writing the problems of the *polis* were ceasing to be the major ones, and were giving way to those of multi-national Empires.

Our own political science is still based on the assumption—understandable enough in a nineteenth-century context—that the proper subject of political inquiry, the equivalent for us, of the *polis*, is the independent nation state. The course of European history, a hundred years ago, seemed set in that direction; only dynastic reaction seemed to be preventing all countries from achieving national self-determination and, with it, the appropriate organs of self-government. Our political language is designed to describe such a state of affairs and when we study other forms of political organization, we do so by treating as a deviation whatever seems to depart from this model. Yet once we extend our horizon beyond the shores of the North Atlantic basin, there seems little value in clinging for instance, to an even earlier, eighteenth-century Anglo-French assumption that the working of government can always best be illuminated by contemplating the eternal triangle of legislature, executive and judiciary. And even a country so central to the Western tradition as France, does not any more lend itself very readily to the classical framework of analysis. It would not be easy for a modern Austinian to describe where political sovereignty lies in the case of such a Frenchman as Monsieur Thorez.

[1] *The Politics of Aristotle*, ed. Sir Ernest Barker, p. xlvii.

But for the *naïveté* involved in holding on to the traditional notions, there is much excuse. For, over the last century and a half, the prestige of Western institutions has been such that their terminology has been borrowed even by systems that formally set out to be the very opposite ones. One can describe the Soviet constitution in language that could not be improved upon by the most rigorous follower of Montesquieu or Madison. There is nothing to prevent the amateur of parlour games from indulging in the pastime of proving or disproving the Soviet Union's claim to be a genuine federation.

It would not be worth while insisting on these obvious elements of sheer verbal confusion were it not that much skill and ingenuity has been devoted to maintaining them. For some writers, the Western tradition in politics is so infinitely expandable that there is room in it for the concentration camp, the secret police and the other indispensable ingredients of trans-Elbian democracy.

It is partly because there is no geographical boundary where ideas are concerned that it is difficult to accept the solution for our problems advanced in some quarters—a solution that can best be characterized as the modern version of the Aristotelean one. We should, it is said, admit frankly that when we say political science, we mean the studies of political societies like our own. Other societies exist with different ways and institutions. But they should be, as were the Barbarians to the Greeks, outside the horizons of scientific curiosity. We cannot know about them; their languages are difficult; their lands hard or impossible to visit; their accessible literature wholly propaganda; why worry? It is simpler to turn in on ourselves, contemplate our own excellences and formulate remedies for whatever minor defects such examination may reveal. At most let the adventurous cross the Channel for a perfunctory and properly guided tour of the institutions of France—a sort of weekend in Paris for the political scientist. The fact is of course, that quite apart from the international implications of such an attitude, our own institutional problems are largely generated by external pressures. This is not always obvious only because the major decisions of politics are not always those over which elections are fought and passions generated. The coming of peace-time conscription as a permanent feature of our social order in Britain is a change of much greater magnitude than will be nationalization of steel; but it has excited far less political controversy.

But as the political scientist breaks down the artificial barriers between the different compartments into which his subject has been divided, he comes up against another problem, that of the relation of his subject, as conceived in this wider fashion, with history itself. How are the two fields to be separated, if at all?

In writing his useful little book on recent British political history, Mr Somervell derived from his studies the conclusion that as his story approached the present 'the men became less and less adequate to the events they had to deal with, not because the men were smaller but because the events grew bigger and bigger and more unmanageable'.[1] Bigness and smallness seem awkward terms to use for events. Was it a bigger or smaller effort that was required to give independence to India as compared with giving self-government to South Africa, to prepare the radar stations that saved us from Hitler as compared with preparing the British Expeditionary Force of August 1914? But when Mr Somervell raises the issue of men becoming less and less adequate, it is arguable that he is dismissing through an oversimplification a problem that, properly pursued, lies at the very heart of our subject and which has been recognized as such since the days of Plato. What he is comparing is not 'intelligence' as measured by the psychologist, or the moral virtues, but political competence which is something that combines these, and adds to them some special quality that is the product of the environment through which political leaders have climbed to power. One cannot know how members of the House of Commons, or the Cabinet or the Higher Civil Service as they existed for instance in the period 1906-10 compared with their successors in 1945-50. But one cannot rule out *a priori* the possibility that the methods of recruitment and training prevailing in the former period may have been superior to those of the latter.

There has been some study of this aspect of modern political systems, in particular by students of political parties.[2] But the study of parties tends to follow too closely the lines laid down by its late nineteenth-century pioneers when what seemed most fascinating was their function in 'getting out the votes'. Writers thus tend to ignore the fact that their primary role is the selection and training of

[1] D. C. Somervell: *British Politics since 1900*, p. 235.

[2] The importance attached to political parties by up-to-date political scientists is so great that one recent book on Australia reverses the usual procedure by dealing with the country's party system before describing the governmental system within which it operates (see L. F. Crisp: *The Parliamentary Government of the Commonwealth of Australia*).

leaders. Only students of one-party systems have this fact forcibly brought home to them. Professor V. O. Key's recent book on the Southern States of the USA shows an admirable awareness of this function, precisely, no doubt, because the South has, for practical purposes, only one party.[1]

One reason why this kind of problem is so rarely formulated in a correct way is the prejudice that political scientists tend to entertain against history and historians. They are determined to prevent their subjects beings absorbed into history, since they know that the economists and sociologists who are usually their nearest colleagues tend to regard history as outside the boundaries of the social sciences altogether. Yet the quickest illumination would often come from seeing such contemporary problems in a different setting.

Had there been a Turkish Somervell in the eighteenth century, he might well have regarded the decline in Ottoman power and prestige as due to external circumstances beyond the control of the country's rulers. Yet the modern historian looks first of all not at the problems to be solved, but at the fitness of those whose business it was to solve them.

No ruling institution could be more alien to our ideas than that built up by the Ottoman sultans in their great period. It was based upon the tribute in children of the subject Christian peoples — children who after conversion to Islam passed through an elaborate system of selection and training, leading to the highest civil and military positions, which they attained and filled without losing their status as slaves. But it is the decay of this institution that seems to be the clue to the Empire's later decay. By the eighteenth century, the ruling institution

had undergone as complete a transformation as was compatible with most of the original forms. Instead of being manned almost exclusively by slave converts, it was now manned entirely by free Moslems. Instead of inspiring its members to earn merit by the exercise of talent and virtue, it taught them that they must look to corruption for advancement, and might safely neglect the duties that should have been concomitant with their privileges. Finally, instead of providing the Sultans with an efficient instrument for the exercise of their power, it was now scarcely strong enough to maintain their authority at home and had become an engine of

[1] V. O. Key: *Southern Politics in State and Nation.*

31

feeble tyranny over those of their subjects that were unable to combine against it.[1]

Or to take another sphere in which the study of a political system as remote as this may help to break the shock of alien modern phenomena, we may consider the problems raised in the study of the Soviet Union by the 'purges' of the 1930s and by the increasing self-isolation of the ruling clique in subsequent years. For, in the case of the Ottoman Empire, it was specifically laid down by the Sultan Mehmed II, the Conqueror, as a method of securing his dynasty from fraternal rivalries, that each of his successors should mark his coming to the throne by the slaughter of his brothers. After the end of the sixteenth century, this injunction was no longer literally honoured, but:

> a substitute was invented. From that time on all princes but the sons of the reigning Sultan were confined in special pavilions in the palace and were denied all communication with the outside world. Their lives were spent in the company of a few eunuchs, slave-girls and pages, from whom they gained what knowledge of the world they could. . . . Moreover any children born to them . . . were not allowed to live. All the princes living therefore were the sons of the reigning Sultan or his predecessors.[2]

Yet another twist was given to this extraordinary system in 1617, when Ahmed I died with none of his sons yet of age. His brother Mustafa I was given preference over these minors despite the fact that he was mad; and at the same time a decree was promulgated to the effect that when the throne fell vacant in future, the successor should always be the eldest surviving male of the Imperial house. So that for a century and a half, there was a constant succession of brothers, uncles and cousins whose previous life had rendered them so utterly unfitted to rule. Despite this, the Turks were for some time yet regarded as almost as much of a menace to parts of the West as are the Russians today. There would thus seem to be good grounds for suggesting the desirability of obviating the difficulties that derive from our habit of comparing the 'abnormal' with the 'normal', by providing ourselves with a wider reference in time than is usually available to the professional political scientist — particularly perhaps in the United States with its rigid departmentalism in University life.

[1] H. A. R. Gibb and H. Bowen: *Islamic Society and the West*, Vol I, Part I, p. 199.

[2] Op. cit., p. 35.

This is not the usual plea for an historical approach which is based upon the belief in the importance of 'origins'. It is rather that we should study remote phenomena for the light they can throw on the enormous variety of possible forms of political society. We assume readily enough that the historian can find language in which to describe the institutions of the Ottoman Empire, of Byzantium, or of the Heptarchy without the need to bring in approximate parallels from our own times. It should then be possible to grasp the necessity of describing in universally acceptable language, the non-Western non-democratic political systems of the present day. Historical study remains the best cure for parochialism, particularly since the materials for many political systems of the remote past are more abundant and above all more intimate than those available for some contemporary ones.

In the study of alien systems, it is not the structure or working of particular institutions that are most difficult to understand but the system of ideas with which they are inseparably connected. And Professor Gibb and Mr Bowen wisely began their survey of the Ottoman system by an examination of its related set of principles since, as they point out, 'it owed its structure, indeed, to the guidance provided by these principles for those who controlled its destinies in the particular circumstances in which it had grown and maintained itself in being'. The authors are dealing with the period from the sixteenth to the eighteenth centuries but the principles of which they speak are those 'embodied in the Sacred Law of Islam, the Seria, which had been constructed during the first centuries of its history by theologians and jurists from the precepts of the Kuran, traditions concerning the practice of the Prophet and his Companions, and custom sanctioned by general consent'.[1]

It would seem correspondingly appropriate that a study for instance of the Soviet Union should begin with its Sacred Law— the works of Marx—and their interpretation by Lenin and Stalin—an an interpretation which rests, at least in theory, upon 'traditions concerning the practice of the Prophet and his Companions', or perhaps it should be companion; since Engels appears to have been the only contemporary of Marx prepared to put up with his companionship for any sustained period.

The wisdom of such a procedure in this particular case has recently become obvious; just as by about 1939 people in this country were beginning to feel that there might be some point in knowing

[1] Op. cit., pp. 20-1.

what Hitler had said about things in *Mein Kampf*. But although those whose concern is with the real world sooner or later have to learn the right thing to do, since the penalties for failure are so enormous and so patent, the academic student of politics is much less easily moved. And just as we continue to separate 'political institutions' from 'international relations', so we separate it also from 'political theory'.

The study of political theory for its own sake complete with the traditional list of authors, has obviously great value in helping one to see how a coherent set of ideas can be built up on so difficult a subject in some obviously powerful and original intellect. Nor again, providing our selection be far-ranging enough, can we fail to benefit from discovering (as in the world of practice) how varied have been the answers given to the familiar questions. But there is always the risk that we may too readily assume a direct and formal connection between such ideas and the world of active politics.

There is the old story of the script for an historical film which begins with a crowd of men-at-arms being addressed with the words: 'Men of the Middle Ages, we are now setting off for the Hundred Years War.' I have a strong feeling that some of our methods of studying political theory leave in the minds of the student a picture of some eighteenth-century notable exhorting his followers with the words: 'Adherents of the social contract, we are about to do battle against the Divine Right of Kings', in fact the connection between political theorists and their fundamental concepts on the one hand, and political institutions on the other is a highly complex one. This does not mean that the appropriate way of dealing with the problem is to explain it away as the Marxists explain everything away: by imputing purely self-interested class motives to the various thinkers preceding their own revelation, except of course those few whom they discover as their own precursors and proceed to dishonour in their graves by distorting their teachings. (As has happened for instance to Winstanley, and some other seventeenth-century figures.)

What it does mean is that from the point of view of understanding political institutions and political behaviour in any society, past or present, what we need to know is not the political philosophy of its most prominent or gifted figures but the set of political assumptions upon which it actually worked or works; and these will tend to be both less obvious and simpler than the refinements of theory usually permit. The degree to which these assumptions will be the product of some direct impact of a particular creed will vary with the self-consciousness of different societies and the effort that has gone into conditioning them. One of our difficulties in understanding the nature of the political outlook of Soviet Communism is that we have to deal with a particularly articulate set of assumptions, whereas our own, although no less real, and no less firmly held, are particularly inarticulate. Seventeenth-century Englishmen would perhaps have found much less of a psychological barrier.

So too, even when the assumptions are formulated from above and conveyed to the mass of the people with the full sanctions of political authority behind them, their reception may well depend upon their conformity to pre-existing beliefs, even if these have not hitherto been effectively formulated. It may be supposed that the doctrines of Hitler or Rosenberg, with their dogma of German racial superiority, met with little resistance because the long history of German contacts with eastern countries of a generally lower standard of material achievement had already given to most Germans a belief in this superiority, even though they had no scientific or pseudo-scientific terminology in which to phrase or justify it. The task of inculcating the principles of British or American democracy has been, as we have suggested, a much tougher one.

Nor when we consider the relations between the accepted great political thinkers and the political presuppositions of their own or subsequent periods, is the line of descent always so easy to trace as in the case of Marx and Soviet Communism. In as far as a single thinker was important in setting the pattern of political debate in the Anglo-Saxon world in the eighteenth century, it was presumably John Locke. And yet, as Professor Guttridge has shown so cogently, the English and the Americans each used his central doctrine for almost precisely opposite purposes—the English to reinforce the notion of parliamentary sovereignty, the Americans in order to substantiate their claims that the British system was one of limited government.[1]

This kind of political analysis would fall into neither of our two principal categories—institutions and theory—but would instead endeavour to restore a unity that in the real world is never wholly severed, except at the expense of the political system in question. For the essence of political revolution is a fundamental disharmony between existing institutions and the political presuppositions of those elements whose consent is necessary to its survival. Some systems

[1] G. H. Guttridge: *English Whiggism and The American Revolution.*

will depend upon the consent of the whole people or a major part of them—as is probably true of most modern democracies—others depend only upon the loyalty of an *élite*. But in either case, there must be this correspondence between idea and fact. Political analysis must therefore concern itself always with both.

Nor has much been done effectively to determine what lines the inquiry into political presuppositions must take; our descriptive technique has been developed far more effectively on the institutional side. But it is clear that it will be concerned not only with what people expect their government to be like, the kind of claim to authority they respect—whether derived from birth or the ballot-box—but also, and most important, what they expect government to do. And 'to do' includes 'not to do'.

I suspect indeed, that it is the latter kind of inquiry that is at present likely to be the more fruitful. It is I think increasingly clear that one of the divisions between ourselves and the countries of Western Europe at the present juncture is our different conception of the proper functions of government, and the order of priority that we attach to these functions. It is for instance probable that the current presupposition of British politics—and this is not confined to a single party—includes the belief that it is the basic duty of government to preserve 'full employment'. Indeed so much has this become part and parcel of our political thinking that it is extremely difficult to bear in mind how new a phenomenon this really is, that it is something that would hardly have been imaginable say fifteen years ago. But only if we realize that we ourselves have almost unconsciously acquired a new criterion by which to judge the efficiency of a political system, can we see how considerable is the intellectual barrier between ourselves and other countries where this object is by no means so prominent.

But so new a branch of our studies is bound to have its own pitfalls. For unless one takes the utmost care to avoid all looseness of language, the classifying of political societies in terms of their presuppositions which is the only rational method of classification, may lead one into very curious positions. For if we say, to take the same example, that Britain has come to set the maintenance of 'full employment' as the criterion of satisfactory government, we will almost certainly get the reply that in that case our natural alignment is with the Soviet Union which has been providing full employment for some considerable time and is certainly likely to go on doing so. And then we shall have to elaborate and explain that what we mean by full employment includes the right to choose one's occupation or to continue in a particular trade, to work in one's home town, or the place of one's choice, and so on. And even where we have admitted some derogations from these qualifications, as in our special treatment of coal mining, agriculture and so on, we do so conscious that these are derogations, but explicable again in terms of national interests, defence or otherwise. So that we build up in the end a complex of ideas totally different from Soviet 'full employment', which starts with the idea of the full utilization of resources material and human, and with the use of the governmental apparatus to bring these together, even at the price of the immense uprootings of human beings and whole communities, which have admittedly marked the several stages of Soviet economic planning.

In other words, one has both to define with some precision the language in which one analyses the presuppositions of the several political systems that one studies—and the same would equally be true if one looked not at economic *desiderata* but at such well worn topics as freedom of speech, freedom from arrest and so on—and to fit each single such idea into the whole system of which it forms part. And this is not easy; for as we have seen, these ideas and their interconnection are never static, but are in all societies changing all the time, even though at various speeds. Indeed it is possible that the variation in speed which makes changes in our own lifetime seem so much more rapid than in past centuries is in fact an illusion comparable to that of perspective in the physical world. So that here too history may be our guide. And furthermore with the ideas the institutions change also, if not formally, at least in their working; so that in fact, all efforts of political analysis tend to be outstripped by the event; and the description of the present remains an unattainable ideal.

Nevertheless it can hardly be doubted that if our political studies are to be taken seriously, and be accepted as relevant to the understanding of the real world, something of the kind I have been trying to suggest is essential. We require a shifting of the present frontiers of political analysis to include both phenomena usually dealt with under other heads, and the problems of societies usually neglected as outside our competence.

This conclusion is of course an ominous one for those who are determined to keep away from unorthodox methods as well as from unorthodox subjects. If our descriptive techniques have been developed to a greater extent in America than in this country, it is not merely that students like Professor Key have had placed at their disposal the financial resources without which detailed field work and statistical analysis are not possible, it is also because, as he explains, he and his workers met with a general readiness on the part of many people concerned to discuss their own political institutions, freely and without fear. But what is possible within the one-party American South, is not possible when dealing with the Peoples' Democracies or the USSR. This does not mean that there is no real evidence, but rather that the evidence is of a kind harder to co-ordinate and check than is usual in the experience of the political scientist. For instance, our most important potential source for information about the Soviet Union has been the so-called 'new emigration' that resulted from the German invasion and defeat. And this evidence is at its most important not when it comes from a single individual—a Kravchenko for instance—but when it can be generalized from the experiences of many individuals which can be compared and collated. What can be done in this respect can be seen from Professor Merle Fainsod's article in a recent number of the *American Political Science Review*.[1] But in this country, anything like the 'Harvard Russian Research Center' appears, alas, to be beyond our means in both money and manpower; one could wish at least it was not outside our mental horizons as well.

For in the world as it is, we cannot adopt the Aristotelean solution of keeping to the *polis* and letting the barbarians look after themselves. Political analysis cannot be confined to the study of the Western democracies. But this need not, and should not mean that we should neglect the vital differences between the Western liberal democracies and the other societies now within our range. We are entitled to say, if we believe it to be true, that although there are other forms of political structure that work, that give the minimum of order and protection without which no society can function, yet from the point of view of the promotion of those virtues that men have sought for in political society, these other structures are inferior, that political life in a liberal democracy has certain positive qualities that other systems ignore. But such a conclusion should certainly come at the end rather than at the beginning of an inquiry.

[1] M. Fainsod: 'Tensions and Controls in the Soviet System', *American Political Science Review*, June 1950.

3

Historians in a Revolutionary Age[1]

THERE would probably have been a reaction against the Versailles settlement in any event. The hopes placed upon it were too high. But this reaction was converted into doubts about the justice of the war itself and the value of the victory, and by a radical revision of the views held about its causes. This revision was largely assisted by the more or less fortuitous fact that the Germans were first in the field with their diplomatic documents of the period, and that the first diplomatic histories of the years in question were perforce written on the basis of these documents and by more or less Germanophile historians. Repudiating the view in the Peace Treaty that the war was one 'imposed upon the Allied and Associated Governments by the aggression of Germany and her allies' these historians, even when they kept clear of the German version of 'Allied encirclement', presented the period in terms of an international anarchy: all nations sought selfish ends — Germany no more than others and less than some — and having no means of settling such disputes except by force or the threat of force, they were bound sooner or later to end in general war.

This is not the occasion to reopen that debate except for one observation which has a wider relevance. It is that the theory of equal responsibility is one which is rendered highly plausible by any technique of historical writing that confines itself to diplomatic documents and ignores the internal life and politics of the countries concerned. So long as one talks in the favourite abstractions and personifications of the diplomatic historian about 'the Wilhelmstrasse', 'the Quai d'Orsay' and so on, it is not difficult to regard all the countries concerned as following policies of the same kind and hence as bearing an equal responsibility for the outcome. It is only when one looks at the internal structure and ethos of the societies concerned that one can differentiate between them, and see the gulf which in

[1] Copyright by The Council on Foreign Relations.

39

fact separated Asquith's England or Wilson's America from the Kaiser's Germany.

This doctrine of equal responsibility which contributed so much (along with some of its offshoots like the alleged wickedness of armament manufacturers and bankers) to the moral and material disarmament of both Britain and the United States in face of the revival of German aggressiveness was, of course, largely unable to hold its own when aggressiveness merged into overt aggression. As soon as it became evident that the object of the Germans was to reverse not the Versailles settlement but the victory which gave it birth, it became possible to review the pre-history of the First World War and to make use at the same time of a wider range of historical materials than had at first been available. If full use is made of the German archives now in Allied hands for the earlier period as well as for the inter-war years, a further revision in the picture may be required.

Now, after the Second World War, we talk very often as though the causes of that conflict were already patent and as though we had only to avoid our previous errors in order to avoid renewed disaster. Just as the choice of 'unconditional surrender' as the leitmotif of our peacemaking projects was based on our determination to prevent a new German 'stab-in-the-back legend', so a great deal of the current political argument turns on the belief that the fundamental cause of the Second World War was 'appeasement' and that the avoidance of 'appeasement' is the sum of true statesmanship. It should be clear that on logical grounds alone 'appeasement' can never be a prime cause, for before there can be 'appeasement' there must be threat of aggression, if not aggression itself to appease. But historians have actually helped the growth of these and other facile stereotypes, for reasons which have again been partly outside their own control.

For the vast bulk of the material available to the historian has come from the Western European countries and in particular from France. And the apologias of Western statesmen, particularly French statesmen, are necessarily concerned primarily with their own share in the events they record, even though from a wider point of view that share was a relatively minor one. The correction of such stereotypes, such automatic reactions to the mention of particular events in the recent past, is an essential but neglected task of the academic student of politics.

The professional historian of the inter-war years as of the previous period still falls too easily into the routine of treating the

Great Powers as so many roughly similar units whose fundamental interests and policies are of the same family. The pieces in the great game of international relations are not like the pieces in draughts or checkers; they are not identical and interchangeable. They are like the pieces in chess with individual habits of their own. Some can travel one way along the board and some another; and the limitations are real and constitute the essence of the game. But unlike even chess, international relations has the awkward characteristic that the values and dispositions of the pieces are not permanent, but changeable. Soviet Russia did not just begin where Tsarist Russia left off. The America of Roosevelt was not the America of Wilson. Hitler was not the Kaiser.

There is, of course, the contrary and equally oversimplified view of the Marxists, who regard the world of the inter-war period as sharply divided between the peace-loving Soviet Union on the one hand and the warring imperialist States on the other — the latter prevented only by their internecine rivalries from joining together to crush the Soviet Union and the hope of emancipation which it presented to their own and the colonial proletariats. But the patent inadequacy of the Marxist analysis should not blind us to the inadequacy of the viewpoint which holds that everything has all been done wrong up till now, but this time we shall show the world how it is to be done. Many of us may have felt like that in 1944-45, and already we see how wrong we were. Human affairs being the tangled mess of rationality and irrationality that they are, it is unlikely that in these great matters any generation should be wholly right. What history seems to reveal is not a succession of errors followed by a flash of final and total illumination, but rather a succession of partial insights and partial blindnesses, leaving us something to learn from both. In our present mood it has become fashionable to contrast the relative solidity of the Vienna settlement with the rapid collapse of the Versailles order. And no doubt there were aspects of politics into which Metternich saw more deeply than Wilson; there were also aspects of politics into which Wilson saw more deeply than Metternich, and more deeply, too, than some of his successors and critics. The contempt for Wilsonian principles that seems to be one of the few meeting places for right and left has yet to be proved a productive form of reaction.

II

What, then, are the particular lessons to be drawn for a study of the history of the inter-war period?

In the first place, it seems that sufficient allowance must be made for two facts which distinguish that period from preceding ones. The first of them is one that has been gaining ground as a result of recent events but is still not altogether accepted as applied to historiography. It is the simple fact of change of scale. After 1917—the crucial year of America's entry into the war and Russia's withdrawal—the European framework of modern history finally collapsed. It was possible to write the history of modern times up to that date around Europe as a nucleus, with the other continents coming into the main story only when, and in as far as, they were affected by European events.

The illusion was not merely an example of European egocentricity. Indeed it would not be too much to say that it has died harder in the United States than in some parts of Europe itself. The whole rationale of American isolation—in so far as it had a rationale—was based on the idea that a European equilibrium could be restored and preserved by the efforts of European nations themselves. Even today the same fundamental illusion underlies the unthinking support given in the United States to the totally unreal notion of West European federation. The British resistance to this idea is not (as some people appear to think) the product of a simple desire to retain certain special benefits of the Commonwealth relationship, but rather of an awareness which the Commonwealth relationship fosters—an awareness of the total unsuitability of a West European unit (or even of a wider European framework) as an instrument for providing a solution for any of the problems, political, economic or even cultural, that such a federation would be supposed to solve.

Any study of the inter-war years which does not give major attention to the changes in the status and outlook of non-European Powers, American and Asian alike, is a parish pump affair, and pre-destined to superficiality. But the historian clinging to his documents which tell him a lot about the Rhine and the Danube, but little about the Ganges or the Yellow River, who finds a comforting familiarity in the interchanges between European diplomats and a discomforting unfamiliarity about the names and aims of Asian statesmen and movements, is normally content to leave these questions as sideshows for specialists.

Important as this question of scale undoubtedly is, it is both easier to understand and simpler to grapple with than the other major particulars in which the years after the First World War differ from the years before it. For we are here dealing with a change of spirit and temper reflected in changing institutions; and such immaterial changes present much harder problems to the historian, particularly the contemporary historian, than do changes in the relative weight and importance of different areas or states. It is indeed precisely the difficulty which those who still took for granted the temper of the preceding age had in understanding the age into which they had now come that explains the extent of their failure. Neville Chamberlain's failure to understand Hitler (dare one add Franklin Roosevelt's failure to understand Stalin?) was not the failure of individuals but of a civilization. And we are still far perhaps from having plumbed the full depths of this gulf. Indeed it is too early to be sure that we shall not be swallowed up by it in our turn.

The gulf is symbolized most obviously and dramatically by what can best be described as a growth in callousness in the Western world—a growth in indifference to murder. In the late nineteenth century or the early years of the present one, public opinion could be moved, and political action to some extent swayed, by revulsion against Turkish ill-treatment of Bulgar or Armenian minorities, or by Russian pogroms against the Jews. Yet the victims of these world-shaking horrors as they were then regarded could have been numbered easily in thousands. In the course of the Second World War, the Germans as a matter of public policy put to death some 5,000,000 to 6,000,000 Jews and further millions of Poles, Yugoslavs, Russians and others. Yet within five years of the overthrow of the regime that ordered murder on a scale unknown since the times of Genghis Khan and Tamerlane, the revulsion against it seems almost to have vanished. Of course the inhumanities of the Soviet rulers have absorbed our attention, yet in discussions about policy with regard to various degrees of partnership with Germany in America, in Britain and even in France, should not the memory that we are dealing with a nation that has recently practised genocide as an instrument of its political programme continue to be a factor in reaching decisions?

It is no doubt true, as Socialists will remind us, that we are more sensitive than our grandparents to some evils, that we accept social responsibility for individual welfare to a greater extent than any previous society. But a public conscience that demands free spectacles all round (in both senses) but is indifferent to the gas chamber and the incinerator seems oddly proportioned to anyone inheriting the simple standards of religion and ethics as the Western world has known them.

Yet this blunting of the public conscience—a theme that could be pursued—is only a reflection in a partly non-political sphere of the impact of the major political event of the period we are considering: the twentieth century revolution. The word revolution is used in the singular of set purpose. It helps to emphasize the necessity of clearing our minds of yet another all-pervasive stereotype that makes a proper understanding of the immediate past (and of the present) quite unattainable. It is the stereotype of political division into right and left. This bore some relation to the political circumstances of an earlier age when it could plausibly be argued that the semicircular arrangement of European legislatures corresponded to some real divergence of fundamental views, so that on the extreme right one would have adherents of the traditional legitimist order, on the extreme left those of pure democracy, with various gradations in between. But since 1917—again the crucial year—all this has been quite irrelevant, and has been kept alive by certain elements who have thought to make political capital out of the resultant confusion.

It has been useful for Communists in their 'popular front' periods —and such periods are recurrent features of Communist tactics—to pretend that as the 'extreme left' of the political amphitheatre they are suitable partners for 'democratic' Socialists and even liberals on the benches next to them. At other periods, it has suited Fascists or National Socialists to claim that they are 'the extreme right', and can thus be regarded as defenders of tradition and legitimacy against the extreme left. Both these claims have paid handsome dividends from time to time. But both are obviously spurious. In everything that matters, Fascism and Communism are far more alike than either is like liberalism or conservatism. In other words, the whole of this right-left dichotomy is now a dangerous irrelevance. Any test one applies will demonstrate the truth of this conclusion. In the days when the right-left division had meaning, it was generally agreed, for instance, that a sympathy for Socialism (in some form) and with internationalism (in some form) was a characteristic of the 'left' as contrasted with the devotion of the 'right' to property and patriotism. Today it is clear enough, at least in Britain, that Socialism can be combined with the very extremes of nationalist insularity. There is thus no logical link whatever between Socialism and internationalism; and the right-left division obviously breaks down.

44

Presented in a highly abstract and schematic form, what has in fact happened appears to be more like this. In the century of the Vienna settlement, the European States-system, then the core of world politics, was run on the assumption, generally if not consciously held, that liberalism was making its way under the shadow of the old legal order. This liberalism had as its expression in the field of international relations a respect for the sovereignty of individual States, and a growing tendency to regard as the proper foundation of such States the principle of national self-determination. Although over much of Central and Eastern Europe this principle was violated in fact, it generally commended itself to what were regarded as forward-looking minds. It was held, too, that nations based upon this principle would be able to compose their differences without the resort to war which was still accepted as the ultimate sanction of national sovereignty. Meanwhile, however, peace was actually preserved by the self-restraint imposed upon the Great Powers by the balance of forces between them, and by a certain realization, perhaps, that under modern conditions a major clash between them might lead to far-reaching and undesirable consequences for their internal structures. For structures of government and society were in many parts of Europe proving less and less capable of giving a proper place to the demands of new classes for political self-expression. Yet there were even in darkest Russia some stirrings of reform; and nowhere in Europe was it possible to take the same gloomy view of the future that the present generation has come to regard as almost normal. It might perhaps be added that the fact that overseas emigration, particularly to the United States, still held out opportunities to vast numbers of those who by reason of political, religious or economic discrimination had least to look forward to in Europe, and was a safety valve of inestimable importance.

Above all, however, the characteristic of this last period of the old Europe was something which can best be described as the rule of law. It was the feeling that people were living within a social and economic order which, whatever its injustices and pressures, could at least be trusted to endure, in which, to take the most telling symbol, the value of money could be expected to remain stable and in which in consequence planning for oneself and one's family was still possible. Under such an order, personal responsibility and personal initiative made up in part at least for obvious social defects. And something in the field of international relations corresponded to this feeling about the internal order. There might be wars as there had

45

been in the past, and some people would suffer; but the basic pattern of civilian life would go on. Statesmen might regard each other with suspicions that were justified, but on the whole they were men in whom a certain degree of self-control, in whose ambitions a certain measure, might be presumed.

This is the order that was destroyed by the First World War, and by the European revolution of which the 1917 revolution in Russia was the first step. In retrospect we can measure its magnitude better. For we have seen in more recent years how the Japanese conquest of South-Eastern Asia and its aftermath have ended the domination of the Western Powers in those lands, and have broken up a great deal of the apparatus of law and order upon which any kind of productive and civilized life must depend. Americans who have been prone to applaud the weakening of 'imperialism' and 'colonialism' can now see in Burma, Malaya, Indonesia and Indo-China how hard it is to supply the place of everyday machinery of government when it is withdrawn, along with the habits of obedience upon which it rests; how easy it is for anarchy to rear its head, and how much may have to be suffered by the peoples of these areas before a substitute is found for the British, French and Dutch rule that would-be 'progressives' have bespattered with so much unjustified contempt.

The difference is, however, that whereas we have so far discovered no clear formula for the current problems of Asia, the problem of the collapse of the old European order seemed in 1919 to have a solution ready-made for it in the principles of Wilsonian liberalism. This solution rested on the belief that what had happened could be regarded as the speeding-up of a natural historical process that had been going on over a long period. Europe was being remapped at last, in terms of national self-determination; those countries which did not already enjoy liberal-democratic institutions were being endowed with them (that 'liberal' and 'democratic' were possibly antipathetic was normally overlooked); and finally an organization was to be set up in order to assure respect in the international order for the rule of law. To replace the balance of power and the self-restraint of autocrats that had failed the world, Wilsonian liberalism provided a new machinery of international co-operation and conciliation, and the hoped-for impact of world opinion mobilized in defence of peace.

With all allowances made for national selfishness and the still greater force of national fears based upon historic experience, the statesmen of Western Europe, of Western-minded Central European nations like the Czechs, and of the Americas (where these participated at all) were for the next two decades governed by the Wilsonian complex of ideas. The new Wilsonian order failed, and with that failure, contempt for these principles grew. But the point here is, surely, that for the most part the wrong reasons were given, and still are given, for their failure.

It is of course true that in action the confinement of statesmanship to Europe proper had the same deleterious effect as the confinement to the European framework has had upon historical thought. But the other reasons were for the most part very wide of the mark. Ignoring the fact that politics nearly always has a primacy over economics, the argument was that the greatest flaw was the multiplication of economic barriers that the practice of self-determination was shown to entail, and the creation of a multitude of warring and autarchic little States. But it was not the little States that went to war; and the whole of this argument seems to rest rather on some intellectuals' love of bigness and power for their own sake than on any reasoned analysis of the course of events.

It was argued, too, that the weakness was that the principle of national self-determination itself was not carried out to its logical conclusion, that its teachings were overtly disregarded in some areas. This of course is not altogether consistent with the first argument, though it was quite often advanced by the same people. But the real point is again that war did not come over an attempt forcibly to rectify an injustice of this kind. The dispute over Danzig and the 'Corridor' was the occasion rather than the cause of the final breakdown. What had made it inevitable was the German march into Czechoslovakia. Wilsonian principles did not demand that Nazis should rule in Prague; and once they were there, there was no reason not to regard the demand for the 'Corridor' (so-called and of set purpose) as more than a stepping stone to German rule in Warsaw, and beyond.

At any rate, criticism of the Versailles settlement for paying too little attention to the principle of self-determination is hardly compatible with the approval of the principles of Potsdam. Self-determination has never until the last decade been held to mean the tidying up of the map of Europe by mass murder — or by mass expulsions. The Russians and their satellites (not without some early connivance in other quarters) have been almost as adept at the latter as were the Germans at mass murder.

The real point is surely that the Versailles settlement was destroyed not by events or causes in the field of international relations proper, but by the advent of the European revolution. In Russia, and then in Italy and Germany, regimes came into power which did not simply demand a revision of the existing structure, but repudiated it altogether. These regimes seeking their support from the lower depths of society, and from the lower depths of human nature, could not be fitted into any system based upon respect for law and upon self-restraint because they recognized no law and no limitations. This was clearer at first internally than externally; it was not at first seen that to deny human rights to 'bourgeois' or to 'kulaks', to Socialists or to Jews, to treat individuals as merely units in the balance sheet of national power can never have a purely internal significance. States which repudiated all law in favour of mere will could not form part of any international order. They were as out of place in the new Europe as they would have been in the old.

It is not surprising that this was not at first realized. As far as Russia was concerned, there was the feeling that it was a government of the 'left' and therefore deserved the support of 'progressives'. Forgetting the circumstances that had led to Allied intervention against a regime that was making peace with the German enemy, and simultaneously stimulating the forces of revolution everywhere, people rapidly developed a guilt complex over the whole episode and this helped to blur the picture still further. But the fundamental point was that certain spurious historical analogies tempted people to believe, after the earlier years were over, that the regime would settle down, that in Russia too, after a fashion, normalcy would return. The complete misconception (that still bobs up here and there) about the meaning of Stalin's famous, or infamous, 'Socialism in one country' provided an intellectual excuse for ignoring the fact that 'permanent revolution' was not simply the heretical doctrine of an outlawed sect, but something inherent in the Soviet regime by its very nature. Violence breeds violence; and a regime which is ready to sacrifice its own people for the sake of its blueprints of future happiness and the more concrete temptations of present power will hardly hesitate to repeat the process at the expense of foreigners when opportunity affords.

And all this of course was equally true of Germany, and to a lesser extent of Italy. It was somewhat concealed from the outside world by the fact that instead of coming into power as a result of a violent revolution against the old order, Fascism and National Socialism each came into power with the connivance of part of the old ruling elements. In Germany particularly, where the existing settlement had never seriously been accepted, soldiers, civil servants and industrialists saw no reason why they should not exploit the dynamic of the revolution for their own purposes. But in a contest as to who should exploit whom, a revolutionary movement with its fewer scruples is almost certainly bound to win against its more traditionalist and intellectual opponents. And so one had in Germany the series of pathetic and foolish manœuvres which ended in the plot of July 20, 1944.

In Italy, the dynamic of Fascism was more artificial and much weaker, the old order, strengthened by the survival of the monarchy, correspondingly stronger. Fascism's malignant hatred for it is shown in Mussolini's *Memoirs*. His final endeavour to build himself up as a revolutionary hero (even if it owed something to the example of Napoleon as the myth-maker of St Helena) was in essence a shrewd appraisal of the reason for his failure.

Only in Russia, where the crust of civilization was thinner and the pent-up dark energies of the people more fully exploitable for the evil purposes of Lenin and his successors, has a twentieth-century revolution really fulfilled itself. There, almost every barrier against naked politics has been swept away—and the prospect is the more grim. In Russia the creation of a people acknowledging no limitations upon human action other than technical ones, and certain of its ultimate mastery over the latter, has gone further than anywhere else. To read the Soviet press is to be reminded that the visions of an Aldous Huxley or a George Orwell about conditioned minds are not pure fantasy. The real problem of our times may prove to be not how to get rid of the Soviet regime (for such a regime is bound to carry within it the seeds of its own destruction) but how to find anything to put in its place. Are there any healthy shoots in the Russian soil ready to sprout up when this vast jungle growth of Communist bureaucracy no longer shuts out the light of the sun?

III

But this is to anticipate events. Our immediate purpose is with the past and particularly with the 1920's and 1930's when the Communist menace was rightly regarded as secondary to the menace of National Socialism and its allied Fascisms. Rightly, because although the universality of Communism makes it in the long run a more dangerous creed than the parochial frenzies of the German master race, it did not seem as though its adherents could rebuild the Russian state and advance its strength to the point at which its military might could seriously weigh in the world, or even the European, balance of power.

Some of the neglect of Russia's possibilities as an ally against the Nazis had nothing to do with any ideological prejudice but was the result of a purely technical appraisal of Russia's weakness. And this weakness was of course realized by the Russians themselves and acted on accordingly. Indeed if the term 'appeasement' is to be applied in its contemporary meaning to the foreign policy of any country in the 1930's, it would seem best of all to fit the policy of the Soviet Union toward Fascism. The whole series of events from the sale of the Chinese Eastern Railway in Manchuria to the non-aggression pacts with Germany in 1939, and Japan in 1941, carries the story of Russian appeasement of the 'aggressor States' well past the point at which Great Britain and France, and in a different way the United States, had abandoned the effort.

If the Russian appeasement was more wholehearted than that of the Western Powers, it was because it was the conscious policy of a government that knew what its object was, that had not renounced the belief in force as the universal arbiter but was concerned to see that no arbitrament was resorted to at a time unfavourable to itself. It did not spring, as did Western appeasement in large part, from the pressure of populations wedded to the ideology of peace as never before in history, and between governments who were caught without a valid doctrine of international relations for the revolutionary world in which they had to function.

In as far as the Governments of Great Britain, the United States and France had a doctrine, it was surely essentially Wilsonian. On the whole, and with the deviations in favour of specific national interests of a traditional kind which were to be expected only in a human and hence imperfect world, they still adhered to the ideas of national self-determination as the proper foundation of a world order. The remodelling of the international relationships of the British Commonwealth to which the Second World War gave an added impetus rather than a new direction was testimony enough in one sphere, as was the revision of the policies of the United States in Latin America in another. And even more important was the belief that such changes in the political order of the world that had to be made by consent and not by force.

The problem was how to apply principles of this kind and to operate the type of international machinery that they demanded in a world in which were at work revolutionary forces that denied the principles themselves. The statesmen of the Western Powers—encouraged as they were by the support of the majority, indeed the vast majority of their fellow-citizens—were bound to assume that time was on their side, that if they could only delay the catastrophe by timely concessions, the revolutionary movements (where they recognized them as such) would undergo a process of stabilization, and gradually fit themselves into the existing framework of world politics. On at least three occasions in the history of the Soviet Union —the last being in the early years of its participation in the Second World War—it has been widely argued in Western countries that the regime was settling down, that its revolutionary impetus was slackening, and that it could henceforth be treated along the lines of the traditional diplomacy. In a similar way in the 1930's, people were prone to clutch at every suggestion that Hitler or Mussolini, as the case might be, were acting as a check upon their 'extremists' and were ready to come into an all-round peaceful settlement.

All these were illusions—but illusions honourable to the heart if not to the head. Is it healthy to treat the heads of great States, the accepted rulers of great Nations, as perjured criminals until proof positive and incontrovertible has been obtained? Would any country having reached the level of humanitarian and pacific feeling of the Western democracies and after the experiences of World War I have agreed to what would have been in effect a preventive war?

And there was in the 1930's a further dilemma of a perfectly genuine kind. The balance of military strength—actual rather than potential—so favoured the revolutionary Powers at the time when the far-reaching nature of the threat they presented became apparent that it was hardly possible to resist one without the help of the others. And it was not obvious in such a case what action would in the long run be most desirable. The British and French Governments have been blamed rightly or wrongly for not doing as much as they could to bring the Soviet Union into a common front against German aggression. But if they are to be blamed for this, should they not also be praised for refusing to have any truck with the idea of joining the Axis Powers in an anti-Bolshevik crusade against the Soviet Union? For despite all Communist propaganda to the contrary, there is not a shred of evidence that this was a part of the policy of the Western Powers, not even to the extent of passive connivance in German designs—though a certain number of individuals may well have felt that the best thing that could happen would be for the different revolutionary regimes to destroy themselves in internecine strife, just as the Communists on their side hoped to see the capitalist world destroy itself in warfare for their own ultimate benefit. One could say that the Anglo-French guarantees to Poland and other countries after the occupation of Czechoslovakia had precisely the contrary effect, providing as they did a cover for the Soviet frontiers.

Indeed one could say that both the negative policy toward the idea of close association with the Soviet Union and the hostile attitude towards the idea of a limitless eastward expansion of Nazi Germany sprang from the same fundamental concept of what was proper to the foreign policy of twentieth-century democracies. In the end, the decision was made for them by the pressure of events; and for a period the Atlantic democracies became the allies of the Soviet Union. It may well be that this alone made the defeat of Germany possible; it can scarcely be said in the light of subsequent events that the forebodings of those who would have preferred if possible to do without it have not in part been justified.

In this perspective, it might well be argued that the statesmen of the Western world in the inter-war period were faced with a dilemma that had all the elements of classical tragedy, since it was ultimately insoluble. There was perhaps no path that could have combined adherence to principle with practical achievement. It is easy to see how in fact the actions of such statesmen contributed to the circumstances in which war came; it is much harder to see how a situation could have been created in which the war might have been avoided.

This does not mean that the historian of the inter-war period should now embark upon a defence of those reputations—Mr Chamberlain's, Monsieur Daladier's, and so on—that have suffered most heavily at the hands of recent writers. There is plenty of evidence that such men lacked even the limited insights of some of their wiser contemporaries—though not all those who criticize them today, such as Socialist opponents of British rearmament, were among these wiser contemporaries. There is plenty of evidence that even their own principles were not always adhered to fully, that they were weak, vacillating and above all unimaginative. Rather it should be realized that these facts and the abundant documentation that increasingly serves to illustrates them are of very secondary importance, that the traditional interests and techniques of the diplomatic historian have little relevance to a revolutionary age.

It may be, of course, that even this level of the argument is not the final one, that if it be true that the historian for the next few generations will see our age in terms of conflicting ideologies and of the movements generated by them, a still more long-range judgment will regard all this activity as superficial compared with underlying changes in technology, in population and in the major question of the relation of the human race as a whole to the resources of the planet it inhabits.

No one can tell. But to those who argue this way, it is possible to answer that such questions lie outside the province of the historian in the accepted sense. His business is with those parts of the historical process that take their form from the conscious activity of the individual or the planned activity of the group. His efforts must be to comprehend so as to narrate the story of each generation within the terms of the problem it set itself at the time. To judge by such historical works as the inter-war period has so far called forth, that is enough and more than enough for most people. It is, as has been here suggested, a problem that is far from having been solved. It is perhaps presumptuous to say that it can be. There may be human tragedies that the human mind is too small to grasp.

PART II

PROBLEMS OF INTEGRATION

4

Self-determination Reconsidered[1]

CRITICISM of President Wilson and the other peacemakers of 1919 has ranged across a wide field: they have been accused alternatively of having adopted principles incapable of translation into practice, and of having betrayed those principles for the sake of national aggrandizement or sheer vindictiveness. Sometimes the roles of the individuals are separated, and Wilson, the transatlantic innocent, is spoken of as though he had been fooled by wilier Europeans; as though he had indeed been a 'blind and deaf Don Quixote', in the foolish and damaging phrase of Maynard Keynes, a man whose literary skill so concealed the poverty of his political thinking that he was able to fasten his opinion of the Peace Conference on a whole English-speaking generation. In fact, neither of the charges is true. The peacemakers — all the major ones — were men of principle; all of them, as the recently published notes of their private meetings show, sought conscientiously to mould stubborn reality a little closer to their own ideals. Wilson was not the dupe of his colleagues, nor indeed, except in some relatively detailed aspects of the problem, was he very far removed from them. His importance was that he gave voice more clearly than anyone else to the principles that all men of goodwill believed to be essential to an enduring peace. And who are we, living in the unease of a temporary settlement based upon the confrontation of sheer opportunism with a dogmatism harsher and narrower than Wilson's, to reject these principles? What do we offer instead? Would it not be fairer to look again at the most celebrated of them, the principle of self-determination, and see what it still has to offer, or what modifications it needs after almost forty years?

It is important to cut loose from the legends that still pass for

[1] This essay comes from one of two special numbers of the Harvard journal *Confluence* which were devoted to commemorating the centenary of the birth of President Wilson.

history in some circles. The most fantastic of these is that there were in Europe in 1919 great areas of free political and economic co-operation—notably the Habsburg Empire—which Wilson relentlessly carved up into competing national States in order to fulfil some purely theoretical commitment of his own.

Why this particular legend has survived and how it is that it still crops up over and over again is a question which would take long to answer. But what is surprising is that it still finds acceptance despite the triumph of two obvious historical truths which few people today would seriously dispute. The first is that the World War itself was to some extent the result of the fact that the European Empires —particularly the Habsburg Empire—had failed to provide for the expression of the sentiment of nationality. This idea had worked itself out in Northern and Western Europe in the preceding centuries, but was still frustrated in the east and south-east. The second obvious truth is that the nationalities of these parts of Europe did not wait for President Wilson or anyone else to grant their demands, but once the imperial dynasties had gone down to defeat, set about getting for themselves what they could. Nothing could have stopped the fragmentation of Eastern Europe except the imposition of force to a degree that neither Wilson nor any of his associates could countenance. Nor indeed had they the means to make another policy effective supposing that had been their intention. Only a Hitler or a Stalin could have done it; and it has yet to be seen whether the Soviet attempt at solving the 'nationalities question' has given a permanent answer to these claims, or has merely 'frozen' them as Bohemian nationalism was 'frozen' for three centuries after the Battle of the White Mountain.

We cannot look into the future; but that is no excuse for distorting the past. Whatever one may think of various acts of Wilson's, he at least understood even before coming to Europe that this was the kind of problem with which he had to deal. He may have been been surprised that national claims were so numerous and so conflicting, that history provided so obscure an answer on the rights and wrongs of particular frontiers, but at least he believed that on the whole, and with due regard to other considerations such as those imposed by geography which he perfectly well understood, the closer one approached a map of Europe based upon the consent of the populations the more hope there would be for peaceful development. Since, in those far-off and civilized times, no one seriously considered mass murder (as practised by the Nazis) or mass transfer of populations (as practised by their conquerors), this meant in fact that by and large the map of Europe would follow the lines of nationality. As Wilson said in his Mount Vernon speech on July 4, 1918: 'These great objects [of the peace] can be put in a single sentence. What we seek is the reign of law based upon the consent of the governed, and sustained by the organized opinion of mankind.' In other words, Wilson saw clearly that no system of international law could work if important groups were profoundly and irrevocably at odds with their political sovereigns. Nor would world opinion—by which Wilson did not mean that travesty of democracy, 'public opinion' as measured by the pollsters—give its support to political settlements imposed in defiance of the wishes of the peoples concerned. For those reasons, Wilson put it in his message to Congress of February 11, 1918: 'all well-defined national aspirations shall be accorded the utmost satisfaction that can be accorded them without introducing new or perpetuating old elements of discord and antagonism that would be likely in time to break the peace of Europe and consequently of the world.'

Wilson was correct in realizing that the map of Europe as it existed in 1914 expressed very different principles, and was in fact largely the legacy of a dynastic system now outmoded. People and provinces had, in his own words, 'been bartered about from sovereignty to sovereignty as if they were mere chattels and pawns of the game.' This was no longer reasonable. Therefore, in the words of his Mount Vernon speech, he stood for 'the settlement of every question, whether of territory, of sovereignty, of economic arrangement, or of political relationship, upon the basis of the free acceptance of that settlement by the people immediately concerned, and not upon the basis of the material interest or advantage of any other nation for the sake of its own exterior influence or mastery.'

II

It would be beyond our present purpose to explore the reasons why the peace settlement, which in fact came nearer to producing a map of Europe in accordance with this principle than any of its predecessors, survived less than twenty years. A nation—Germany—nominally actuated by Wilsonian principles, but in fact dedicated to their destruction, did indeed 'desire a different settlement for the sake of its own exterior influence or mastery'; it could have been prevented from carrying out its purposes only by the operation of a principle which Wilson mistakenly condemned—the principle of the balance of power. And even here it is not clear that Wilson, once he had seen that the League system failed to substitute for the balance of power, would have been as unwilling to return to it as his successors in the United States and abroad.

This again is speculation. The Second World War did not come about because of the application of the principle of self-determination, or because the settlement was not fully applied. Power was mobilized only belatedly, and the German tyranny, established on the basis of a denial of the Wilsonian principles, was eventually overthrown. What we have known since this task was accomplished scarcely lives up to the Wilsonian ideal.

In our time, the challenge to self-determination does not come from the atavistic claims of particular nations to racial superiority nor from fantastic appeals to set the clock back to an age before nationalism assumed its modern form. It comes essentially from those who wish to further self-determination or to complete it in some way; in other words, from those who accept Wilsonian principles but claim that in 1919 they were not carried far enough.

This best can be explained by examining the way in which the original Wilsonian diagnosis came to be made. There are two fundamental points about Wilsonian self-determination. In the first place, although it was no doubt coloured by memories of the American Revolution, and was to that extent American, its frame of reference was essentially European. There has perhaps been a tendency to suggest that nationalism as a source of political energy is a relatively recent development. In fact, it came into evidence as soon as a secular literate class developed in medieval Europe. The Reformation could scarcely have followed the course it did had not distinctions of nationality already existed. For Wilson and his contemporaries, the problem presented itself as it had developed during the democratic age since the French Revolution, and was intimately connected with two dominant aspects of that age; democracy itself, and the growth of State intervention in many aspects of economic and social life.

Both of these were at once cause and consequence of a further development of literacy. As the State machine grew, and literacy with it, the importance of having one's own language recognized—and of being able to take State employment or deal with the State machine unhandicapped—became increasingly obvious. At the same time, the growing self-consciousness (largely attained through literacy) of classes hitherto wholly passive politically except for rare outbreaks of violence, prompted demands for political enfranchisement. But if in the future political decisions were to depend on popular votes and not on a dynasty or ruling class whose outlook might well be supranational, it became vital for national groups to avoid or to escape from incorporation in a State dominated by some other national group. The demand for self-determination was thus a natural consequence of the whole course of Europe's social and political development; Wilson was being thoroughly realistic in accepting these facts. However, in many parts of Europe, no adequate geographical line could be found to separate rival nationalities into homogeneous blocks; and those other valid criteria for State boundaries — economic viability, strategic demands and historic claims — did not always coincide with the lines of nationality. Hence, a Europe based upon the principle of self-determination meant a Europe of minorities; only Switzerland, for a variety of reasons peculiar to itself, avoided the notion that State and Nation, the latter defined primarily in terms of language, ought always to be coterminous.

III

Since Wilson's day, this type of development has ceased to be confined to Europe. Some of the familiar features have been reproduced in other and very different parts of the world; as self-government approaches, the fears of minorities grow. India, united under the British Raj, split when independence came; and even the truncated India of Nehru is threatened by further scissions based largely on differences of language. The language issue threatens the State structure in Ceylon, one of the least immature of the newly-enfranchised States of Asia.

But the application of the idea of self-determination outside Europe does more than reproduce the old problems; it is not just a question of 'plural societies' in Asia or Africa reproducing in an exaggerated form the tensions of Danubian or Balkan Europe. Over most of Europe, the plea for self-determination was made by countries which had at least the elementary requisites for successful self-government: an understanding of the role of law, habits of civil discipline, and the elements of an educated elite. Outside Europe, on the other hand, the demand for self-determination was often exploited by ruling groups who wished to fortify their own position, and had little interest in democratic government, for which the pre-

61

conditions scarcely existed. It was not simply a case of good government being sacrificed for self-government, for by a sheer calculus of material gain this may also have happened in parts of Europe; it was a question of government itself in the modern sense giving way to direct and corrupt personal rule. Yet the pure doctrine of self-determination makes difficult the drawing of distinctions as between a Masaryk and a Nasser.

The other fundamental point about Wilsonian self-determination is that it was essentially political; it was not an accident that Wilson belonged to the traditional party of free-trade and laissez-faire. The assumption prevailed that all that the peoples of Europe asked was the right to govern themselves. Left to themselves, it was taken for granted that they would do the best they could with the resources available to them; it was not expected that self-determination by itself would suddenly make Bulgaria as prosperous as Belgium, or Albania a second Sweden.

Here too, the spread of nationalism outside Europe has been accompanied by a major change in emphasis. The State is thought of increasingly inside and outside of Europe as an economic provider. Self-determination now implies outside Europe not only the absence of foreign control, but a positive accretion of economic well-being. The notion of equality as between individuals, which has haunted generations of Utopian speculators, has been transferred to the field of relations between whole peoples. To some extent, no doubt, Communist propaganda is responsible; backwardness is asserted to be the fruit of imperialist exploitation and not of natural inequalities of endowment, whether material or human. Imperialism, by such a reckoning, will be considered destroyed only when inequalities disappear. The pressure of population on resources — the experience of which has brought about the almost instinctive Malthusianism of the European peoples — is a problem whose very existence Communist propaganda denies. But it would be a mistake to think that Communist propaganda alone is responsible for the state of mind of many among the new devotees of self-determination. Rather, it is that the ideas are there, and the Communists have known best how to exploit them for their own purposes.

The ironical result of this development is plain enough on any reading of the history of the last fifteen years. Franklin Roosevelt — a Wilsonian, though an inconsistent one and a man much shallower than Wilson in his understanding of non-American politics — did his best to make the restoration of self-determination in countries where the dictators had done away with it the prelude to enforcing the principle on a world-wide scale. Roosevelt, a pragmatist, did not carry this to extremes, and other of the possible evil fruits of such a course were staved off by the stubborn good sense of Sir Winston Churchill. But, in Indo-China for instance, the French were successfully prevented by the United States from restoring their authority until it was too late to check the spread of Communism. A weaker British Government gave way largely to American pressure over the evacuation of Suez, with possibly fatal consequences to the authority and influence of the non-Soviet world in the whole Middle East.

While it is easy enough to dwell upon these short-term ironies, this is not the best way of appreciating the dilemma which faces the contemporary exponent of Wilsonian self-determination. The difficulty today is that by general consent the whole idea of a world of tight-knit and self-reliant national units is out of harmony with the demands, and in particular the material demands, made by man on his world. Technology dictates interdependence; prosperity is unattainable except through the organization of resources which nature has not seen fit to arrange according to the dictates of nationality. So we have countries which in one and the same breath denounce all 'foreign' intervention in their affairs and demand that the rest of the world channel its resources in such ways as to obliterate their own backwardness. In few instances will national madness go so far as in the case of the Arabs, who are disbanding the machinery of locust-control because it is 'British'—a fact which will not prevent them from blaming 'imperialism' for any subsequent famines. But the dilemma is always present and can hardly be solved by Western programmes motivated solely by the desire to compete with Communism.

In demanding self-determination, a people, as Wilson understood, interprets its needs correctly, but alas, only certain of them. Short of a merging of the nations into some undifferentiated mass—a sort of esperanto or 'basic-English' culture—the national units deserve preservation, for much that is most valuable in the history of civilization has come out of their interplay. One has only to think of the perpetually renewed miracle of the impact of Mediterranean civilization on the North European mind. And there is no reason to believe that national units can fructify only in Europe. But nations cannot reasonably expect that this demand for an unimpeded enjoyment of their own cultural inheritance, of their own tongue and soil

—landscape is a part of culture—must necessarily involve control over all the machinery of the modern State.

It was the work of the democratic age in whose perilous aftermath we live to unite the two different concepts of Nation and State; Wilsonian self-determination lay at the end of that secular process. We now need some guidance on how to separate these concepts. In this field, which is still largely unexplored by the social psychologists and the political scientists, a great deal of thinking remains to be done. But nothing will be achieved by those who dismiss the Wilsonian liberal phase as a mere record of illusion, or by those who repeat in quite different circumstances slogans not relevant to their own needs, as they themselves define them. There is really no reason to go on repeating *ad infinitum*: what the nineteenth century hath joined, let no man put asunder.

5

(a) European Association

(*The Times*, May 4, 1950)

IT is a platitude that no one ever learns from history; people forget to add that, when some lesson of history is quoted, the conclusion drawn is generally false. At a time when Americans are urging upon the countries of Western Europe some closer form of association, it is to be expected that they should point to the advantages that they have undoubtedly derived from the federal system, and commend to Europeans the example of the Founding Fathers. Such parallels are easily drawn upon also by British enthusiasts for the federal idea and by its continental partisans — the latter the more enthusiastically in that they come from countries without experience of genuine federal institutions and without a very clear idea of their implications. When a French professor writing in 1949 includes the Commonwealth in that part of his treatise on political science dealing with federalism, one may well feel a sensation of despair, even though his actual description of the Commonwealth's institutions leaves little to be desired.

The problem with the Americans is different. The continental partisans of European federation are often such because they are unaware of the significance of the federal formula, particularly under modern conditions, when the parallel would be not the American Constitution as framed in 1787, but the American Constitution after a century and a half of judicial and conventional interpretation. When Frenchmen say that they wish to see federal institutions set up at Strasbourg, it is not because they wish to see Paris reduced politically to the status of Albany or Harrisburg. The Americans know what it is they mean where the present is concerned, but employ a false analogy from the past to insist that what was possible for the United States is possible and indeed essential for Western Europe.

Not all of them limit themselves to Western Europe. In 1948 so eminent an American writer as Mr Carl Van Doren could call his account of the making and ratifying of the constitution of the United States *The Great Rehearsal* and be thinking of the federal problem of today as one not on a European but a world scale. Yet when one reads Mr Van Doren's admirable narrative or other recent more strictly scholarly works on the period, and still more when one reads the writings of the Founding Fathers, above all the *Federalist* itself — and no one should be allowed to go to Strasbourg who could not pass an examination on that text — what one is struck with is not the parallel with the present but the immensity of the difference.

Some of the differences are obvious and generally admitted. The thirteen States had in common language, cultural tradition and, to a large extent, race and religion. At least the Protestant Anglo-Saxon element was universally predominant. Even more important was the fact that, since all of the States had been British colonies (some for a century and a half), they had all had roughly the same political and legal institutions. The delegates at the Philadelphia Convention or to the first Congress did not settle their procedure across the historical gulf which divided at Strasbourg the parliamentary experience of, say, M. Spaak from that of Sir Gilbert Campion. When the Founding Fathers assigned a function to the executive, the legislature or the judiciary, their decision had for them a perfectly definite and concrete significance.

Furthermore on some important matters, in fact in the all-important spheres of defence and foreign relations, the separate units had always been ruled from a single centre. When the ties that bound them to Whitehall snapped they did not acquire sovereign independence, but found themselves at once in a subordinate status towards the Continental Congress under which they fought the war to its successful conclusion. As Abraham Lincoln was to remind his fellow-countrymen in the Union's hour of crisis, there was a very real sense in which the Union was older than the Constitution. And this war-time improvisation was itself the basis of the first written Constitution, the Articles of Confederation — an instrument of government much less ineffective, as Professor Merrill Jensen, of Wisconsin and Oxford, has shown in a remarkable study, than its opponents at the time alleged, and than subsequent writers have been content to assert, in echo of these partisan allegations.

The popular memory of these events as transmitted to current enthusiasts for federalism has thus a tendency to confuse the achievement, or better still the perpetuation, of American Union with the framing of the second and definitive Constitution. In doing so it has obliterated not only these obvious differences between past and present but some less obvious and no less important. The advocates of European federation rely on two main arguments—first, the obvious common interest in defence against the Soviet *bloc*; and second, the presumed salutary effect upon Western Europe's economy of the creation of a single economic unit, a single large market. Of these, the second—whatever its current plausibility upon which a possible caveat might also be entered—was not seriously in the minds of the Founding Fathers, dealing as they were with areas where agrarian and mercantile interests were overwhelmingly more important than any industrial interest, except for the obviously special case of ship-building.

In so far as they were concerned to prevent the growth of tariff barriers in what had (under British rule) been a single free-trade unit, it was because they thought that such barriers might lead to political strife, and hence to the danger of foreign intervention, and a possible relapse into a colonial status. Their primary concern was political—the fact that the financial resources available to the central authority under the Articles of Confederation were insufficient to enable it to fulfil its responsibilities under the head of defence, and the fact that its lack of control over the commercial legislation of the States handicapped its diplomacy.

It is hardly irrelevant to remark that in so far as the Council of Europe itself is concerned today, the approach has so far been precisely the opposite to this. Having been precluded from discussing defence, it has not had the healthy experience which the Philadelphia Convention enjoyed of considering federalism from the core outwards. The question which the Founding Fathers were asking themselves was this: what powers does a federation require in order to present a single front to the outside world, while allowing the units of which it is composed to retain the maximum of autonomy in their purely internal affairs?

One could close the discussion by pointing out that this has been the central theme of all in the subsequent constitutional history of the United States, and that there can be no advance anywhere along the federal road unless the question is tackled in this form. But to close the debate at this point would be to omit one aspect of the matter that has preoccupied American historians for a generation, without, it seems, producing any notable effect upon the public mind. What has been said hitherto relates to considerations upon which there was a fair measure of unanimity at Philadelphia. The real discussions there were over means rather than ends. But this unanimity was not representative of the country as a whole.

Quite apart from the issues already dealt with there were other grounds upon which the Americans of the day, particularly propertied Americans, might wish to recast their existing federal institutions. It was a fact that the weakness of the existing federal authority diminished the value of its bonds which were an important element in the structure of credit generally, and which, having been bought at depreciated prices, might yield a handsome profit to the holders if financial stability could be ensured. In the second place there was the fact that within many of the States strongly democratic tendencies had been at work, and that their existing institutions were such as to give popular majorities political power which might well be used against the interests of the better-off minority of the citizens. A strengthening of federal authority might be the best way of curbing democracy in the States, since popular movements were less likely to make themselves felt at the centre than on the circumference.

There is no need to follow some of the late Charles Beard's followers in suggesting that this element of self-interest stamps the Founding Fathers as selfish hypocrites. When Madison identified 'public good' with 'private rights' there is no need to think he was insincere. Nor was he necessarily wrong. If the American Revolution had gone all the way to pure democracy at one step, it might have ended as did the French. From our present point of view the important thing is that this common interest, binding together the propertied classes, whether southern planters or northern businessmen, helped to create what was in fact a political party organized across State lines. It was this party which organized the movement to revise the Constitution and which saw to it that the States accepted the idea of a Convention for the purpose.

Even more decisive was its role during and after the Convention. It needed a party with clear aims in view to turn the Convention from its proclaimed object of revising the Articles of Confederation to the different one of writing a totally new document. And when the new Constitution was framed it was this party — the Federalists, as they came to be called — who fought the elections to the ratifying conventions in each State, and then struggled within the ratifying Conventions themselves to secure an affirmative vote.

It is here that the real difference between the situation in America then and that in Western Europe now becomes most apparent.

There are, so far as one can see, no powerful groups in Western Europe passionately convinced that their interests would be served by federation, no political parties whose organizations are not bounded by national frontiers, and none in any country prepared to fight the cause of federalism in the Parliaments and on the hustings. Until such a party exists no useful parallel can be drawn, and those who believe in furthering European unity must seek for inspiration elsewhere than in American federalism.

(b) Britain and Europe

(*The Times*, December 7, 1951)

POLITICAL institutions if they are to be durable and to fulfil their purpose must be the product of acknowledged needs and strongly felt sentiments. They cannot by themselves create a unity where exists, or produce consent where it was previously lacking.

They may, it is true, given time, permit a latent and limited feeling of community to establish itself and take root; and this aspect of federalism is the one most generally stressed by those who point to the American example as suitable for imitation on a European or an Atlantic scale. Yet the partisans of such solutions are too apt to overlook the number of conditions that must be fulfilled before their hopes can be realized.

Nevertheless, scepticism is not enough. However powerful the arguments against a federal scheme for Western Europe, however convinced one may be that the word 'federation' has come to signify utopian hopes far beyond its powers to fulfil, however muddled and inadequate the explanations offered by its European advocates, however irritated one may be by the attempts to arrive at it by roundabout means—for 'federation without tears' is still federation—the debate has now gone too far for it to be closed by a British negative.

By now we have certain moral as well as material commitments. In our own interest we cannot afford either to reject altogether the Continental plea that we should do something to assist its painful gropings towards a new system or the rising American insistence that we should accept a greater integration of our own and the Continent's resources as a price of further aid.

In these circumstances there is something to be said for a new initiative on Britain's part which should endeavour to take into account what is genuine and indeed desirable in such proposals, while providing at the same time for the special needs of Britain. Only by transferring the argument from a negative to a positive basis can European and American opinion be persuaded that British criticism of federal panaceas is based on something more than a selfish and self-defeating isolationism.

Britain's special position arises from her traditional concern with oversea rather than with narrowly European matters. Today these world-wide interests are linked together with the existence of the Commonwealth, that is to say, of a group of self-governing nations who pursue their common purposes (or attempt to) through the machinery of consultation.

They do not form in any sense a federation but rely upon the sovereign effectiveness of their several Governments. It is not merely a question of the existing members of the Commonwealth, but of those other countries whose development towards a similar status is the declared aim of British policy.

Britain cannot sacrifice those elements of her sovereignty which are needed to enable her to fulfil this purpose nor can she by herself alienate other nations concerned.

It is not too much to say that every development towards a wider self-governing Commonwealth makes the entry of Britain into a European federation more and more unthinkable. A Britain ruling her Empire through a sovereign Parliament as George III attempted to do was a possible component of a federal union; the Britain of George VI is not. Nor is it at present conceivable that the other nations of the Commonwealth which have rejected federation among themselves would accept it with others — even if an equally warm welcome were extended to them all.

The experience of the Commonwealth itself suggests, however, that the federal method is not only one through which greater unity in action may be achieved. On the political side the problem which at present demands solution is fairly straightforward. The heart of the matter is the different interpretation placed upon the events of 1940 in Britain and in France.

For France, the outstanding facts are that the metropolitan squadrons of the RAF were not thrown into the battle, and that the British

Army was withdrawn from the Continent under the cover of
Britain's air and naval power. Some Frenchmen believe that this was
responsible for the catastrophe, and even those who do not hold this
view may feel an obscure resentment at the geographical good fortune that made the withdrawal possible.

For Britain, the outstanding fact was that our ultimate control
over the destinies both of the RAF and ultimately of our ground forces
made possible our own survival and eventually the liberation of the
Continent.

Both in Britain and on the Continent, however, it is appreciated
that this sequence must not be allowed to recur, and that Europe is
seeking means of being defended and not another chance of 'liberation'. Machinery must be devised, supplementing the machinery of
the North Atlantic Pact, which will convince Europeans that Britain
has accepted the fact that the defence of Western Europe is now
inseparable from her own security.

In this sense, Britain's role is not dissimilar from America's. What
is required, therefore, is a tripartite structure of command and
responsibility. The Supreme Commander must have at his disposi-
tion an American, a European, and a Commonwealth force, whose
three commanders would be operationally responsible to him.

On the political side, the arrangements for a Committee of
Ministers to control the European army may eventually result in an
agreement for the standardization of contributions in men and
money, without which progress towards a truly federal authority
would seem to be unthinkable; but in any event it would be desirable
for the other two components of the allied force to have a political
link with the European organization.

This could take the form of a Committee of three Ministers
(working in Paris), of whom one would be the chairman of the
Committee of European Ministers. They could advise the Standing
Group in Washington in the light of their knowledge of the European situation, and thus contribute to giving the feeling in Europe
that general planning was giving sufficient place to Europe's primary
needs.

It would be the special task of the British and American Ministers
to determine with their European colleague the extent of the commitment involved in the common defence scheme allotted to the
troops for whom they are responsible, and to represent within their
own Cabinets, and before their own public opinion, the special
needs of West European defence. One would assume that the British

71

member would maintain contact with the countries of the Commonwealth, and particularly with any of them directly represented in
the Commonwealth force itself.

In such a scheme no obstacle would be placed by Britain in the
way of the countries of the European army progressing as fast and
as far as they wished and, in fact, could, while the existence of the
tripartite structure on both the military and the political side would
assure them that no plans were being made, or were likely to be
made, which contemplated a repetition of 1940.

More than this, on the military side, could not reasonably be expected of any British Government, but there are two other directions
in which much might be done to dispel suspicion. In the first place,
if the strategic-political aspect of the demand for federalism were
disposed of in this way — and one might envisage some parallel
device to get over the problems presented by the Schuman plan — it
would be possible for the Strasbourg assembly to abandon those attempts at extending its functions which have caused alarm not only
in this country but also in Scandinavia.

Strasbourg could then again represent those things in which
Britain is truly a part of Europe. It could become the expression of
the common cultural heritage that Britain shares with her continental neighbours, and devote itself to practical methods by which
this may be furthered, in the shape of a freer movement of men and
ideas.

In this setting, Britain — the classical country of individual freedom — might find it possible to play a more active role in establishing certain international standards in the matter of human rights, a
question far less academic for many people than more fortunate
nations always realize.

If Britain is to share, in this sense, in a European community it is
also necessary to convince that community, as it has not so far
been convinced, that the Commonwealth is neither a simple excuse
for inaction in Europe nor a deep conspiracy against the liberties or
interests of others. And this is something that cannot be done
through mere exposition.

It would be better to prove the non-exclusiveness of the Commonwealth family by inviting to the now fairly frequent meetings of the
Commonwealth Ministers a non-British representative of the Committee of Ministers of the Council of Europe.

Other devices to link the Commonwealth practice of regular consultation with the European preference for incipient federalism

can readily be imagined. The important point is that all machinery should reflect clearly where responsibility lies, and that Britain should show what is in fact the case, that the share of responsibilities that her people have assumed, and are carrying, in the post-war world is not inferior to that of any other free country.

6

Europe from Lorraine

THE movement for the federation of Western Europe is often misunderstood, particularly in Great Britain and the United States. We tend, and Americans still more so, to think of it in pragmatic terms, to argue as to its value as a measure of military security or as a means of reproducing in the Old World some of the economic advantages of a large single market. There is a tendency to assume that the motive power behind the movement is similarly rational and the product of relatively recent developments. The over-simplification of political issues prevalent in America makes a large-scale change of this kind particularly appealing. At last, they feel, those Europeans are showing some kind of sense; at last they are willing to forget the past feuds and wars; at last they are beginning to behave like sensible Americans: the Council of Europe is something like the great Constitutional Convention; Strasbourg is a modern Philadelphia; and Dr Adenauer and M. Schuman are the Hamilton and Madison of the twentieth century.

How plausible it all sounds — and how misleading it all is! So far from being a simple acceptance of the logic of contemporary economics and strategy, the movement for European Union is made up of diverse and complex strands; its supporters are moved by hates as much as by loves. So far from being a streamlined twentieth century 'solution' to Europe's problems, it has historical roots that go back at least to Charlemagne and to the tripartite division of Charlemagne's Empire. There is not one single broad highway to Strasbourg but a multitude of separate roads — some of them very unlikely ones. Until this is appreciated, those who play with the idea of European Union, especially in the English-speaking world, are in the same position as children playing with an unexploded bomb, under the impression that they have found some new and interesting mechanical toy created specially for their enjoyment.

Let us look at one such road to Strasbourg, that of the Count Jean de Pange.[1] Monsieur de Pange comes from a long-established noble family of Lorraine. His wife is a member of one of the most remarkable of French families, that of de Broglie, and so a descendant of Madame de Staël and of Necker. He himself was trained at the turn of the present century as a medieval historian at the Ecole des Chartes. He is an ardent Catholic and well acquainted with the great figures in the Catholic hierarchy in more than one country. He is not, in this account of his own intellectual and political journey towards the idea of a European federation, writing of experiences felt from the outside, but with something of the authority that comes, if not from the exercise of power, at least from easy familiarity with those who do exercise it. It is a book which deserves to be treated seriously. Of M. de Pange's absolute sincerity, there can be no doubt at all. The middle of the book is taken up with passages of description of his experiences on the Western front in the first world war — experiences which no man of any sensibility could undergo and not feel a genuine horror of war, and a genuine desire to find some means of ending the national feuds which have hitherto been at the root of so much of Europe's suffering. Since his family home lay within the part of Lorraine annexed by Germany in 1871, the meaning of being subjugated to another nation is for him also a vivid one, and not a mere paper concept. And although the mainspring of his ideas can be traced far back in his career, he has the final honesty of admitting when he was wrong. Thus although his teachers at the Ecole des Chartes were revisionists in the Dreyfus case, de Pange, like most men of his kind, was anti-Dreyfus, on the ground that injustice to an individual was better than calling into question the honour of the French Army, thus deflecting it from its task of preparing for the reconquest of the lost provinces of Alsace and Lorraine. He now admits that, having seen where such ideas lead, he was wrong; that individual rights must be central in any civilized State.

On the other hand, although he repudiates the 'integral nationalism' of the Action Française, he remains essentially a monarchist, believing that State power based upon popular will rather than some immanent right can only lead to totalitarianism of one kind or another. The French Revolution and the Napoleonic Empire remain for him the great disasters, the diplomacy of the *Ancien Régime* the example of wisdom. Despite the passion he felt

[1] *Les Meules de Dieu: France—Allemagne, Europe* by Jean de Pange. (Paris. Editions Alsatia, 1951.)

75

for the undoing of the wrong of 1871, he hates Clemenceau, the father of victory, more than any other political figure who crosses these pages. His hero is the great royalist, Marshal Lyautey, whose empire-building on a basis of the peaceful diffusion of French culture he admired in his youth, in Morocco, and whom he would have liked to see exercising not dissimilar functions in regained Alsace. And Lyautey, too, hated the Republic. One chapter consists entirely of a description of the coronation of George VI, which M. de Pange attended—and its irrelevance is only apparent, since M. de Pange sees in the British Monarchy, and in the link with the Commonwealth which it provides, that spiritual sanction which is for him at the root of all healthy political organization.

Sincerity, the avowal of opinions, some of which will be unpopular, is a great merit; what of M. de Pange's range of knowledge? It would be an impertinence to insist upon his deep and loving knowledge of his own Lorraine, of neighbouring Alsace and of the Saar (whose surrender to Hitler in 1935 he regards as the real blunder of pre-war diplomacy), of the German Rhineland, and of Austria where he lived as a boy and where in the Habsburgs, the disappearance of whose Empire still fills him with immeasurable regret, he saw primarily the Dukes of Lorraine. The United States scarcely exists except as a contributor to victory in two world wars. Of its role in world politics—indeed of world politics as distinct from European politics—there is no mention. With Great Britain the position is different. M. de Pange is friendly to this country and in the early months of the war was deeply involved in informal discussions which may have played their part in the abortive Anglo-French Union project of June 1940. It is difficult to see quite how M. de Pange reconciles his apparent enthusiasm for this scheme with his present advocacy of a European Federation on quite a different basis, and on one which would be more likely to separate the destinies of Britain and France than to unite them. One suspects that his real knowledge of British politics and recent British history has its lacunae. (No profound student of British history would repeat the legend that the Entente with France at the beginning of the century was the personal work of Edward VII. Nor was it Cecil Rhodes's intention that the number of German Rhodes Scholars should be equal to those from the English-speaking world. Rhodes's last will added in a codicil fifteen scholarships for Germans to the sixty provided for the Commonwealth and the two for *each* American State.) It is more than the passing factor of a Socialist Government—as events indeed have shown—that has prevented Britain from marching in step with the advocates of a real federal system for Western Europe. As for Russia, if the Americans are tolerated but ignored, the Russians are feared and detested. M. de Pange quotes with approval Tocqueville's prophecy of the coming might of Russia and his advice to France to unite with Germany to resist it. He condemns the French Government for having brought Russia into the League of Nations in 1934, which he regards as the death-blow to that institution. For him the European Union movement means that 'Europe has already regained consciousness of herself before the menace of the Slav world, in which she has recognized her unconquered enemy of the past fifteen centuries, since the period when its pressure against the Germans provoked the great invasions'. For it is not only Communist Russia but all the Slavs who are thus put under the ban. The Czechs in particular. No words are too harsh for Benes, and every accusation brought by the Nazis against Czechoslovakia as an oppressor of minorities seems readily acceptable to M. de Pange, despite his proclaimed aversion for the principle of nationality which he regards as one of the unhappy progeny of the French Revolution A United Europe committed to a crusade against both Communism and Slavdom, cut off from the resources of the eastern half of the Continent, seems a poor guarantee of either peace or prosperity. Yet this would appear to be what M. de Pange is advocating.

Let us look more closely at this creature of his imagination. The war of 1914-18 was a war, he shows, to remedy the wrong done to Alsace-Lorraine. But the French in their turn were wrong to insist on treating Alsace as an integral part of France and forcing her to accept the entire system and outlook of the Third Republic. That such an attempt was made was the fault of the anti-clericals. The separate culture of Alsace, centred round its deeply Catholic religious feeling, should have been encouraged and given institutional expression. Regionalism in Alsace might have helped to revive regionalism elsewhere in France. In his regional and anti-centralist tendencies, M. de Pange shows curious affinities with the Vichy outlook, despite his severity at the expense of Vichy's collabora-tionism. Alsatian autonomy is thought of, then, as a model for France. But it is to be more than that. Alsace is to be a bridge for the entry of French ideas into Germany. So, too, could have been the Saar, and finally the Rhineland itself. If, instead of pursuing reparations into the *impasse* of the Ruhr, France after the first world war had given proper political and economic encouragement to the Rhineland autonomist movement, then flourishing under the Mayor of Cologne, a certain Dr Adenauer, it could have been a bridge between France and Germany. If the Popular Democrats, the precursors of the MRP, and founded on the model of the Catholic party of Alsace, had had power in France in the inter-war years, they could have linked up with the Centre Party in the Rhineland and with Catholic Bavaria, with the Catholic parties of Italy and Austria 'to discuss projects of European Union which took shape only a quarter of a century later.' Instead came Hitler, backed by the new Protestant industrialists.

Yet this notion of a federal Europe is presented alongside another which stands in some contradiction to it, that of a resumption of French influence in Germany. For the German Empire created by Bismarck and its Emperor—quel parvenu!—M. de Pange has nothing good to say. For him Prussian militarism is rightly odious, and the Reich itself, whose only common possession was Alsace-Lorraine, a merely transient phenomenon. Not only did M. de Pange regard as possible after its fall the revival of the separate kingdoms and principalities—the old French illusion of 'The Germanies'—but also the possibility of France playing an active role in German affairs. How right in his view were the French negotiators at Westphalia in 1648 to insist that the links between Alsace and the Empire should remain, that thereby France might have a place in the deliberations of the Imperial Diet! But can the methods of 1648 mean anything in an age when the balance of forces has shifted so profoundly and when the sentiment of nationality has come to exercise so profound an influence? What can be build upon dynasticism in the twentieth century?

It would be unfair to M. de Pange to press the point too far, for clearly this argument is a secondary one and is partly brought in to criticize those Frenchmen who in his view were led by an exaggerated nationalism, and a wish to maintain an exclusive and narrow French outlook, to lose a chance of reconciliation with Germany on the morrow of 1918. The heart of the matter remains his particular view of European federation. Its military, economic and political institutions are hardly touched upon. From some asides on the proposed Anglo-French Union and its similarities with the Austro-Hungarian Monarchy, from his comparison of the Commonwealth with the League of Nations, and other references to federalism, one must assume that M. de Pange is no clearer than are most Continental students of what is implied by the acceptance of federalism under modern conditions. What is important to him, however, is not the institutions but the idea: the binding force is essentially a cultural one; and the cultural unity is that conferred by the common Catholicism of the lands in question. Republicanism of the French radical and anti-clerical variety, and continental socialism, which is close to it in spirit, are thus the principal internal enemies. It is a point of view which anyone is perfectly entitled to hold. But a few comments upon it will suggest themselves. It would mean not merely the direction of political development in France itself along certain lines, but also the maintenance of the division of Germany. For the Catholic majority which is Dr Adenauer's support is, of course, largely the accident of Germany's division along lines which leave the core of Protestant Germany on the Soviet side of the line. Much of the current support for the Bonn Government, and much of the opposition to it, are only understandable if this is kept in mind. It explains, too, the not surprising lukewarmness of the Dutch towards the federation scheme—they are nowhere mentioned in M. de Pange's book, but they can scarcely be excluded from the organization of Western Europe; and the Dutch Protestants can hardly feel at home in a union inspired along these lines. Something of the kind may also affect the attitude of Switzerland, a country which is mentioned, though somewhat obliquely. Finally, of course, the lack of a political movement in Britain corresponding to the Continental parties in which M. de Pange puts his trust adds another difficulty to those of fitting Britain into the scheme.

M. de Pange's views—and a summary must do them some injustice—are not of course shared by all those who support the movement for European Federation. But the preponderant roles of the Catholic Lorrainer, M. Schuman, and of the Catholic Rhinelander, Dr Adenauer, are a pointer to where some at least of its strength lies. It is a point of view which must be considered; and it will be obvious that to consider it and assess its potentialities it is necessary to take a much longer view of European history than is often customary. Centuries have gone to making up the complex of issues of which the problem of Alsace is typical. The difficulty is to keep this long history in perspective with the newer developments, the rise of Russia and the United States, the development of the British Commonwealth, the claims of new secular ideologies. There is a genuine unrest in Western Europe, a genuine dissatisfaction with existing political institutions, a genuine readiness for radical experiment. But it is not clear that this demand can be met by going behind the French Revolution. For better or for worse, the Reformation, the French Revolution, and for that matter the Russian Revolutions, are facts of history. Statesmanship must reckon with them if the remedies it proposes are not to be worse than the disease.

7

The 'Federal Solution' in its Application to Europe, Asia, and Africa[1]

IN the preface to his study *Federal Government*, which is dated July 1945, Professor K. C. Wheare referred to the fact that much of what he had written might soon be out of date because 'under the impact of war federal government was undergoing such strenuous testing, and such radical adaptation'.[2] What he failed to suggest was that in the post-war years the federal idea itself would enjoy a widespread popularity such as it had never known before.[3] While it is true that the war did bring about important changes in the practice of federalism in the four classic federations to which Professor Wheare's definition of federal government substantially though not entirely restricted his attention, and while it is significant that these changes were all in the same direction, namely, in favour of the central authority at the expense of the separate States, Provinces, or Cantons, all the three belligerent federations, the United States, Canada, Australia, and neutral Switzerland emerged from the war with political systems of the same fundamental kind as they had enjoyed (or tolerated) before. But in the subsequent eight years a number of new governments have arisen which at least claim the designation federal; and other federal structures are in process of construction.

[1] This paper provided the substance of a lecture given before the University of Leeds on March 12, 1953. It was originally printed in *Political Studies*, Vol 1, No 2, and is reproduced here by permission of the editor and The Clarendon Press, Oxford.

[2] K. C. Wheare, *Federal Government* (1st ed. 1946, Oxford University Press for Royal Institute of International Affairs), p. v.

[3] See for example, László Ledermann, *Fédération internationale: Idées de hier possibilités de demain* (Neuchâtel, 1950), and its useful short bibliography.

In the western hemisphere where the federal idea has made its modern home ever since the founding of the American republic there has been little room for it to expand. Brazil recovered in 1946 the federal form of government which it had lost through the *coup* of President Vargas in 1937; but nowhere in Latin America does genuine federalism flourish.[1] On the other hand, the movement towards federation among the British Caribbean colonies looks the most promising of all the potential federations in the Colonial Empire.[2]

In Europe the new federal constitutions are those of Western Germany and Yugoslavia.[3] In Asia, the constitution of the Republic of India is a federal one based on the Government of India Act of 1935.[4]

The constitution of Pakistan now being shaped will also be a federal one. Pending its adoption, Pakistan has also been using the machinery of the Government of India Act.[5] The most obvious reason for a federal system in the future lies in the separation of East Bengal from the rest of Pakistan by more than a thousand miles of land. But the diversities of race, language, and history are also factors which would probably have made for a federal system in any event. The recognition of Urdu as a State language for the whole country, although it is not the native language of any of its provincial units, is intended to provide a compensating national link. Even more

[1] A federal constitution may be, in practice, unitary, as indeed are the so-called federal constitutions of Mexico, Venezuela, Brazil and the Argentine': Wheare, *Modern Constitutions* (OUP, 1951), p. 30. The constitutions of Mexico (1917), Venezuela (1947), and Brazil (1946) will be found in Russell H. Fitzgibbon, ed., *The Constitutions of the Americas* (Chicago UP, 1948). The constitution of Argentina (1949) will be found in A. J. Peaslee, ed., *The Constitutions of the Nations* (Concord, NH, 1950), vol. i, pp. 63ff.

[2] The scheme now under discussion will be found in *Report of the British Caribbean Standing Closer Association Committee, 1948-9* (Col No 255, London, HMSO, 1950). See A. H. Birch, 'A British Caribbean Federation: The Next Dominion?', *Parliamentary Affairs*, vol iv, No 1, 1950.

[3] The Fundamental Law of the Federal Republic of Germany of May 23, 1949, and the constitution of the Popular Federative Republic of Yugoslavia of January 31, 1946, can conveniently be studied in B. Mirkine-Guetzévitch, ed., *Les Constitutions européennes* (Paris: Presses Universitaires de France, 2 vols, 1951). The latter was of course modelled on the constitution of the USSR of 1936 and was replaced by a new federal constitution voted on January 13, 1953.

[4] See *The Constitution of India* (Delhi, 1949). Cf. B. N. Banerjea, 'Le Fédéralisme dans la constitution indienne', *Revue française de science politique*, July-Sept. 1951.

[5] Richard Symonds, *The Making of Pakistan* (London, 1950), chap. vii.

important is the religious link of Islam.[1] Indeed, Pakistan will be unique among federations in formally deriving its constitutional and legal systems from the dogmas of a religious faith.[2] Burma also claims to be a federal State, and a nominally federal constitution has been promulgated for Malaya.[3]

On December 27, 1949, sovereignty in what had hitherto been the Dutch East Indies was transferred to the United States of Indonesia, created with a draft federal constitution apparently agreed upon between the Dutch and the Indonesians. The subsequent outbreak of a series of revolts in which the Indonesians suspected the Dutch of being indirectly concerned strengthened their feeling that the federal constitution had been imposed on them in order to weaken their control over outlying areas for the benefit of the Dutch. On August 14th the federal constitution, which had never gone into effect, was abandoned for a new unitary one, and the United States

---

[1] Ajit Kumar Sen, 'The New Federalism in Pakistan', *Parliamentary Affairs*, vol iv, No 1, 1950.

[2] The future constitution will presumably be based upon the *Report of the Basic Principles Committee* (Karachi, 1952). The Committee was appointed by the Constituent Assembly on March 12, 1949, and reported on December 22, 1952. The proposals bear a close resemblance as regards machinery of government and the allocation of functions to the constitution of India. The geographical division of Pakistan is recognized by the fact that both in the popularly elected House of the People, and in the House of Units, to be elected by the provincial legislatures, it is provided that East Bengal as a whole should have as many members as the nine units of West Pakistan taken together. The residuary powers which lie in the Union in India were to lie in the Federation in Pakistan, though four members of the Committee dissented on this point. The report does not deal with the vital question of the allocation of financial resources between the Federal Government and the Units. On the situation in the transitional period see the paper read by Dr S. M. Akhtar at the Third All-Pakistan Economic Conference at Karachi, February 11-13, 1952, and published as *Distribution of Revenue Resources between the Centre and the Provinces* (Lahore, 1952). I am indebted to Professor Gerard M. Friters, Professor of Political Science at the University of the Panjab, Lahore, for providing me with copies of the report and of Dr Akhtar's paper and for other information on recent developments in Pakistan.

[3] The constitution of the Union of Burma adopted on September 24, 1947, is given in Peaslee, op. cit., vol i, pp. 250-93. Burma's independence was proclaimed on January 4, 1948. See Peter Calvocoressi, *Survey of International Affairs, 1947-8* (London, OUP for RIIA, 1952), pp. 439ff. On developments in Malaya see ibid, pp. 414ff. The basic document is *The Federation of Malaya Order in Council 1948* (No 108, London: HMSO, 1948). This replaced the Malayan Union of April 1, 1946. The working of the federal constitution has been arrested by the 'emergency' due to terrorist activities by Communists.

of Indonesia became the Republic of Indonesia.[1] In Africa, Nigeria has now a federal constitution in operation despite the fact that it has not yet attained full self-government.[2]

In all these instances the impetus to change has arisen from the war and its consequences. The choice of a federal form for Western Germany was not merely a return to some of the external forms of the Weimar Republic swept away by Hitler.[3] It also reflects the view of some Germans, and of the Western Allies, that over-centralization was a definite factor in accelerating the warlike tendencies of the Third Reich. In Yugoslavia the war swept away the royal dictatorship which King Alexander had instituted in 1929 as a check upon the centrifugal tendency of his multi-national realm.[4] By so doing it opened the way for experiments in Communist constitutionalism in both its orthodox and its Titoist form.[5] In Asia, the Japanese conquest

[1] For information on the constitutional development of Indonesia I am indebted to Mr C. A. Fisher, of University College, Leicester. Cf. O. Renier, 'Towards the United States of Indonesia', World Affairs, October 1949.

[2] See Nigeria (Constitution) Order in Council June 29, 1951 (London: HMSO, 1951). On this constitution see 'Nigerian Democracy: Federal Aspects of the New Constitution', The Times, July 2, 1952; 'Nigeria under the Macpherson Constitution', The World Today, January 1953.

[3] It must be noted that a study of the workings of the Weimar constitution of 1919 leads Professor Wheare to the undoubtedly correct conclusion that 'the Weimar Republic does not provide us with an example of federal government' (Federal Government, p. 26).

[4] On the Yugoslav position before the war see Hugh Seton-Watson, Eastern Europe between the Wars (Cambridge, 1945), pp. 217-21.

[5] From the point of view of the amateur of federalism, the most important change in the constitution of Yugoslavia is the replacement of the Council of Nationalities as the second chamber of the federation by a Council of Producers. A number of deputies to the first chamber will, however, be elected in future by the legislatures of the constituent units of the federation, and these will meet separately as a Council of Nationalities whenever the agenda of the Federal Parliament contains proposals affecting the constitutional position of the republics. The new executive, the Federal Executive Council, will, under the constitution, have to contain members from all the republics. This point is of particular interest since, although no such provision exists in the 'classic' federal constitutions, their conventions have tended towards a federalization of the executive. Canada is perhaps the best example: 'The Canadian Cabinet by convention is federal in being always designed to represent the principal races, religions, and regions of the country': Alexander Brady, Democracy in the Dominions (Toronto, 1947), pp. 76-7. I am indebted to Mr A. Sokorac, Press Counsellor to the London Embassy of the Federative People's Republic of Yugoslavia, for documents on the constitutional changes in Yugoslavia.

84

and occupation helped to bring about the conditions for Burmese and Indonesian independence and quickened the pace of constitutional change in Malaya. The experiences of the war also had their impact on the constitutional development of the Indian sub-continent despite the fact that the Japanese were turned back at its gates. And even in tropical Africa outside the war zones altogether, the distant repercussions of the conflict must be reckoned among the factors leading to a weakening of direct colonial rule and hence to the necessity for new constitutional experiments.

Even this enumeration of new federal constitutions does not exhaust the contribution of the last few years to the material available to the student of federalism. It is unlikely, indeed, that anyone will be found in this country who would accept the French Union as being a product or an extension of the federal idea. And scepticism on this point is hardened when one finds that it is classified in this respect with the British Commonwealth.[1] If there is any political concept that does not assist one to understand either the machinery or the spirit of the Commonwealth, it is that of federalism. And although in the High Council and Assembly of the French Union there exist what might be described as embryonic federal institutions, nothing in the post-war history of the relations between France and its overseas territories suggests the possibility of a solution for their problems being found in the establishment of a genuine federal link. It is, however, within the Commonwealth that the most conspicuous efforts have been made or proposed for applying the idea of federalism to the problems of the multi-national, or, as it is now styled, the plural society.

The use of the federal formula to solve the problem of how to give any kind of self-government to societies in which different races mix but do not mingle is often dismissed in a relatively cavalier fashion.[2] History does indeed provide a number of examples where federal proposals have had to be abandoned in favour of the outright partition of the country concerned. One example could be taken

---

[1] For a defence of the treatment of the French Union and the British Commonwealth under this head see Georges Burdeau, *Traité de science politique* (Paris: Librairie Générale de Droit et de Jurisprudence, 1949), vol ii, Part III, chap. 3, 'Les extensions du fédéralisme', pp. 501-39. Part VIII of the French Constitution of October 27, 1946, which deals with the French Union will be found in Mirkine-Guetzévitch, op. cit., vol ii, pp. 435-7.

[2] See, for example, *Problems of Parliamentary Government in Colonies* (Hansard Society, 1953), pp. 64-6.

from the history of Palestine under the British mandate.[1] Another and on a larger scale is that of British India. The Provincial Governments set up in 1937 under the 1935 Act put Moslem minorities under Hindu majorities; it was the experience of this situation that brought the Moslems round from joining in the demand for an independent India to insisting upon a separate State of their own. It is not surprising that some students of colonial affairs regard every attempt to solve the problems of a plural society in this way or indeed in any constitutional way as foredoomed to failure:

> In all the plural societies (writes an expert on Malaya), in Asia as well as Africa, we seem to be expecting radically different peoples to co-operate peaceably and rationally to make adjustments in their societies which in the extremely chequered histories of most nations, were almost always made by a resort to force. Peoples of different cultures, who neither inter-marry nor inter-dine, will not co-operate within a single political unit simply because we want them to co-operate.[2]

But it is hard to see what alternative there is to some form of constitutional device, at least drawing inspiration from federal sources, in those cases — and they are the most common — where the rude surgery of partition is wholly impracticable. It was possible to divide off Pakistan from India at terrible cost in human suffering.[3] But in Malaya geographical separation of the races would not be possible: and in the plural societies of Africa the economic interdependence of white and black makes a recourse to partition inconceivable. If there is to be a future for the multi-racial societies of Africa, it can only be by discovering some constitutional device which will remove

[1] One of the best accounts of the problems of a plural society from the point of view of devising a government for it is to be found in the Report of the Palestine Royal Commission of 1937 (Cmd. 5479, 1937).

[2] F. G. Carnell, 'British Policy in Malaya', *Political Quarterly*, vol xxiii, No 3, 1952. Cf. the statement by Mohammed Ali Jinnah, subsequently first Governor-General of Pakistan, to the 1940 session of the Moslem League at Lahore: 'The Hindus and Muslims belong to two different religious philosophies, social customs, literatures. They neither intermarry nor interdine, and indeed they belong to two different civilizations which are based on conflicting ideas and conceptions. . . . To yoke together two such nations under a single state, one as a numerical minority, and the other as a majority, must lead to growing discontent and final destruction of any fabric that may be so built up for government of such a state.' Quoted by Symonds, op. cit., pp. 56-7.

[3] For one aspect of the price paid for partition as seen from the vantage point of the Punjab see the article 'The Price of Circumstance', by Lieut-Col D. G. H. de la Fargue, *The Fortnightly*, January 1953.

the fears that all such societies have shown as soon as the prospect of democratic government has appeared on the horizon.

At present, the superior wealth and skill of the white settler populations and to a lesser extent of Asiatic immigrants, where these exist in considerable numbers, have the effect of framing the question of what is to be done in terms of protecting the rights of the Africans —the numerical majority—even if the only method suggested is that of avoiding the whole issue by perpetuating control by the home government. In a longer view, however, and taking Africa as a whole in relation to the rest of the world, it is the white settlers who might seem in the greatest need of guarantees. For the plural societies of Africa differ from those of Asia in the much wider discrepancy in size between the different groups concerned. In Malaya as a whole the Malays constitute 43 per cent of the population, the Chinese 44 per cent, and the Indians 10 per cent. If Singapore be omitted, as it is from the federation, the respective percentages are 49, 38, and 10.[1] But in the Union of South Africa the white inhabitants account for only 1 in 5 of the population, in Southern Rhodesia for 1 in 20, in Central Africa as a whole for 1 in 40, in East Africa for 1 in 400. To undertake to apply the federal formula to a whole or part of this area is thus to use it for a purpose and in circumstances which have no parallel in the past and to which much of the classic discussion of federalism is irrelevant.[2] This fact helps to explain the several unique features of the plans put forward for the federation of Central Africa—that is of Southern Rhodesia, Northern Rhodesia,

[1] F. G. Carnell, 'Malayan Citizenship Legislation', *The International and Comparative Law Quarterly*, October 1952.

[2] The federation proposals for the British Caribbean colonies have also run into the problem of the plural society, though in a less intense form. 'The East Indians', we are told, 'who form almost half of the population of British Guiana and are the second largest racial group in Trinidad view federation with suspicion. In Trinidad, particularly, they are becoming increasingly race conscious. They see the possibility of being swamped in a predominantly African dominion and losing the advantages of a rising birth-rate and spreading literacy': article on 'Closer Caribbean Union', *The Times*, April 13, 1950, reprinted in the pamphlet *The British Caribbean* (London, *The Times*, 1950), pp. 9-10. British Guiana will consequently not take part in the discussions on federation due to be held in London in the early summer of 1953. But this has not been the fundamental issue, and the discussions at the Montego Bay Conference in September 1947 provide an excellent modern example of the classic debate on the merits and demerits of federation: *Conference on the Closer Association of the British West Indian Colonies*, Part 2, *Proceedings* (Colonial No 218) (London: HMSO, 1948).

and Nyasaland.[1] Its proposed form, and the opposition to it from sections of the white settler population and spokesmen for the Africans, have both been influenced by another feature almost without precedent in the history of federalism—the different constitutional and political status which the proposed units enjoy at present and which it is feared would be compromised even under a scheme of federation designed to perpetuate them.[2]

What a federal scheme in such a situation is intended to perform is obviously different from that which is the object in cases where the units of the federation are intended to correspond to racial, linguistic, religious, or other cultural diversities existing between their respective populations. On the contrary, it is taken for granted that there will be more than one racial group in each: and the difference will consist in the different patterns which the relations of such groups to each other will continue to display and in the consequent differences between their policies. It is hoped that the advantages of a larger and more varied economic unit can be combined with the political advantages which such continued differentiation appears to offer from the differing viewpoints of the Africans of Northern Rhodesia and Nyasaland and the settlers of Southern Rhodesia.[3]

[1] The proposal for extending the federal plan to include East Africa—the so-called 'Capricorn Africa' scheme—hardly seems to have reached a stage to warrant consideration as a federal experiment. For the proposals of the 'Capricorn Africa Society' see The Times, December 8, 1952. The existing East African High Commission is simply a device for the performance of certain functions which it is thought can best be managed jointly on behalf of the three territories concerned—Kenya, Uganda, and Tanganyika. See The East Africa (High Commission) Order in Council, 1947 (Statutory Rules and Orders, 1947, No 2863). It is not a federal government in any ordinary sense. For a brief outline of the history of the scheme for a Central African Federation see Report by the Conference on Federation (held in London in January 1953), Cmd. 8573.

[2] There is a distinction in status between the three types of States which are federated in the Republic of India. But the special element of continued dependence upon an external Power is lacking. Malaya affords an even more dubious precedent.

[3] For the constitutional proposals of the London Conference of April-May 1952 see Southern Rhodesia, Northern Rhodesia and Nyasaland: Draft Federal Scheme (Cmd. 8573, 1952) and my own comments in 'Federation in Africa', The Times, June 19, 1952. The draft scheme was expanded by the reports of special commissions set up by the London Conference to study the questions of a civil service, a judiciary, and fiscal arrangements appropriate to the proposed federation. These were published on October 29, 1952 (Cmd. 8673, 8671, and 8672).

As in the case of most other federal situations in the past, the main protagonists of federation in Central Africa—the leaders of the settler communities of the two Rhodesias—could have achieved what they hoped for from federation from a unitary scheme of government. The federal idea was adopted, not for its own sake, but because it seemed to provide the only way of getting round the objections of the British Government to any scheme of union—objections deriving from their unwillingness to see the settlers have the final word in the future treatment of the Africans of Northern Rhodesia and Nyasaland. It did not, however, succeed in disarming opposition on these grounds, nor the opposition of some of the Europeans of Southern Rhodesia who felt that the safeguards adopted in the scheme for the protection of African rights meant an infringement of their own paramount right of self-government.[1]

In view of the fact that no proposal likely to commend itself to the Europeans of the Rhodesias seemed to have any prospect of being accepted by vocal African opinion, or by those in Britain who claimed to represent African opinion, a tendency emerged during the discussions of the draft scheme of June 1952 to argue that the economic objects of the partisans of federation could in fact be achieved without any alteration in the political relations between the three territories.[2] It was also suggested that closer co-operation in the economic field through 'joint executive instruments' might

[1] A brief statement of the argument for federation will be found in the pamphlet *Central African Federation: The only way to Partnership between the Races*, published by the London Committee of the United Central Africa Association (1952). The opposition to the proposals as harmful to the interests of Africans can be studied in the publications and speeches sponsored by the African Bureau. See also the letters from African delegates from Northern Rhodesia and Nyasaland in *The Times*, April 29, 1952 and February 5, 1953. The opposition of some elements among the European population of Southern Rhodesia was voiced by the 'Rhodesia League', whose policy was that Northern Rhodesia should be assisted to achieve the same measure of (white) self-government as Southern Rhodesia and that the two territories should then be amalgamated. See the speech at Salisbury (Rhodesia) by Sir Ernest Guest, reported in *The Times*, November 14, 1952. A memorandum summarizing the League's objections to the draft scheme was summarized in *The Times*, January 1, 1952. For British political opinion see the House of Commons debate on July 24, 1952. A summary of the whole discussion up to the opening of the second London Conference on January 1, 1952, appeared in an article in *The Times* on that date entitled 'Central African Federation'.

[2] See, for example, the letter from the former Secretary of State for the Colonies, Mr A. Creech Jones, *The Times*, January 13, 1953.

form a prelude to an implementation of a full federal scheme by consent at some later date.[1]

This proposal for what is sometimes known as the 'functional' as opposed to the political approach to federation is an interesting example of the limited number of variations that can be played on the federal theme.[2]

The London Conference of January 1953 concerned itself, however, exclusively with amending and amplifying the original draft constitution.[3] A new draft was published on February 5th and in most respects followed closely the lines of the original scheme.[4] The essential reason why the federal form of government rather than amalgamation had been adopted, and the principle followed in the allocation of powers, were made amply clear in the claim that the powers left to the territories included those 'most closely affecting the daily life of the African people.[5] The transfer (between the two drafts) of European agriculture in Southern Rhodesia to the federal list indicated the willingness of the Europeans to use the federal machinery wherever possible.[6]

The institutions of the proposed federation have also had to be devised so as to provide adequate safeguards for the two communities. Apart from the complicated scheme of representation in the Federal Legislature, the main instrument of protection for the Africans is the 'African Affairs Board'. In the original scheme this was an in-

[1] See the letter from Professor Vincent Harlow, ibid, January 12, 1953.

[2] The suggestion that the policy of federation should be adopted in principle, but that some later date should be chosen to implement it, did not commend itself to the second London Conference which went ahead with the revision of the draft scheme. It is possible that the unwillingness to consider delay may have been due to the fear that, if federation were to prove impossible, Southern Rhodesia might fall back upon a policy of closer association with the Union of South Africa with all that this implied in its racial and other policies. This external political aspect of the proposed federation of Central Africa figured hardly at all in the public discussions of the subject for obvious reasons. In so far as it was germane to the issue it provided yet another parallel to the classic federal situation, that of Canada immediately prior to federation, for instance.

[3] Cmd. 8753.

[4] The Federal Scheme (Cmd. 8754).

[5] Cmd. 8753, p. 6.

[6] The legislative powers are dealt with in two lists: the federal and the concurrent. Residuary powers rest with the territories. This suggests also a greater measure of genuine federalism than in, for example, the Constitution of India with its three lists and with the residuary powers retained by the federal Parliament.

dependent board with the primary function of making 'such representations in relation to any matter within the legislative or executive authority of the Federation as the Board may consider to be desirable in the interests of Africans'. This would enable the Governor-General's powers of reservation to be called into play in case of legislation 'differentiating' against Africans. Under the revised scheme the powers of the Board remain unchanged, but it ceases to be an external body, and becomes a standing committee of the Federal Legislature composed of Africans and of Europeans specially elected or appointed to look after African interests. Although the argument that the Board can function better from within the federal legislature is readily understandable, some of the criticisms of the original proposal still stand. Except for some rather ill-defined advisory powers in relation to the Territorial Governments, the Board remains a brake on bad government rather than a driving force for good government: and for the proper performance of even its negative functions the inclusion of a Bill of Rights and of 'Directive Principles of State Policy' on the Indian model would have been desirable, particularly since such measures of 'differentiation' as the 'colour-bar' lie at the root of much of the African objection to the federal scheme.[1] Whether these objections and opposition among the Europeans of Southern Rhodesia will prevent the scheme being implemented, and thus cause the British Government to abandon all its efforts at promoting such a federation for the present, cannot be foreseen at the time of writing.[2] It is worth pointing out that an attempt has been made to allay some fears by making it impossible for the federation to amend the distribution of powers under the federal scheme for ten years without the consent of all three territorial legislatures having previously been obtained for the introduction of such an amendment in the usual form of a Bill before the federal legislature. A conference for the revision of the constitution is to be called within not less than seven or more than nine years of the present one coming into force; the constitution must therefore be thought of as no more than a transitional one.

Whereas in Asia and Africa federalism has been thought of as a solution to the political problems of countries which have previously been held together by external imperial rule, in Europe it has been

[1] The 'Directive Principles' in the Indian constitution were derived from Republican Spain via Eire. (Ivor Jennings and C. M. Young, *Constitutional Laws of the Commonwealth*, 1952, p. 365). They have thus no necessary connection with federalism.

[2] For the attitude of the United Kingdom Government see Cmd. 8753, p. 7.

a question of bringing within a federal framework units of government hitherto separate and sovereign. There has been widespread
acceptance of the dictum of John Stuart Mill that 'when the conditions exist for the formation of efficient and durable Federal Unions,
the multiplication of them is always a benefit to the world'.[1] The
positive attempts at embodying this belief in new federal institutions
have been confined to Western Europe; but if we may judge from
the war-time negotiations between some of the exiled East European
countries, and from developments in the Balkans prior to the split
between Yugoslavia and the Soviet Union, similar efforts might
well have been now in progress in Eastern Europe as well but for
understandable Soviet opposition.[2]

The main purpose of such efforts at federation by agglomeration
is clear enough and was again clearly stated by Mill:

> By diminishing the number of those petty States which are
> not equal to their own defence, it weakens the temptations to
> an aggressive policy, whether working directly through arms,
> or through the prestige of superior power.[3]

In so far as the problem has merely been one of creating new
federal or quasi-federal institutions, the amount achieved and the
speed of the achievement, particularly since the hardening of relations between the Soviet Union and the West in 1948, have been
impressive enough. By the end of 1952 there were, in addition to
the Council of Europe, the Coal and Steel Community (the Schuman
Plan Organization) and the still unratified European Defence Community. Discussion was also in progress on draft constitutional proposals for a Political Community to absorb the Coal and Steel and
the Defence Communities and thus to create out of 'Little Europe' —
France, Western Germany, Italy, Holland, Belgium, and Luxembourg
— what would be something approaching a genuine federal system.[4]

[1] J. S. Mill, *Representative Government* (ed. R. B. McCallum, Oxford, 1946),
p. 305.

[2] See on this point Hugh Seton-Watson, *The East European Revolution*
(London, 1950), pp. 354-8.

[3] Mill, loc. cit.

[4] See the diagram illustrating the interrelationship of these organizations,
actual and proposed, in the article 'Big Europe and Little Europe', *The Econo-
mist*, January 10, 1953. On the Council of Europe and the Schuman Plan see
the account in G. Schwarzenberger, *Power Politics*, 2nd ed. (London, 1951),
pp. 782-803. The Council of Europe Statute of May 5, 1949, is printed as Cmd.
7778; cf. *Concise Handbook of the Council of Europe* (Strasbourg, 1951).
The Schuman Plan was first proposed in a note from the French Government

The draft treaty or statute for a Political Community had been drawn up by a committee appointed in September 1952 by the Coal and Steel Assembly, which had expanded itself into an *ad hoc* Assembly for the purpose of framing such a scheme by admitting nine observers from countries outside the Schuman Plan.[1] It was published on December 19, 1952.[2]

The statute described the proposed European Political Community as 'an indissoluble supra-national political community, based on the union of peoples' which would 'in international relations . . . possess the juridical personality necessary for the exercise of its functions and the attainment of its aims'. Its 'Parliament' was to have the typical federal structure: a 'Chamber of Peoples' directly elected by universal suffrage and a 'Senate' elected by national parlia-

to the British Government on May 9, 1950. Subsequent interchanges of views failed to persuade the United Kingdom to adhere to the organization, although a considerable measure of co-operation was envisaged. See *Anglo-French Discussions regarding French proposals for the Western European Coal, Iron and Steel Industries, May-June, 1950* (Cmd. 7970). The six countries of 'Little Europe' signed the Schuman Plan Treaty on April 18, 1951. Cf. 'P. R.', 'Quelques aspects constitutionnels du Plan Schuman', *Revue du Droit Public et de la Science Politique*, vol lxvii, No 1, January-March 1951; Paul Reuter, 'La Conception du Pouvoir politique dans le Plan Schuman', *Revue française de science politique*, July-September 1951. There are useful examinations of the tensions that have developed over attempts to use the Council of Europe as a step towards a federal system in J. Boulouis, 'Les Rapports de l'Assemblée Consultative et du Comité des Ministres du Conseil de l'Europe', *Revue du Droit Public et de la Science Politique*, vol lxviii, No 1, January-March 1952, and M. Mouskhély, 'Le Mandat des Représentants à l'Assemblée Consultative du Conseil de l'Europe', ibid, vol lxviii, No 3, July-September 1952. The idea of a European Defence Community was given official form in a Declaration of the French Government of October 24, 1950. The treaty for a European Defence Community was signed at Paris on May 27, 1952. Extracts from it are printed as an appendix to the useful analysis by G. Héraud, 'La Communauté européenne de défense dans ses relations avec l'alliance atlantique et le "fédéralisme fonctionnel" du continent', *Revue du Droit Public et de la Science Politique*, vol xvliii, No 4, October-December 1952. A summary of the treaty and of related documents is given in the Appendix to *Chronology of International Events and Documents* (RIIA), vol viii, No 11.

[1] *Council of Europe News* (Strasbourg), October 1, 1952. The development was not out of harmony with the essential idea of the Schuman Plan, which was, in the words of the French Government's communiqué of May 9, 1950, to 'build the first concrete foundation of the European federation which is indispensable to the preservation of peace' (Cmd. 7970, p. 4).

[2] *Assemblée Ad Hoc*, Doc AA/CC (3) PV 10, Annexes 1, 2, 3 (mim), Paris, December 19, 1952. The substance of the plan was reproduced in *The Times*, January 7, 1953.

ments. In each house the number of seats for each country was to be fixed in an agreed ratio. There was to be a dual executive composed of a European Executive Council responsible to the Parliament of the Community, and exercising its allotted functions independently of the national governments like the High Authority of the Schuman Plan, and a Council of Ministers to replace the Councils of Ministers of the Schuman Plan and of the European Defence Community. The Council would consequently require a two-thirds majority for most of its decisions, and unanimity when its functions went beyond those of the Councils of the Coal and Steel and Defence Communities. The powers would in the first place be confined to the co-ordination of foreign policy and to the progressive establishment of a common market. The former would be exercised through the conclusion of agreements (on subjects allotted to it by the Statute and by subsequent amendments to the Statute) and by the exercise of a veto power over agreements inconsistent with its purposes entered into by the member-States.[1] The question of the Community's powers in regard to the creation of a common market would be the subject of a special protocol which would be submitted for ratification separately from the Statute, and which would not form part of it.

These proposals were vigorously discussed by the *Ad Hoc* Assembly at Strasbourg at a meeting at Strasbourg from January 7 to 10, 1953, and it approved certain amendments for the drafting committee to take into consideration before presenting their final report to the Assembly on March 1st. These included a provision that representation in the Lower House should be on the basis of population, which meant reducing the number of members from the smaller countries. The Executive Council, enlarged from seven to ten members, would be the sole executive: the Council of Foreign Ministers would be outside it, though it would still have to be consulted. The Council of Europe also discussed the draft statute at a special session at Strasbourg from January 14th to 17th. It approved various proposals for closer co-ordination between the proposed Community and the Council of Europe, in addition to any specific

---

[1] The question of how far federal governments can extend their internal authority by the use of the treaty power has increasingly exercised students of federalism with the great growth of international organizations of different kinds. See J. P. Nettl, 'The Treaty Enforcement Power in Federal Constitutions', *Canadian Bar Review*, December 1950. Under Art 253 of the constitution of India the Federal Parliament is given specific powers to legislate to give effect to international agreements irrespective of the division of powers between the Union and the States.

arrangements that the Community might enter into with other States. This move met with opposition from those who, like M. Paul-Henri Spaak, of Belgium, the President of the Coal and Steel Assembly and of the *Ad Hoc* Assembly, feared that the progress of the new Community towards a genuinely federal structure would be slowed down by those members of the Council of Europe who had always resisted attempts to turn that body in a federal direction.[1]

It is not possible in this paper to take the story of Europe's attempt towards a federal system farther: but enough has happened already to suggest that many of the preconceptions which were held by its sponsors have proved ill founded.[2]

In the first place, the main object, that of creating a barrier to aggression, is clearly something beyond the strength of Western Europe, even supposing Great Britain were to withdraw its objections to full participation in the proposed federal institutions. This barrier cannot be created without the United States, and is, in fact, being created in co-operation with it through the machinery of the North Atlantic Treaty of April 4, 1949, which followed upon the Brussels Treaty of March 17, 1948, between Great Britain, France, and the Benelux Powers.[3] Despite expressions of American approval of federalism in general, there is no reason to dispute the conclusions of a recent study which declares that 'nothing that has happened in the history of NATO so far shows either a conscious desire or an

---

[1] The position of M. Spaak, who had resigned from the Presidency of the Council of Europe on December 11, 1951, because of such resistance, was curious inasmuch as he was on record as hostile to the idea of a 'Little Europe', that is to say, a federation excluding Britain. Speaking in London on October 30, 1950, he said that if 'Great Britain remained outside, the Scandinavian States would do the same and probably the Benelux countries also; it would mean that the union of Europe would amount to a triple alliance between Italy, France and Germany. I am absolutely opposed to this idea. Such an alliance could not be considered as representative of Europe, it would be a caricature of Europe, a dangerous triple alliance, an unbalanced fraction of the whole': P.-H. Spaak, *Strasbourg: the Second Year* (Stevenson Memorial Lecture, No 2, London, 1952), p. 24.

[2] A useful compendium of British opinion on the whole question will be found in 'Aspects and Problems of European Union', the title of the September 1952 issue of *The Twentieth Century*.

[3] See *Collective Defence under the Brussels and North Atlantic Treaties*, Cmd. 7883 (1950). The genesis of these arrangements is dealt with in *Defence in the Cold War*, a report by a Chatham House Study Group (London, 1950). The original structure of NATO, with relevant documents, can be found in *The Nato Handbook*, prepared by the Nato Information Service (London, January 1952).

unconscious tendency among members to develop federal institutions or to imitate the forms of previous confederations'.[1] Serious American opinion does not expect to see the merging of American sovereignty to any degree in a supra-national body. On the other hand, there is obviously a strong conviction in some quarters that efficiency in using the common resources of the free world 'demands the closest kind of political and economic co-operation, particularly in the area of Western Europe. For if the free nations of this region were really a unit, tremendous benefits would accrue to them individually and to NATO.'[2]

For this reason, the argument so often drawn from the experience of the Founding Fathers of the United States of America has a double irrelevance.[3] The objects which they sought to achieve could not now be achieved by the only grouping of nations for which federation is conceivable: and this is as true of the economic as of the military needs of Western Europe.[4] In the second place, they were seeking to give a common government to States which had till recently owed allegiance to a common Crown and been subordinate to a single imperial government and between whom some form of link had never ceased to exist.[5] What is now being attempted is to place under a Federal Government a group of nations with different histories, different and often conflicting interests, different relations with the non-European world, and widely different political out-

---

[1] *Atlantic Alliance*, a report by a Chatham House Study Group (London, 1952), p. 43. Cf. ibid, pp. 102-7. On the more recent functioning of the organization see the two articles 'NATO Defence Structure' (*The Times*, December 12, 13, 1952).

[2] Supreme Allied Commander Europe, *First Annual Report* (Paris, SHAPE, April 2, 1952), p. 25.

[3] The argument is constantly drawn upon in the series of works in which Mr Lionel Curtis advocates a federal solution to current international problems: *Decision* (1941); *Action* (1942); *Faith and Works* (1943); *The Way to Peace* (n.d.? 1944); *World Revolution in the Cause of Peace* (1949); *The Open Road to Freedom* (1951). The philosophical and historical background of the argument will be found in the same author's *Civitas Dei* (new ed. 1951). In changing circumstances Mr Curtis has been compelled to envisage different memberships for his proposed union; but he has never shifted from the principal point that nothing but a real surrender of sovereignty on the major issues will suffice.

[4] See for a British expression of this view, Lionel Robbins, 'Towards the Atlantic Community', *Lloyds Bank Review*, July 1950.

[5] I have dealt with the fallacies of this analogy in my article, 'European Association', *The Times*, May 4, 1950, reprinted *supra*, pp. 65 ff.

looks. For such a task history appears to provide no precedent.[1]

On one point only there seems to be some approximation to the conditions applying to successful movements towards federation in the past. The latter have all been the work, in effect, of a party organization extending across the boundaries of the several units. The strongly Catholic-Democratic flavour of the politics of the three principal architects of the 'Little Europe' scheme, M. Schuman, Dr Adenauer, and Signor de Gasperi, has obviously proved of great assistance in providing them with a common meeting-ground. But this very fact is also a source of weakness in arousing party and doctrinal suspicions to add to the existing national ones: and the difficulty of overcoming such objections is enhanced by the fact that the present strength of Catholic influence in the German Federal Republic is a consequence of the partition of Germany and would disappear if the Germans were to be successful in the struggle for reunion. Nor do the affiliations of the three political parties concerned imply anything like the same intimacy as existed between the leaders of the movement towards giving the American Confederation the additional powers of the new constitution.

If it were merely that precedents for success were lacking, there would be no reason for the enthusiasts for federation to lose heart. They could continue to repeat their slogan: 'No Europe without a Common Sovereignty', and brand as reactionaries all who dissented from their claims.[2] More serious is the question of whether their own advocacy of the federal solution has not been based upon a misconception of what is entailed by a federal system under modern conditions.

[1] Switzerland comes nearest to providing an example of federation by the agglomeration of separate units not previously in political connection with each other: but the actual origins of the original Confederation remain obscure. See E. Bonjour, H. S. Offler, and G. R. Potter, *A Short History of Switzerland* (Oxford, 1952). The more recent constitutional development of Switzerland is dealt with in detail by W. E. Rappard in his *La Constitution Fédérale de la Suisse, 1848-1948* (Neuchâtel, 1948).

[2] 'Pas d'Europe sans souveraineté commune', the title of an article by Jacques Chaban-Delmas, a member of the Strasbourg Assembly, in *La Vie Française*, January 4, 1952. Cf. the pamphlet *European Federation Now*, published by the European Union of Federalists (Paris, December 1951). The monthly publications, *Fédération* and *Le Bulletin fédéraliste*, both published in Paris, give an adequate presentation of the federalist approach to current political problems in France and abroad. For the expectations held of the federal approach in the immediate post-war period see the symposium, *La Bataille de la Paix: Les Chances du Fédéralisme* (Paris, Éditions du Monde Nouveau, 1947).

G   97

In the nineteenth century it was still possible to believe that a federal system could make a logical distinction between matters appropriate for dealing with at the federal level and matters suitable for the units to continue to handle. One could say that 'a Federal Union, in short, will form one State in relation to other powers, but many States as regards its internal administration';[1] or even more simply: 'whatever concerns the nation as a whole should be placed under the control of the national government'.[2] All this was perfectly acceptable so long as governments were substantially concerned only with the preservation of the peace against internal and external troubles and with providing the minimum legal framework within which individual economic enterprise could function. But with the abandonment of *laissez-faire* in favour of collectivism under one name or another this situation has ceased to exist. The modern democratic electorate takes no such narrow view of the responsibilities of its rulers. They have to provide not merely law and order and defence, but also social welfare services and above all 'full employment'. The latter objectives can hardly be achieved unless governments have full powers of legislation over the whole economic and fiscal field. It is for this reason that each new federation created has tended to allot more powers to the centre than its predecessors and that within every existing federation the centralizing tendency has been steadily at work and with ever increasing speed.[3]

It is not at all surprising that societies that expect so much from their governments should demand that these governments be as efficient as possible, nor that they should act upon the implications of the dictum that 'federation is an extravagant and inefficient form of government to be justified only where a closer form of organization is politically impracticable'.[4] It seems strange at first sight, therefore, that this argument should not be applied to the international field. In part the explanation would seem to be that the lessons of federation in the internal field have not been assimilated in international thinking. When in 1949 the Assembly of the Council of

[1] E. A. Freeman, *History of Federal Government*, vol i (1863), 2nd ed., 1893, p. 3. A constitution for an international federation on this basis has actually been drafted by Professor H. G. Hanbury and is printed as an appendix to Lionel Curtis's *The Open Road to Freedom* (1950).

[2] A. V. Dicey, *The Law of the Constitution*, 7th ed., 1908, p. 139.

[3] For an examination of this tendency with special reference to Switzerland see Otto Kirchheimer, 'The Decline of Intra-State Federalism in Western Europe', *World Politics*, April 1951.

[4] Jennings and Young, *Constitutional Laws of the Commonwealth*, p. 343.

Europe committed itself to the view that a European political authority was desirable 'with limited functions but real powers' or when in 1950 this was interpreted to mean that specialized authorities should be set up within the framework of the Council to be 'competent respectively in the political, economic, social, legal, and cultural fields', it was not at all clear that the supporters of such resolutions understood the interdependence under modern conditions of almost all the aspects of government.[1] It has yet to be seen whether the Governments of Little Europe can fulfil their own plans in the economic and social field when deprived by the Schuman Plan of direct control over such a great sector of the economy as is represented by coal and steel, or whether, conversely, the Schuman Plan's objectives can be attained when the High Authority lacks powers to deal with the social and fiscal repercussions, for instance, of any major changes it may wish to bring about within its own sphere of competence

On the defence side the position is even more paradoxical, as is shown by the delay in ratifying the EDC treaty whose future remains obscure at the time of writing. Here the real impetus has come from outside Europe altogether, from the decision by the United States that the defence of the West demanded a measure of German rearmament, and from the resistance of opinion outside Germany to the prospect of a German national army. And quite apart from such direct fears of a repetition of past events there is the fact that a unification of defence seems almost meaningless without a unified foreign policy; nor can this be achieved without the Federal German Government abandoning its hopes of re-unifying Germany within the frontiers of 1937 if not of 1939 or 1940.[2] It seems not unlikely that the United States has been pressing for the creation of a European Federation under the twin illusion that it would create an area of

[1] Recommendations of the Assembly of the Council of Europe, September 6, 1949, and of November 23, 1950. The latter recommendation and others relating to proposed extensions of the powers of the Council in a federalist direction will be found in vol i, No 5, of the *Summary of the Debates in the Consultative Assembly of the Council of Europe 1950* published in London by the Hansard Society. A useful and critical account of the first three years of the Council leading to the conclusion that federalism is inapplicable to the situation in Western Europe and that 'the twentieth century is not the eighteenth century' will be found in an address given at Chatham House by a prominent member of the British delegation to Strasbourg, Mr Robert Boothby, MP, on February 19, 1952. See *International Affairs*, July 1952.

[2] See the two articles by Raymond Aron entitled 'La Fédération des Six', *Figaro*, December 3 and 4, 1952.

economic prosperity equivalent to that of the United States, thus lessening Europe's dependence on America, and that such a federation would enable a stronger policy to be adopted towards Soviet Communism.[1] The latter objective is hardly reconcilable with the obvious fact that some of the support for the federal idea in Europe itself has sprung from the expectation that such a federation would enable Western Europe to take up a more independent line in foreign policy and to avoid its present commitment to what is thought of as an unnecessarily rigid anti-Soviet position.[2] The purely doctrinaire aspect of the American approach is best seen, perhaps, in the repeated evidence of American belief in the view that Great Britain could also merge her identity in such a unit despite the world-wide character of her interests and outlook.[3]

But it is too easy to dismiss the whole federal idea in Europe as simply the result of the United States' pressure or of the reaction towards it.[4] The early discussions at Strasbourg confirmed what a study of the federal movement as a whole reveals, namely, that it sprang largely from the conviction in much of Western Europe that the national governments in the area were not strong enough to solve their post-war problems by traditional methods or within the traditional framework of the nation-state: 'None of these

[1] See, for example, the article by the US Ambassador to France, Jefferson Caffery, 'Les États-Unis devant le fédéralisme européen', *Fédération*, May 1949.

[2] On 'neutralism' see Marina Salvin, 'Neutralism in France and Germany', *International Conciliation*, June 1951.

[3] The question of Britain's special position is outside the scope of this article. It is discussed in the pamphlet *Britain and the Cold War* (Oxford Radical Association, 1952). The possibility of Britain assisting in such schemes was discussed in my article 'Britain and Europe', *The Times*, December 17, 1951, printed *supra*, pp. 69 ff. The 'Eden Plan' presented to the Committee of Ministers of the Council of Europe on March 19, 1952, represented a step in this direction. One definite move was the signature on May 27, 1952, of the Treaty of Guarantee between the United Kingdom and the European Defence Community, though later developments were to show that it did not go far enough in dispelling French fears that Germany would come to dominate the Community.

[4] The Americans, declared Mr Boothby in February 1952, 'have attempted to batter the unfortunate countries of Western Europe, just trying to stagger to their feet again, into solutions of the rearmament problem which are bound to take time to work out. They have made the fatal mistake of assuming that political unity can be achieved by means of rearmament. The process should have been completely reversed' (*International Affairs*, July 1952, p. 335). After the first visit of President Eisenhower's Secretary of State to Europe at the end of January 1953, it looked as though the new Administration was even more determined than the old to pursue this policy.

countries,' wrote an eminent British observer early in 1951, 'which formerly played such leading roles on the European stage, has yet recovered its self-confidence and internal cohesion. That is why they are attracted by the notion of a federation, which would give a new inspiration and to some extent supersede their unstable regimes.'[1] What is lacking is any reason why the crisis of authority, so obvious in France for instance, should be circumvented through demanding allegiance to an international rather than a national body, or why the Dutch should entrust the handling of the grave problems which they face in consequence of the war to a Parliament in which they would only be entitled (in the case even of 'Little Europe') to one-fifteenth of the seats.[2] The dispute between 'federalists' and 'functionalists' seems unimportant compared with the fundamental issue of whether or not a European community exists. If it does, then obviously federal institutions would be appropriate at least for a period in its constitutional evolution: if it does not, it is hard to see how their creation could bring the community into existence or how they could function in its absence. Would anyone argue with confidence that there were smaller differences between France and Germany in 1953 than between the Northern and Southern States in America at the time of Lincoln's election?

To understand the drive behind the federal idea it is necessary perhaps to discard the purely analytical approach. It is worth remembering that it is not merely the longing for international peace that moves its adherents. The wish to set up supra-national institutions of a federal kind cannot be dissociated from a lingering or perhaps growing antipathy towards the Leviathan of the national State in its purely domestic aspects. It is a movement for breaking down existing units as well as for building new ones.[3] It is not an accident that the name of Proudhon occurs with such regularity in the literature of contemporary federalism.[4] The word 'federal' in its French context has, after all, a long history in this sense from the

[1] Sir Harold Butler, 'Strasbourg in Retrospect', *The Fortnightly*, February 1951.
[2] The unwillingness of Holland to enter an organization of which Great Britain is not a member is understandable both in political terms and in the light of the dominant position which the Roman Catholic Church holds in 'Little Europe'.
[3] See, for example, Michel Berveiller, 'Fédéralisme interne et fédéralisme international', *Fédération*, August-September 1949.
[4] See in particular the numerous writings of the French exponent of federalism, M. Alexandre Marc.

Fête of Federation of July 14, 1790, to the federalist notions of some of the Communards of 1871; not to mention some of the more far-fetched constitutional notions of Vichy.

Federalism in Asia and Africa, then, appears in the middle of the twentieth century in its classical connotation as providing a solution for a political problem of a particular kind: though that is not to say that the solution will prove everywhere workable or even acceptable. Federalism in Europe is more of a sentiment than a programme; but in the first half of the last century this was equally true of Socialism. The historian may warn the political scientist not to discount too much the role of sentiment in human affairs.

8

Problems of International Government

IT is a curious fact that the academic organization of particular studies may influence the relations of their subject-matter in the real world. In our universities we have tended over the last generation or two to divide a subject known as 'political science' from a subject known as 'international relations'. This both reflects the state of affairs which existed at the time when these two studies were first professionally developed and contributes to its perpetuation. One result of this is that both subjects are nowadays pursued in an unreal atmosphere and that in consequence much of the literature is of surprisingly little use to people trying to clear their minds about the real issues involved.

Political science in its descriptive form has been concerned with the internal governmental and administrative systems of sovereign States; and the functions which arise from the relations of these States to each other have been thought of as falling within the province of particular Government Departments, or as involving, as for instance in the case of the United States, special responsibilities on the part of the legislature. Political theory, which has in a sense a longer history, has also concerned itself with the single community; and its central problem, the problem of obligation, has been thought of as a discussion of the relations between the individual and the community of which he happens to have been born a member. Whether this community be as small as a Greek city state or as large as a modern nation the fundamental problem has been no different, and in consequence political philosophers find no difficulty in following through a single line of thought from Plato or Aristotle to the thinkers of our own day. It is true that the idea of a possible dual obligation or of a conflict of allegiances has not been unknown at any period of human history. But almost invariably this conflict has been between two authorities acting on different human levels, the spiritual and the secular. The problem of Church and State is, therefore, one which is familiar to thinkers on politics, and for which various solutions exist. It is a problem that can be embraced within the general field of political theory, and its institutional expressions, State churches or voluntary religious associations, can be dealt with within the descriptive framework of political science.

International relations is a newer subject in the academic sense, though it presupposes simply the existence of a number of political communities which together make up a single society. It has, of course, close links with international law, a subject of respectable antiquity whose purpose is to develop rules the observance of which will minimize the consequences of friction between the interests of citizens of different communities or States, or even in the case of the 'rules of war' between these States themselves. International relations might indeed be thought of as simply a descriptive and naturalistic method of handling problems with which the international lawyer is familiar from a more limited and formal standpoint. But for the student of international relations the important thing is that there should be a number of separate units whose relations form the subject of his study. In order that they should have such relations with each other their existence as political units must not be called into question; but there is no absolute reason why one form of State should be more susceptible of entering into such relations than another. The interest of the student of international relations thus stops outside the national frontier and the interest of the political scientist stops just within it. One study explains to us what foreign offices are, the other what they do.

Two major developments of the last half-century have made the fundamental assumptions of such an approach untenable. In the first place, for reasons primarily technological, there has been a growing conviction that human society itself cannot afford the cost of war, and that since war has hitherto been the final sanction in all questions of international relations these relations must now come to an end, in the sense that communities or States hitherto distinct must cease to have a separate and independent existence, in the same way in which the warring States or principalities of the Dark Ages were incorporated into larger units within which the royal peace was maintained. The second change which has its technological aspects also, has been the development and diffusion of conflicting claims to allegiance which are all on a secular basis. The essence of modern totalitarianism indeed, as Dr Hannah Arendt has shown in her remarkable, and to my mind neglected, book, is that the movement to which loyalty is demanded has no necessary connection with territory or even race.[1] It is something, therefore, which cannot be fitted within the chequerboard pattern of national sovereignties bequeathed to us by the nineteenth century, and which raises problems that neither political science nor international relations is competent to handle. All governmental systems and social systems have their own particular set of attitudes towards the exterior world and from these flow policies. Nothing is to be gained by simple labels like 'war-monger' or 'imperialist' which simply confuse the issue. It was possible for the minority groups at the time of the Wars of Religion to argue that their loyalty to their sovereigns was unaffected by their divergence in religious faith, because the demands made on them by Rome or Geneva were demands in a different sphere from those made by the secular State. But this answer is hardly possible for a French Communist upon whom the demands made by Moscow may easily conflict directly with those which his government claims the right to make upon him. In these circumstances it is difficult to see either how France, for instance, can be described in terms of political theory and traditional political science, or how relations between France and the Soviet Union are international relations in the sense in which this was true of relations between, say, Bismarckian Germany and the France of Napoleon the Third.

It is the neglect of these fundamental questions of theory that seems more responsible for the disappointments and disillusion of the last few decades than the mere inadequacies of the international institutions that have been created. It is a fundamental unwillingness to inquire into them that seems to be the major weakness of nearly all the recent thinking on the subject.

It is curious to reflect how innocent the peacemakers of 1919 were in this respect. Indeed neither of these problems seems to have worried them very considerably, if at all. They adopted as a fundamental article of faith the view that the conflicts which had arisen in the past between human associations were the product of the selfishness and greed of small minorities who had power within such societies and whose prestige or wealth was actually added to by conflict. War, for them, was the product of militarism, not militarism of war. There was, therefore, no discrepancy for the Wilsonians between internal and external objectives of their policy. Democracy

[1] H. Arendt, *The Burden of Our Time*, 1951.

in the primary sense of the diffusion of political power to the widest possible extent would produce, as an almost inevitable by-product of its own growth, an increase of the desire to solve disputes between separate communities by non-violent means. And institutions such as the League of Nations were thought of as necessary only for an interim period, during which this general forward movement might still be challenged by undemocratic survivals from the past. In this way it was thought possible to avoid changing those sentiments which would react in a violently hostile fashion to a merging of communities and States into a wider system, so that no one would have to fulfil the function of the early medieval kings in extending the peace by force of arms. At the same time the two functions of conciliation and coercion, exercised through international institutions, were not thought to involve any serious possibilities of contradiction.

It cannot be said that the makers of the United Nations Charter departed in principle from this naïve approach to the problems which they faced. There were, of course, modifications in the outlook of the peacemakers as a result of the experience of the world between 1919 and 1945. The most obvious of these was the greater emphasis upon economic and social progress as the solution of those problems in international life making for conflict. A more positive and universal effort to raise standards of living now occupied something of the place which the spread of parliamentary and democratic forms of government had occupied in the Wilsonian ideology. In the second place, greater recognition was given to the rule of force in international relations by a generation which was less pacifist in outlook than that of 1919. The working of the United Nations was predicated on the continuing unity of the great victor Powers rather more than the League of Nations had been predicated on the authority of the victors in the first world conflict. Even so, however, the General Assembly of the United Nations which has come to play perhaps a more important role than was expected of it, reflects accurately the older notion of the equality of independent sovereign States in its voting system and general procedures. For the second time the idea of a super-State has been rejected, and international relations are still thought of as those between units whose fundamental daily life goes on in an autonomous fashion, merely safeguarded against the risk of external aggression by such international institutions, and by their own diplomatic and military resources. Even on the non-political side, the continuity between the League of Nations and the United Nations has been greater than is always appreciated.[1]

In fact, however, the development of world politics, particularly in the last fifteen years, has produced yet another phenomenon which calls into question the utility of thinking of this kind. The differences in the status of different countries arising from differences in size and technical efficiency have become increasingly marked and the number of States capable of a fully autonomous existence in the old sense is now clearly very small. We have, therefore, in the very heart of the civilized world the kind of thing which previously existed only on its fringes, that is to say, a quasi-colonial relationship between Powers of different orders of magnitude. We have, in effect, communities whose affairs are obviously intermingled in many different spheres and between whom at the same time some obvious element of hierarchy exists.

This has to some extent been concealed by the delayed action which some of the older concepts have had outside Europe. Countries like Egypt or some of the nations of Southern Asia are demanding a measure of independence and sovereign self-determination which European countries may have enjoyed in the nineteenth century but which is hardly compatible with the state of affairs anywhere today.[2] There is little disagreement that such relations involving loss of sovereignty on the part of the subordinate partner exists between the Soviet Union on the one hand and a number of the so-called satellites on the other. It is, however, often considered politically injudicious to call attention to such relations between countries outside the Soviet sphere. But attention ought in fact to be directed to such relationships where they exist because unlike those of the Soviet sphere they do not represent a mere surrender to superior force and therefore something likely to be temporary, but, on the contrary, developments which are in a sense natural and inevitable and which probably therefore throw light on the future development of world politics as a whole.

Just because we are dealing with countries capable of at least an element of self-determination, the relations between them, however one likes to classify them, are much more varied and subtle than the

---

[1] Cf. F. P. Walters, *A History of the League of Nations*, 1952, Vol II, Chap 60: 'The Renaissance of the Economic and Social Agencies'.

[2] There seems to have been little critical study if the attitudes of the newly enfranchised States to the question of the modern meaning of political independence. See, however, W. Levi, *Free India in Asia*, 1952.

simple one of a patron and its satellites. Despite the overwhelming predominance of American power, particularly economic power, in the non-Soviet world, there is more than one centre from which influence radiates, and more than one grouping of Powers between whom relations are not strictly those of an atomized diplomatic system. At least four such groupings other than the surviving combinations of a metropolis and its colonial dependencies suggest themselves for consideration. There is the United Nations itself; or rather the United Nations without the countries of the Soviet *bloc* whose participation in its everyday work has hitherto been limited precisely by this unwillingness to surrender even a particle of sovereignty. There are the countries of the North Atlantic Treaty Organization (NATO) who are dealing in perhaps more favourable circumstances than those that confronted the makers of the League of Nations or the United Nations with the task of squaring the circle, that is to say, with the task of producing organs capable of framing and pursuing common policies in defence in its widest sense, without the formal surrender of authority to supranational institutions. Thirdly, there are the various institutions whose common denominator is a belief in the capacities of non-Soviet Europe for integration. These last present a bewildering complexity at the moment partly because of the fact that the membership of the different existing organizations is not identical. Those that like the Organization for European Economic Co-operation (OEEC) are a legacy from the Marshall Plan period and are primarily economic include countries (and in particular Great Britain) which are unwilling to participate to the same extent in organizations which look forward to a future situation in which their several sovereignties will be absorbed into a federal system. Finally, there is the British Commonwealth, a system which is almost wholly without common institutions and which works only through the practice of frequent and intimate consultation.

The reason why such groupings have come into existence, or in the case of the Commonwealth have continued to exist, are not difficult to formulate and are indeed commonplaces. No one disputes the inability of the countries constituting them to stand entirely on their own feet economically, or the necessity of pooling their resources against the possibility of further Communist aggression. In the Commonwealth there are of course the additional ties of history and sentiment. In the case of Europe there is to some extent a belief in the existence of a European civilization which would find its proper expression in a greater measure of political unity. All these organizations profess on the part of their members a common devotion to liberal-democratic forms of government. But the most important immediate common factor is the preponderant role in all of them of the United States. This, paradoxically enough, is as true of the European organizations and of the Commonwealth from which the United States is by definition excluded as of the United Nations or of NATO. Indeed all of them represent methods by which the achievements of the United States in the production of wealth and military potential are channelled in the direction which the Americans and their partners think most likely to achieve the common good. If this is disputed, and it still is half-consciously perhaps, by ardent patriots in many parts of the world, one has only to think of what the position would be if there were a number of countries at the present time with similar productive capacities to those of the United States, if, that is to say, the whole capital for the development and defence of other countries could be furnished from non-American sources.

But if the reasons for this state of affairs are by now commonplaces this is not true of its consequences. Much of the uneasiness which exists in the relations between the countries making up the non-Soviet world can best be explained either by an inability to grasp what is implied in this state of affairs, or by a reluctance to grapple with the problems which it raises. Since the United States is the focal point of all these systems it is not surprising that the strain has told most heavily upon that country, or that the tensions which must necessarily arise often find their most dramatic expression in its internal political conflicts.

The two main forms of tension may be broadly outlined as follows. In the first place there is the fact that people working within such systems are trying to live in two worlds at once. In their day-to-day activities they are concerned with what is, at least formally, still a world of sovereign States where the relations of one community to another are still international relations as we have defined them. But inasmuch as they accept and even desire the permanence of these more intimate relations, and regard the mingling of interests as something to be encouraged and developed, they are living in a future in which the significance of such national boundaries will largely have been obliterated. This issue can be seen at its crudest in the question of European federation and in particular in that of the proposed European Defence Community, since the ability of a country to command its resources for warlike activities has always been the ultimate test of sovereignty. It is clear that it is difficult to know how to behave as a Frenchman or a German today when one believes that one is going to be a European tomorrow.[1] Certainly no analogies from the past history of federal institutions are of much help in this respect. The conflict of allegiances may not be as dramatic as in the case of Western European or North American Communists today, but it is no less genuine because of the existence of a time factor which does not exist in the other case. For Americans the realization of dependence upon them by others has meant a mental adjustment almost as great as that involved in the recognition by Europeans of the passage of supremacy across the Atlantic. Even in the relatively limited sphere which has hitherto been taken up by the non-security activities of the United Nations an element of dissatisfaction has appeared. The refusal of the United States to be a party to such things as the proposed Convention of Human Rights or the Convention on Political Rights of Women is supported by arguments which suggest that the social progress of the United States is not thought of as a suitable field for international action; and if not of the United States why of other countries? The support for the proposed Bricker Amendment to the Constitution would suggest that many Americans are prepared to go much further than the present administration in making sure that there is no substantial mixing up of American affairs with the affairs of other countries; and the Amendment would really have the effect, if enacted, of re-creating as far as the United States is concerned the older system of international relations.[2]

This brings one to the second main source of tension, namely that between the idea of democratic self-government and the surrender of some governmental functions implied in the recently established international organizations. One can dismiss the thinking behind the Bricker Amendment as merely an up-to-date expression of the historic rivalry between Congress and the President, an attempt to make certain that the Treaty Power is not invoked at the expense of the law-making functions of Congress. But this is to obfuscate the issue with mere cynicism. For it is a fact that if these wider

[1] There is an admirable analysis of the French side of this dilemma in D. Pickles, *French Politics*, 1953, Chap 13: 'The Pursuit of Europe'.

[2] See the texts of S. J. Res. 1 and S. J. Res. 43 with the statement on them by Secretary of State Dulles in 28 *Department of State Bulletin*, No 721, April 20, 1953.

communities are to develop, not merely the representative bodies within existing national systems but the electorates too must resign themselves to a certain surrender of power. It would certainly be wrong for Western Europeans to criticize Americans under this head. For one of the reasons for the political uneasiness which manifests itself in so many of their countries is precisely the realization that their domestic policy is today something which is largely outside the control of their own governmental institutions however devoted they may be to the principle of government planning. The joke that was current in Europe in the autumn of 1952, that the best way to amend the American Constitution was to have the American President elected by European voters represents a real political truth. Because of the American preponderance in power and wealth, American decisions must affect even the intimate day-to-day matters which are the concern of other national governments. Resentment against this or that appearance of American dictation, against, for instance, suggestions that American economic aid might be affected by the choice of this or that political party to govern the European countries concerned, conceal this more fundamental fact. For the stronger as for the weaker partners in all these groupings the ability to make independent political decisions has to a great extent been lost. Three courses only are open. Either there must be a retreat to earlier conceptions of self-sufficiency and independence which would run counter to the whole technological and economic development of recent times, or there must be progress to something like a super-State, that is to say, the creation of a political community capable of giving direction to the organs of international government as national communities have given direction through representative institution to the organs of domestic government or, finally, we shall witness the growth in what might be called the authority of international bureaucracies. This last would mean that decision-making power would pass, bit by bit, into the hands of persons who although nominally responsible to national governments would in fact be attempting all the time to reach corporate decision using the national governments merely as instruments for obtaining the consent of the administrations and peoples concerned. The Schuman Plan and NATO both present, perhaps, prototypes of this relatively new international phenomenon. One is inclined to think that the reaction against this development, of which the Bricker Amendment would appear to be a symptom, will be far too strong to permit it to succeed; but since politics dislikes clear-cut conclusions we may go on for years yet, uncomfortably and irritably balancing between all three theoretical possibilities.

It may be helpful here to look at the matter from the point of view of the Soviet-dominated sector of the world. We have seen, notably in the disarmament discussions of the United Nations, how difficult it is to devise a system of control and inspection of the uses of atomic energy which will not involve a scale of investigation by external observers which is totally unpalatable to the Soviet Union.[1] Even supposing the Soviet Union were quite willing to see a fool-proof system of inspection devised for which adequate reasons in terms of enlightened self-interest could, without difficulty, be adduced, it is obvious that enormous difficulties would remain. The industrial ramifications of atomic energy which are likely to increase would be so mixed up with other aspects of the Soviet economy, labour-system and so on, as to make inspection involve a total breach of the secrecy with which the Soviet Union has thought it proper for many years past to shroud its economic operations, and would make its notorious statistical reticence almost pointless. A matter which, on the surface, appears to be one of international security becomes, therefore, one intimately involving the whole economic and social structure of the country. If this is true of a country which clearly retains its sovereign powers to decide upon its course of action, it is truer still of those countries whose policies are dictated by their relationship to Soviet needs. The Soviet refusal in 1947 to permit Poland and Czechoslovakia to share in the benefits of the Marshall Plan was used at the time as an indication of the political determination of the Soviet Government to prevent the establish-ment of new ties between its satellites and the Western world. It was, however, much more understandable if one accepted the fact that the economics of those countries would be replanned to suit the needs of a wider economic system of which they only formed part, and which could not, therefore, allow for the new set of in-fluences which acceptance of American aid must entail. We are not familiar in detail, of course, with the methods by which the economic relations of the Soviet Union and the East European countries are regulated; but such devices as joint companies for the exploitation of particular resources suggest that the relationship is a much more intimate one than just a mere set of political controls.

Under a system of planning, in other words, decisions must be

[1] There is a useful summary in A. Martin, *Collective Security: A Progress Report*, 1952, Chap 1.

taken by a single centre of authority and it is hardly possible for such an authority to admit of the derogation from its powers inherent in full membership of international institutions. This is true, of course, of such matters as human rights and cultural freedoms, and, for all these reasons, the abstention of the Soviet Union and the countries which it controls from nearly all of the non-political side of the work of contemporary international institutions is readily understandable. The Soviet Union and the other countries concerned can take part in the work of the Security Council, as at present organized, because it means no more to them than a forum for discussion and, of course, propaganda. But if the original intention to proceed to the creation of an international force of any kind in support of the Security Council's decisions were to be proceeded with, the same obstacles in an even sharper form would almost certainly arise.

The fact that most of the countries of the free world find no difficulty in participating, at least to some extent, in such non-political institutions is not, therefore, primarily the result of the fact that they enjoy a greater or lesser degree of democratic self-government. It merely means that the national governments demand a lesser degree of control over some aspects of their citizens' activities and are, therefore, prepared to see these aspects, at least to some degree, regulated by international action. If the State does not both own and plan the entire economy but relies for its general policies on such more flexible agents as tariffs and the control of credit it can afford at least to discuss the use which it makes of them in an international gathering. Similarly, if it makes no positive attempt to decide what its citizens shall learn or think it can participate in a body like UNESCO. But, as we have already seen in the case of the United States, there arise even in the non-political field important barriers as soon as international action threatens to impinge upon a sphere which a particular government regards as of vital concern to itself. These examples could, of course, be multiplied indefinitely, and the choice of the United States is justifiable merely because it is the United States which was the primary protagonist of the creation of such organizations in their formative period at the end of the Second World War. But one could draw the same conclusion from the defiant attitude of the Union of South Africa to any suggestion that its treatment of immigrants or of native Africans is of international concern.

In the light of such considerations it is not as self-evident, as some people assume, that a transformation of the present regimes in the Soviet Union and associated countries would put the development of international organization back on the straight highway, which was thought of as open to us by optimistic persons before the beginnings of the cold war. For democratic majorities would appear to be almost as unwilling as totalitarian dictators to let go of any activity other than the most inessential. The problem, therefore, becomes in a way diplomatic once again, that is to say, one of discovering the best techniques for regulating by agreement and through negotiation such matters as the individual sovereign Powers realize cannot, in fact, be dealt with in isolation. Useful work of this kind is obviously not outside the range of contemporary statesmanship where a sufficiently compelling reason exists for agreed solutions to be sought. Because Europe could not afford to forgo American economic aid, success up to a point was achieved in both OEEC and the European Payments Union (EPU), though in both institutions there have been occasions when one or other sovereign State has been subjected to criticism because it felt obliged to put some internal emergency of its own before the interests of the Group as a whole. It is obvious from the history of such institutions that a great deal depends upon the intimacy attained in the course of their working between the persons responsible for domestic policies, and the extent to which they are willing to be frank about their own prospects. On some matters frankness has its dangers, since a currency devaluation, for instance, can hardly serve its purpose if it is made public beforehand. But as one contemplates the wider use of such negotiating techniques, it becomes evident that further obstacles exist in respect of the internal arrangements of the States concerned. It is not always the case that a particular Foreign Minister, Finance Minister, or Minister of Commerce is in a position to answer precisely for the actions of his own Government, and even where he can answer for its policies there are obvious possibilities of friction in detail because of the administrative complexities involved. It has been recognized that it is not merely legislation on United States' tariff levels which requires revision in order to fulfil the declared policy of the United States Government: to free the channels of international trade. Congress has in fact considered a Bill revising in detail the administration of the American customs system. But this is to be done not by international agreement, but as an exercise of domestic sovereignty.

Consideration of this kind of problem tends to come about at two levels, the administrative and the constitutional, though it becomes apparent if one attempts to confine oneself to the former that it is the latter which may ultimately prove decisive. The difficulties arising from administrative considerations were realized very generally at an early date in the history of the present set of international institutions, and there was obviously a good deal of experience to draw upon from the League of Nations period. As early as 1947 UNESCO set on foot an inquiry into the administrative problems arising from the new developments in international collaboration, and in 1951 published, as the result of series of national inquiries, a report entitled *National Administration and International Organization: a Comparative Study of Fourteen Countries.*[1]

This report dealt with two main topics, the co-ordination of policy within national governments so that the views they expressed in different international organizations and their several organs should be in harmony with each other, and with the governments' general policies, and, secondly, the implementation of the recommendations made by international organizations through the domestic machinery of the States concerned. On the latter point the national reports were apparently not very informative. But it was clear that considerable difficulties existed in the way of such implementation and even in the way of discovering to what extent it had taken place. The report noted a particular difficulty in the case of federal States such as Australia, Brazil, India and the United States, where matters like those dealt with in labour conventions and in the UNESCO educational programmes fell wholly or partly within the orbit of the unit governments rather than of the federal authority. The fear that the federal authority might by-pass such constitutional divisions of powers is indeed one of the reasons put forward in support of the proposed Bricker Amendment to the United States Constitution, which have already been referred to. This amendment would make State legislation necessary in every case of this kind and would effectively cripple the power of the Federal Government to negotiate meaningful international conventions. One is indeed assured, probably correctly, by students of American politics that no such amendment can possibly be enacted. But the proposal itself indicates how difficult it is to put on top of the pyramid of a federal system a further pyramid of international organization without

[1] Published by UNESCO and the International Institute of the Administrative Sciences, 1951.

reducing the constituent parts of the original federation to mere administrative units.

On the first point the UNESCO study concentrates very largely on devices for inter-departmental organization such as the British Steering Committee on International Organizations set up in May 1946 whose functions were described in the British report.[1] But it is made clear ultimately that the efficacy of such co-ordinating devices depends upon the constitutional structure. In the British case it is the ultimate responsibility of the Cabinet which makes it possible to have flexible institutional devices at lower levels.

The United States, with its lack of an effective Cabinet system as well as the division of powers between executive and legislature, presents the most difficult problem of all. A great deal of thought, both official and unofficial, has gone into its solution in the last few years. An important symposium on 'The Impact of Foreign Commitments on Administrative Organization' was held at the December 1948 meeting of the American Political Science Association with the participation, among others, of Professor W. R. Sharp, who was the rapporteur of the UNESCO inquiry. The papers read at this symposium illustrate many of the difficulties of formulating and executing American policy in international organizations.[2] Two points, in particular, deserve notice. On the political side there is the particular difficulty arising from the American tradition of regulating defence and the planning of defence as a technical, military matter unsuitable for civilian control, a belief which seems to be even more firmly rooted among civilians than among the military themselves. In the second place, on the non-security side there is the enormous weight attached to the expression of particular opinions through pressure groups, not only by their action on Congress, but by direct and sometimes formalized contact with those actually engaged in representing the United States or in operating foreign programmes. Professor Sharp pointed out the tendency in the principal functional agencies of the United Nations for national delegations 'dominated by enthusiastic subject-matter specialists' to press for their pet projects and to get them adopted very often by 'the familiar process of vote trading' without regard for the 'limited

[1] *United Kingdom Administration and International Organization*, a report by a Study Group of the Institute of Public Administration, 1951.

[2] See *International Commitments and National Administration*, published by the Bureau of Public Administration, University of Virginia, 1949.

human and financial resources now available for international organizations'.

The main official contribution to the study of this problem has been the work of the Hoover Commission, whose report on foreign affairs was presented to Congress in February 1949 and was the prelude to a large-scale reorganization of the State Department.[1] The general line taken by the Hoover Commission was to try to restore the position of the President as the co-ordinating authority for all policies with a clear line of command through the departments and other organizations concerned. It was thus against the setting up by legislation of statutory bodies entrusted with particular tasks in the field of foreign policy and against the assumption by the State Department of operational responsibilities overlapping those of other departments. The State Department under this system would be confined once more to its traditional functions of formulating the broad lines of policy and negotiating on the political level with foreign governments. President Eisenhower's first moves towards reorganization in this field were along these lines. The difficulty of achieving a fully rational reorganization of the executive is obvious in the absence of the political attitudes, particularly in Congress, which would be needed to make executive leadership effective. The question was gone over again in an important Study Group report under the chairmanship of Professor W. Y. Elliott, who was one of the participants in the 1948 symposium already referred to.[2] This again emphasizes the need for executive leadership and the extent of reorganization in the executive office which would be necessary effectively to institutionalize the President's powers. For if everything must depend on the President's own constitutional and political authority, the organization of the 'White House' side of government becomes all-important. This Study Group seems to have been working towards the idea that the National Security Council, set up in 1947, might for foreign policy purposes come to act something like a British Cabinet. To some extent President Eisenhower's mind seems to have been moving in this direction. Even so, of course, the difficulty involved in the necessity for following accepted Congressional procedures would still be there. The State Department would still be vulnerable to Congressional inquiry.

---

[1] Commission on the Organization of the Executive Branch of Government. Report to the Congress, 27 *Foreign Affairs*, 1949, and Task Force Report, 27 *Foreign Affairs*, (Appendix H), 1949.

[2] *United States Foreign Policy. Its Organization and Control*, 1952.

It is possible, of course, to point to periods of crisis when important steps in foreign policy have been taken on a bipartisan basis. But there are obvious limitations to bipartisanship in a country fundamentally committed to the idea of a working two-party system and increasingly aware of the interpenetration of domestic and foreign policy.[1] It is all very well for academic students of government to talk about the executive-legislation relation as being the 'Achilles heel of United States foreign policy.'[2] It is possible to suggest even within the framework of the division of powers amendments to the Constitution which would make it function better, such as replacement of the two-thirds majority requirement for treaties by a requirement for a joint resolution of the two Houses together. It is, however, extremely unlikely that any such amendment could be got through. Suggestions for improving co-ordination between Congress and executive departments while clearly worth consideration in themselves would, as already indicated, demand a very considerable change of attitude on the part of some Congressmen before they could be effective. The temptation for the Executive to keep what power it can in its own hands and not to reveal more of its intentions than necessary is almost bound to continue so long as a professional foreign service is encouraged or at least permitted to call to its attention those obstacles to the free play of the American democracy's desires which are inherent in the present world situation.

It is proper, as has already been pointed out, that attention should concentrate on the United States because an effective, responsible and, above all, continuous American foreign policy is the most important single prerequisite of a stable world. It is obviously not possible for countries to base their defence programmes and economic planning upon the vagaries of an annual system of appropriations over which the American Executive has no direct control. It can be argued that a greater measure of independence on the part of other countries is anyhow desirable. But this could simply mean a retrogression away from the idea of a greater mixing up of the affairs, at any rate, of friendly countries and towards the more autonomous situation which such countries occupied in the nineteenth century.

[1] On this see the material in A. H. Vandenberg, *The Private Papers of Senator Vandenberg*, 1953.

[2] D. S. Cheever and H. F. Haviland, *American Foreign Policy and the Separation of Powers*, 1952, p. 172.

Such reflections suggest the conclusion that political movements, particularly in the democracies, are today tending in one direction; and technological and, consequently, economic tendencies in the other. This simple fact may indeed be at the root of most of our current problems in foreign policy. The international history of the last decade or even the last fifty years would seem well worth rethinking from this point of view.

9

The Russian View of European Integration

THE difficulty of describing the Russian view of European integration derives not from any ambiguities in Soviet policy towards the European institutions that have come into existence or have been proposed since 1947, but from the fact that the attitude which this policy expresses is a product of a general outlook on world affairs which tends to relegate the whole question to a very secondary position. This is true both from a long-range and from a short-range point of view. From a long-range point of view, the Soviet regime has never swerved from its original ideological commitment to the spread of world communism or from its belief that only the triumph of communism could put an end to international conflict and bring about a genuine era of peace and co-operation between different peoples. The extent to which Soviet policy has actually been attuned to the pursuit of this goal has varied from time to time according to the relative strengths of the Soviet world and of its capitalist environment. It is true indeed that 'peaceful co-existence' — meaning by this a *temporary* condition of normality in the political and economic relations of the Soviet State with other States — has repeatedly and sincerely been proclaimed to be a guiding principle of Soviet foreign policy ever since the time when the rulers of the Soviet Union first accepted the fact both that world revolution was not coming immediately, and that their own regime could survive without it. Nevertheless, even in the periods of relative stability which have existed, the Soviet Union has been able neither to abandon the cause of communism outside its borders nor to contemplate any intimate relationship with non-Communist countries. Thus European integration could not include the Soviet Union itself (or in the more recent period the Popular Democracies); on the other hand, any movement towards European integration excluding the Soviet Union must always appear as part of that solidifying of the capitalist world in opposition to the Soviet Union which it is the prime purpose of Soviet diplomacy to avoid.

From the short-range view—that is in relation to the Europe of the post World War II period—the Soviet attitude has been dominated by its consistent hostility to and fear of the United States which has replaced Germany (as Germany replaced the Entente Powers) as the Power believed most likely to head an anti-Soviet combination created for aggressive purposes. Ever since the crushing of Nazi Germany it has been the principal object of Soviet foreign policy to exclude the United States from all say in European affairs, partly because the removal of American military strength from this side of the Atlantic would dissipate all fear that the Soviet Union has felt for the security of its own territory or of the territories of its satellites, and partly because a Western Europe, not protected by the umbrella of American air-power, would offer no serious resistance to a further extension of the Communist frontier when the time should seem ripe.

The Soviet belief in the aggressiveness of American policy was not merely the product of the disagreements that arose between the victorious allies over the shaping of post-war Europe; it was also the product of Marxist dogmatism which has interpreted American foreign policy in the light of 'imperialism' in the Leninist sense and has seen American diplomacy as the instrument of American 'capital' dominated by a search for markets and intent on reducing its capitalist competitors, that is the countries of Western Europe, to a condition of economic vassalage.

Zhdanov put this view forward at the meeting in Poland at the end of 1947 at which the Cominform was launched. He said:[1]

The end of the war confronted the United States with a number of new problems. The capitalist monopolies were anxious to maintain their profits at the former high level, and accordingly pressed hard to prevent a reduction of the wartime volume of deliveries. But this meant that the United States must retain the foreign markets which had absorbed American products during the war, and moreover, acquire new markets. . . . Whereas, before World War II, the more influential reactionary circles of American imperialism had adhered to an isolationist policy and had refrained from active interference in the affairs of Europe and Asia,

---

[1] *Informatsionnoe Sovestchani Predstavitelei Nekotorikh Kompartii.* Moscow, 1948. pp. 17-19.

in the new, post-war conditions the Wall Street bosses adopted a new policy. They advanced a programme of utilizing America's military and economic might, not only to retain and consolidate the positions won abroad during the war, but to expand them to the maximum and to replace Germany, Japan, and Italy in the world market. . . .

The purpose of this new, frankly expansionist course is to establish the world supremacy of American imperialism. With a view to consolidating America's monopoly position . . . the new course of United States policy envisages a broad programme of military, economic and political measures designed to establish United States political and economic domination in all countries marked out for American expansion, to reduce these countries to the status of satellites of the United States, and to set up regimes within them which would eliminate all obstacles on the part of the labour and democratic movement to the exploitation of these countries by American capital. The United States is now endeavouring to extend this new line of policy not only to its enemies in the war and to neutral countries, but in an increasing degree to its wartime allies. . . .

The movement towards European integration in its recent form, deriving as it did such a notable impetus from 'Marshall aid', has been pictured by the Soviet leaders as simply one of the methods through which the European countries have been subordinated to American policy.

Everybody is familiar with the stir raised in Europe over the Marshall Plan. This plan is advertised as the factor of salvation for the post-war recovery of Europe's economy. To listen to certain British or French statesmen, without American credits under the Marshall Plan the economic recovery of the European countries is impossible. However, the American dollars which flowed this year into the pockets of the European capitalists under the United States credit plan were not productive of any real revival of industry in the countries of capitalist Europe. Nor can they result in such a revival—because the American credits are not being given in order to restore and expand the industries of the European countries which compete with the United States, but in order to provide a broader market for American goods in Europe, and to place these countries in economic and political dependence on the capitalist monopolies which dominate the United States, and on their aggressive plans, in disregard of the interests of the European peoples themselves.[1]

At no time therefore does there seem to have been any attempt by the Soviet leaders to examine the movement independently or to assess the probable results of any successes it might achieve. The American aspect of the movement has thus far outweighed any particular causes of anxiety which the Soviet Government might have found in the composition and outlook of the movement itself; for instance the strongly Catholic (and hence irreconcilably anti-Communist) outlook of much of its leadership, or the natural reluctance it has shown to disinterest itself from the fortunes of the peoples of Eastern Europe now under Soviet domination. The American obsession has also had the effect of making the Soviet Union quite oblivious to any advantages that such a movement might present even from its own point of view—the fact, for instance, that a not inconsiderable portion of its support has come from 'neutralist' elements that is to say from those who believe that a united Western Europe could to some extent dispense with its current dependence on American aid and protection, or the possibility that a thoroughgoing integration of Western Germany with her western neighbours would help to reduce the drive for German reunification which represents the biggest single obstacle to a perpetuation of the existing political arrangements in Europe.

Whatever our views may be of the consequences of this Soviet hostility to the idea of European integration it is important to avoid seeing in it some important key to the history of Europe, to assert as is so often done that Russia is a country external to Europe, alien to its civilization, 'Asiatic' even. No serious historian would deny that both Russia's Byzantine inheritance and the very different course her history took in the Middle Ages from that of the Western countries have had profound effects upon her political and cultural development. Yet both before and after the period of the Mongol Yoke Russian affairs were closely interlocked with those of the Western and Central European nations. It would be a great mistake to allow the considerable prestige of Professor Arnold Toynbee to force one into believing that the single circumstance of belonging to the Orthodox rather than to the Roman world is enough to have divided Russia for all time from the body of European civilization. The point has been well made by an historian deeply alive to the

[1] V. M. Molotov: Speech of November 6, 1948, in Molotov: *Problems of Foreign Policy*. Moscow, 1949. p. 572.

significance of both Russia and Byzantine history:

Unconsciously influenced perhaps by the legacy of Gibbon's contempt of Byzantium, or by the picture of Slavonic barbarism painted by some German nineteenth-century historians, are we not sometimes apt to regard Western and Central Europe— France, England, Germany and Italy—as the true centres of European civilization, the primary objects of a medievalist's study? On this reading, the countries east of the Carpathians and south of the Danube seem to play the part of an appendage, or at least of an isolated and self-contained unit, in either case admitted only grudgingly and sparingly into our manuals of European history. There can be no doubt that the writing of history has suffered from this one-sided presentation. Nor are the dangers of cultural parochialism limited to the sphere of the technical historian. In the countries of the West the general public is beginning to appreciate how much our common European inheritance has been obscured, and the international life of modern Europe perverted, by the fact that history has so often during the past century been written from a nationalistic point of view. But the tendency to an egocentric reading of history may conceal dangers of a more subtle kind: the view entertained by present leaders of the Western world that in resisting aggressive totalitarianism they are defending the true values of European civilization has much to commend itself; yet it may be asked whether this view would not acquire greater force and conviction if it were rid of two widespread assumptions: the notion that Western culture is identical with European civilization *tout court*, and the belief that there is something perennial and almost predetermined in the present schism in the body of Europe.[1]

Is he not right in suggesting in direct opposition to Professor Toynbee that 'Byzantium was not a wall, erected between Russia and the West: she was Russia's gateway to Europe'?[2]

Furthermore the idea of European integration cannot reasonably be identified with that of recreating some distant and imaginary past unity; it must take its start from the modern nations of Europe; and from this point of view the most important fact about Russian history is that it was precisely in the two centuries immediately preceding the Revolution that Russia moved most rapidly towards an

[1] Dmitri Obolensky: 'Russia's Byzantine Heritage'. *Slavonic Studies*. Oxford, Vol I, 1950. pp. 55-6.

[2] ibid. p. 6.

ever-increasing participation in both European politics and European culture. To argue Russia out of Europe is to sacrifice from Europe's heritage the whole glorious achievement of nineteenth century Russia in literature and music, and not unimportant contributions to the natural and social sciences. A British authority on Russian history put the argument as follows:[1]

It is true that Russia gave an exceptionally distinctive, and often nationalist, stamp to what she borrowed from the West. It is true that increasingly in the nineteenth century the contrasts and antipathies between Russia and the West became strongly emphasized, particularly by Russians. It is also true that her expansion eastward and her great land empire drew her in some respects away from Europe, somewhat like the British Empire in the nineteenth century. But I do not think that thereby Russia, any more than Great Britain, ceased to belong in the main culturally to Europe. The great Asiatic expansion of Russia has not meant that she had been deeply influenced by China, India, or the Islamic world. What of significance have they contributed to civilization in Russia during the past three centuries — unless it be tea? The choice must be made between regarding Russia either as in the main a world to herself or as in the main belonging to Europe. On the whole I should say that the new Europe, which took a variety of shapes in the eighteenth and nineteenth centuries, was in such continuous and increasingly close contact with Russia that by 1900 Russia was perhaps more European than at any other time in her history.

Not only would no one in 1900 have thought of excluding Russia from Europe, but even after the Revolution there was a marked reluctance to regard this event as marking a final repudiation of Europe by Russia. It is true that when in 1929, Briand launched his 'Pan-Europa' scheme Russia was not among the countries covered by his plan. But its inclusion was urged by both Germany and Italy for their own political reasons; and when the Commission of Enquiry set up by the European States Members of the League of Nations met in January 1930 it decided to invite Russia to participate in its deliberations. Despite the suspicions of the scheme voiced by Litvinov in his reply, he duly attended the Commission's meeting in May, and used the occasion to refute charges that the Russians were engaged in 'dumping' on world markets and to point out the importance that the Russian market might offer to the industries of some of

[1] B. H. Sumner, 'Russia and Europe'. *Slavonic Studies*. Vol II. pp. 8-9.

the countries suffering from the world depression.[1]

Litvinov's conduct on this occasion was characteristic of the subsequent Soviet attitudes towards organs of European co-operation; to take part in those where no loss of sovereignty was involved and to use them either for inter-State negotiations or for propaganda purposes if no practical outcome useful to the Soviet Government could be envisaged. Thus in the post-war period the Soviet Government has participated in the work at Geneva of the Economic Commission for Europe of the United Nations, although its general attitude to most of the specialized international organizations of the period has been negative or hostile.[2] Soviet policy towards Europe within its firmly doctrinaire framework has thus shown a limited measure of flexibility, in the sense that it has not been wholly averse to using the European framework as a possible one for negotiation, subject always to its determination to avert any movement towards integration that might threaten itself or help to frustrate its own plans.

In the war years the issue came forward in various forms. In 1943, Churchill put forward the idea of a European Council as one of the regional bodies upon which a future world organization might rest and seemed to have the idea that this, in turn, might partly be composed of federations of the smaller European States. This, however, came up not only against the American preference for a single world organization, but also against Russia's objection to any form of federal organization for Europe. Eden told Harry Hopkins, in Washington in March 1943, of a recent conversation with the Russian Ambassador in London, Maisky:

> Maisky said that the Soviet Government was not enthusiastic about the proposal for a future federation of Europe. He believed that a federation including a number of small countries would have negligible significance, either from the military or the political point of view, although there might be some advantage in an economic federation.[3]

Meanwhile, Britain had encouraged the exiled Governments of the

---

[1] Max Beloff, *The Foreign Policy of Soviet Russia 1929-1941*. Vol I. London, 1947. pp. 42-4.

[2] On the position in the pre- and immediately post-war years see: L. B. Schapiro: 'Soviet Participation in International Institutions', G. W. Keeton and G. Schwarzenberger ed. *The Year Book of World Affairs*, 1949. London, 1949.

[3] *The White House Papers of Harry L. Hopkins* ed. Robert E. Sherwood, Vol II. London, Eyre & Spottiswoode, 1949. p. 711.

Eastern European countries to work out schemes of future collaboration; and agreements for federation were reached between Poland and Czechoslovakia and between Greece and Yugoslavia. Such ideas also fell under the Russian ban. This was made plain at the Conference of Foreign Ministers in Moscow in October 1943:

Molotov read a statement that emphatically criticized the idea of planning federations of small nations at this time. His Government considered the active consideration or encouragement of such schemes as premature and even harmful, not only to the interests of the small countries but also to the general question of European stability. Some of the plans for federations, he said, reminded the Soviet people of the policy of the 'cordon sanitaire' directed in previous years against the Soviet Union.[1]

And the schemes were abandoned.

By the end of 1944, however, Communist Governments were established in both Yugoslavia and Bulgaria and they had begun talks about a Balkan federation. Since it seemed certain that such a federation would be wholly under Soviet domination, this was opposed by both the British and the Americans at the Yalta Conference.[2] However, it became apparent that the Russians were worried about moves of this kind even between communist countries and it is almost certain that the moves for a federation between Bulgaria and Yugoslavia in 1947-48, were among those which led to the breach betwen the Soviet Union and Yugoslavia. A statement by the Bulgarian Communist leader Dimitrov, on January 17, 1948, suggested, indeed, that these talks were concerned with other countries in addition to Bulgaria and Yugoslavia. He said:

If and when this problem becomes ripe for discussion, the democratic countries—Bulgaria, Yugoslavia, Albania, Rumania, Hungary, Czechoslovakia, Poland, and perhaps Greece—will decide how and when such a federation should come about. What the people are doing now is, in fact, to prepare for such a federation in the future. . . . If and when a federation was to be created, the people would not listen to imperialists; they would decide this question for themselves, considering only their own interests and those of international co-operation.[3]

[1] *The Memoirs of Cordell Hull* (London, Hodder & Stoughton, p. 1948) Vol II. pp. 1298-9.

[2] Edward R. Stettinius: *Roosevelt and the Russians* (New York, Doubleday, 1949) p. 257.

[3] RIIA *Documents on International Affairs 1947-1948.* ed. Margaret Carlyle. p. 297.

On January 28th, a Tass communique explained that *Pravda* had felt obliged to publish Dimitrov's statement since it had already been published elsewhere. It went on to say:

That does not mean, however, that *Pravda*'s Editorial Board endorses Dimitrov's attitude on the question of a federation or a customs union of the above-mentioned countries. On the contrary, *Pravda*'s Editorial Board is of the opinion that what these countries need is not a problematical and artificial federation, confederation or a customs union, but the consolidation and defence of their independence and sovereignty by means of a mobilization and organization of democratic forces within their frontiers, as was rightly pointed out in the well-known declaration of the nine Communist Parties.[1]

In this respect it is notable that no federal machinery, even of a formal kind, has been established as part of the measures of consolidation introduced into the Soviet sphere in Europe as a reply to the London and Paris Agreements of 1954. The Treaty of Friendship, Co-operation and Mutual Assistance, signed in Warsaw on May 14, 1955, and setting up a joint command for the armies of the Soviet Union and its European allies, contains no provision for any supranational institutions. Indeed its difference, in this respect, from developments in Western Europe was stressed by the chairman of the Foreign Affairs Commission of the Soviet Union when recommending the Treaty for ratification on May 24, 1955.

'Unlike the Atlantic, Paris and other pacts concluded by the imperialist states for the purpose of creating aggressive military groupings,' said Suslov, 'the Treaty under discussion was noteworthy for its exclusively peaceable and defensive nature. Its lofty purpose was to protect the peaceful labour of the peoples of the States which were Parties to the Treaty. It rested upon the principles of full equality, respect for state sovereignty and noninterference in the internal affairs of the States which were Parties to the Treaty.'[2]

Since the Russians are thus unwilling to contemplate federal arrangements even between countries under their own control, it is not surprising that, as we have already seen, any movement towards integration in other areas has been vigorously opposed by them. The Russian attitude to the offer of American aid in the

[1] ibid. pp. 297-8. The text of the Declaration of the founding of the Cominform is given ibid. pp. 122-138.

[2] *Soviet News*, London, May 25, 1955.

summer of 1947, took the form of opposing any form of European collaboration in handling this aid or in planning its use and tried to limit the functions of the proposed conference of European countries to drawing up individual lists of requirements. After Molotov's failure to persuade Bevin and Bidault of this point of view at the Paris Conference of June 27-July 2, 1947, the Soviet Government refused to attend the subsequent conference and brought pressure to bear on the East European States not to attend either. The Czechs were, indeed, obliged to cancel an acceptance of the invitation which they had already sent off.

We have already indicated the framework within which the Soviet exponents of foreign policy expressed their hostility to the movement towards Western European integration. The work of the Council of Europe was passed over in contemptuous silence, no doubt because of its remoteness from military affairs and the full measure of Soviet wrath was reserved for the proposed European Defence Community. A Note from the Soviet Government to the USA on May 24, 1952, included the following passage:

> Moreover, the Governments of the USA, Great Britain, and France achieve the inclusion of West Germany into the group of powers created by them under the name of 'European Defence Community': France, West Germany, Italy, Belgium, Holland, and Luxembourg. This self-styled 'European community' is supposed to become an integral part of the North Atlantic bloc and the great and so-called 'European army' into which should go the presently created German armed forces in West Germany. It is quite obvious that the aim of the creation of a 'European community' and 'European army' is not only to legalize the remilitarization of West Germany, as is taking place, in fact, but also to include West Germany in the aggressive North Atlantic bloc.[1]

In their campaign against it, Soviet leaders made a special point of attacking its supporters for being willing to compromise the national independence of their countries. In his speech to the 19th Party Congress on October 19, 1952, Stalin said:

> In the past the bourgeoisie was regarded as the head of the nations. It was defending the rights and independence of nations, placing these above everything else. Now no trace is left of the national principle. Today the bourgeoisie sells out its rights and independence, and national sovereignty has been thrown overboard. There is no doubt that this banner must be raised by you—

[1] RIIA *Documents on International Affairs 1952*. ed. Denise Folliot. p. 102.

the representatives of Communist and democratic parties—and carried forward if you wish to be true patriots of your countries, if you wish to become the leading force of nations. There is no one else to raise that banner.[1]

The records suggest that there may have been some misunderstanding on the occasions when British statesmen claimed that they had found the Soviet Government sympathetic to the idea of close links between Britain and her neighbours in Western Europe. In speaking on this subject in the House of Commons on February 21, 1946, Eden said:

> So far as I can remember, no statesman of the Soviet Union has ever raised to me any objection to such a course. I have seen plenty of it in the newspapers, but I do not think any such objection was raised by any statesman of the Soviet Union. On the contrary, I can remember one particular occasion when the Soviet Union took exactly the opposite line and made it clear that they did not take any objection to our making such an arrangement.[2]

Bevin referred to what was presumably the same discussion in a speech on January 22, 1948, when he said:

> We have always wanted the widest conception of Europe, including, of course, Russia. It is not a new idea. The idea of close relationship between the countries of Western Europe first arose during the war, and in the days of the Coalition it was discussed. Already in 1944, there was talk between my predecessor and the Russian Government about a Western Association.[3]

At any rate it is clear that from the time of the proposed Marshall Plan, any such idea of a mutual toleration of each other's security arrangements had been abandoned by Western statesmen because of their conviction that the Soviet treatment of the East European countries amounted to a denial of the right of freedom of choice which was an essential element in the Western view of the form political integration might take.

A final question might perhaps be raised as to whether there was any federal element in the proposals for a 'general European Treaty of Collective Security in Europe', first put forward by Molotov at the Foreign Ministers' Conference in Berlin on February 10, 1954. The nearest it came to it was in the proposed Clause 8:

> For the purpose of holding the consultations among the parties

[1] Ibid. pp. 239-40.
[2] 419 HC Deb 5s Col 1346.
[3] 446 HC Deb 5s Col 390.

provided for by the Treaty, and for the purpose of considering matters arising out of the problem of safeguarding security in Europe, the following shall be provided for:

(a) The holding of periodic and—whenever required—special conferences, at which each State shall be represented by a member of its Government or by some other specially appointed Representative;

(b) The establishment of a permanent consultative political committee, whose task shall be the drafting of appropriate recommendations for the Governments of the Parties;

(c) The establishment of a military consultative body whose terms of reference shall be determined in due course.[1]

An organization of this kind would obviously leave national sovereignty totally unimpaired. Furthermore, the fact that, from the beginning, the Russians suggested that the United States and China might sit in as observers on this organization and that, on March 31st of the same year, they modified their proposals to allow for actual membership by the United States, gave sufficient indication of the lack of any connection between these proposals and the European idea. It is clear that a prerequisite for the re-entry of Russia into the European mainstream is an abandonment of the ideological conflict which, despite all conciliatory moves from either side, still remains the main element in her interpretation of European and world politics.

[1] *Soviet News*, London, February 12, 1954.

PART III

AMERICA

10

Tocqueville and the Americans

IF political philosophers were quoted on 'change instead of in the classroom, the last few years would have seen a steady rise in the price of Tocqueville. It is no disrespect to Mr J. P. Mayer to suggest that it was an intelligent investment (in this case of his talents as an expositor) in the fortunes of Tocqueville's reputation at a comparatively early stage in the boom, that led to his selection for the all-important task of giving to the world a new complete edition of Tocqueville's works and correspondence, the first since the 1860's. This undertaking has had the backing of the Centre National de la Recherche Scientifique in France and of the Rockefeller Foundation through the National Institute of Economic and Social Research in London and represents a co-operative endeavour of international scholarship of which all concerned may well be proud. The National Commission set up by the French Ministries concerned to supervise the project contains the names of R. H. Tawney and Christopher Dawson as well as that of the late Harold Laski who wrote a characteristic introduction to the *Democracy in America*, the first part of the edition to reach publication.[1] Nor is so impressively international an effort unjustified; for as Mr Mayer shows in an interesting appendix—one of his few personal contributions to a commendably unobtrusive piece of editing—the influence of this great book has been of profound importance in almost every country in which the democratic idea has been discussed—but above all of course in France itself, in the United States, and in Great Britain.

Apart from Mr Mayer's notes which are chiefly bibliographical, the new edition is based directly upon that of 1850, the last one to be corrected by Tocqueville himself. And it contains, as that one did, two subsidiary items: a brief disquisition on Swiss democracy presented in the form of a review to the Academy of Moral and Political

[1] *Oeuvres Complètes* d'Alexis de Tocqueville, édition definitive publiée sous la direction de J. P. Mayer. Tome I. *De la Démocratie en Amérique*. Paris. Librairie Gallimard. 2 vols.

135

Sciences in January 1848, and the text of the remarkable speech made by Tocqueville in the Chamber of Deputies on the 27th of that month in which, with uncanny prescience, he foretold the imminent outbreak of the revolution that was to sweep away the July Monarchy. What we have, then, is the *Democracy* as Tocqueville a century ago wished us to have it. And although later volumes of this edition, notably the 'English Correspondence' which is due fairly early on, will contain elements of greater novelty, it is worth having the *Democracy* before us by itself, and considering it for the light it can throw on two great questions of our own day.

The first of these is a matter that will primarily concern the professional historian and student of politics; it is the question of whether and to what extent contemporary history can be studied in a truly scholarly and detached spirit; and whether such studies are possible without some guiding principle of interpretation, without the aid, that is, of what its opponents are apt to sneer at as 'meta-history'. As Mr Christopher Dawson recently indicated in a remarkable little essay in *History To-day*, those who condemn 'meta-history' and laud Tocqueville have their work cut out to prove their consistency.

But it is the second question — the light this great imaginative work of interpretation can still throw on the American scene — that may seem the more important from the practical point of view, even though the two questions are not of course wholly disconnected. Tocqueville's famous prophecy that the future of the world belonged to two races only, the Slav and the Anglo-Saxon, has been all too fully and dramatically justified. And if we tend to look at the Russians more eagerly because with greater uncertainty and foreboding, it is nevertheless far more likely that it is the American side of the balance that will weigh heavier in the long run, and it is to interpreting American democracy that we should still turn if we are endeavouring to understand the dominant trends of our own age.

It may be argued that to examine Tocqueville's book from this narrow angle is unfair not only because it discounts the history of the 130 years that have elapsed since the two young French aristocrats Tocqueville and Beaumont paid their brief but celebrated visit to the America of Andrew Jackson, but because it ignores Tocqueville's own description of his work and its object. As he told John Stuart Mill, America provided only the framework; his real subject was democracy and the laws of its development which he believed to be universal. Nor should one forget the well-known limitations upon

Tocqueville's own sources of information about the America of his day or the errors to which these gave rise. Least of all has this been permissible since Professor G. W. Pierson's admirable *Tocqueville and Beaumont in America* laid a solid groundwork of factual knowledge, upon which Harold Laski drew fully in his introduction to the present edition.

Yet the curious fact remains that, notwithstanding the coming of democracy, as Tocqueville had foreseen, for other countries in the Western world, and more particularly his own and England, the two he knew best, the *Democracy* continues to portray to the modern reader not some undifferentiated democratic scheme, but a living society—and that society is unmistakably American. Of course Tocqueville was right in his belief that democracy in the broadest sense had become an inevitable consequence of the way in which the Western world was developing; of course he was correct in saying that the task of those who cared for liberty was not to combat democracy with a blind hatred—the charge he brought against the Swiss writer he was reviewing on the eve of 1848—but to seek for those things which, within a democracy, might yet act as barriers against the total extinction of the individual in the face of an all-pervading levelling tendency. He could afford to ignore the taunt of Guizot that he was simply a conquered aristocrat who accepted his defeat; because to accept the defeat was a necessary preliminary to transcending it. The fact remains that when these generalities are brought down to earth, it is American democracy we are still concerned with and not simply the democracy of Andrew Jackson, but that of Harry Truman too. It is this quality of relevance, here and now, that gives actuality to Tocqueville, while a book like Bryce's, nearer us in time and the product of a much more extensive and scientific study of the subject, has for us now only an historical not to say antiquarian interest. A United States whose frontier of settlement has extended from the Mississippi to the Pacific, whose population is twelve times as great as in Andrew Jackson's day, and which has seen the British element in that population numerically submerged through decades of intensive immigration from the continent, a United States which has emerged from the self-imposed isolation of a distant and second-rank power to play the dominant role in world politics, a United States which has seen a prodigious accretion of the federal power—this new United States is still essentially, in the things that make it different from Western Europe or from Britain, the United States that Tocqueville saw when he landed in New York after more days on the boat than the slowest 'plane would take hours today. There is no greater testimony to his genius.

Whether this claim is too far-reaching the readers of Mr Mayer's edition must judge for themselves—wishing perhaps that an unabridged and adequate English translation were available also. In a brief article the salient points can be recalled. In the first place, Tocqueville's method of approach would lead one to expect that if he were right in his general conclusions, he would be right not only for his generation but for a long way ahead. For as he himself insisted, institutions which are mutable are of only secondary importance in determining the destinies of a people. These destinies are the product of their national and social characteristics and of the stock of general ideas implicit in their social arrangements or held by them in the form of dogmas. And there can be no doubt that Tocqueville's Americans—with their self-confidence, their touchiness where their own ways are concerned and their tendency to judge all others by them, with, above all their restless energy and the spirit of practical contrivance which Tocqueville regarded as one of the main advantages of a democracy—are well recognizable today in their descendants, and in the descendants of those later immigrants who have been subjected to the powerful process of cultural assimilation.

In a chapter significantly entitled: 'Why the Americans seem so restless in the midst of their prosperity', Tocqueville writes:

In the United States a man builds his house to spend his latter years in and sells it before the roof is on; he plants a garden and lets it just as the fruit trees are beginning to bear; he brings a field under cultivation and leaves other men to gather the harvest; he takes up a profession and gives it up; he settles in some place and soon afterwards leaves it to carry elsewhere his fluctuating desires. If his private affairs leave him any leisure, he instantly plunges into the vortex of politics; and if at the end of a year of unremitting labour he finds he has a few days vacation, he transports his eager curiosity hither and thither within the vast limits of the United States. He will thus cover five hundred leagues in a few days in order the better to provide some distraction from his happiness.

Apart from the fact that politics is a more infrequent leisure occupation as the result of the growing professionalization of politics which Tocqueville's observation missed, one might almost think that the Americans had spent the last 110 years in living up to Tocqueville's opinion of them.

Within this essentially fluid and egalitarian world, knowing none of the barriers of rank and culture that still divided an essentially aristocratic society such as that of contemporary England, cohesion was provided by the acceptance of certain general ideas. Nor would Tocqueville be surprised to find many of them still persisting into a later age; for as he argued, whatever might be true of the small democracies of the ancient world, a constant fluctuation in feeling and sentiment was not an aspect of modern democracy as illustrated by the Americans.

> Two things are surprising in the United States—the mutability of most human actions, and the singular stability of certain principles. Men are in constant motion; the mind of man appears almost unmoved. When once an opinion has spread over the country and taken root there, it would seem that no power on earth is strong enough to eradicate it. In the United States, general principles in religion, philosophy, morality, and even politics, do not vary or at least are only modified by a hidden and often imperceptible process: even the grossest prejudices are obliterated with incredible slowness, amidst the continual friction of men and things. . . . I do not think it is easy as is supposed to uproot the prejudices of a democratic people—to change its beliefs—to supersede principles once established, by new principles in religion, politics and morals—in a word, to make great and frequent changes in men's minds. Not that the human mind is there at rest—it is constant agitation; but it is engaged in infinitely varying consequences of known principles. It is engaged in turning in agile fashion upon its own axis, rather than in moving rapidly and directly forward. Little by little it extends its orbit through small continuous and hasty movements; but it does not suddenly displace it.

Despite the New Deal, and despite the seemingly permanent entry of the United States into the arena of world politics, this analysis seems to shed equal light upon the kind of shift the American outlook has undergone and upon the obstacles to its shifting more rapidly. Above all, it helps to explain the prodigious efforts that American statesmen must always make to convince their public that whatever departures are made can be accounted for in terms of this original stock of general ideas. Nor are these ideas likely to permit of the subtleties which modern politics, particularly international politics, demands. For, as Tocqueville points out in another passage, 'in politics, as well as in philosophy and in religion, the intellect of democratic nations is peculiarly open to simple and general notions. Complicated systems are repugnant to it, and its favourite conception is that of a great nation composed of citizens all resembling the same pattern, and all governed by a single power.' May not this help to explain in part the curious persistence of the American belief in the possibility and desirability of a European federation? But this is perhaps to press on a weak point: 'Do not,' said Tocqueville, 'get an American to talk about Europe. He will normally display great presumption and a rather foolish pride. He will content himself with those general and indefinite notions that in every country are of such great help to the ignorant. But ask him about his own country and you will at once see vanish the cloud which enveloped his intelligence. His language will become clear and precise to match his thought.' Recent experience might cause a modification in the harshness of the former judgement; the second must on the whole be sustained. What then of America's internal polity?

Here the interrogation of Americans today would on the whole confirm what was perhaps the most important of all Tocqueville's insights, namely that with the disappearance of aristocracy and the general percolation of egalitarian ideas, two consequences would follow. In the first place, there would be a tendency to concentrate in education upon the normal rather than the exceptional, so that though few would be wholly without instruction, few comparatively would be impelled to seek the highest honours. Tocqueville at the very beginning of America's industrial revolution foresaw that it would be marked by an extreme ingenuity in screwing the maximum of practical use out of fundamental principles often discovered in other countries. The emphasis would be on the exploitation of the discovery rather than on the discovery itself. One might be having a century's preview of the story of penicillin. From this observation, Tocqueville drew the deduction that still stands, that the real anxiety of democratic governments should be to encourage fundamental research and scholarship; applied science can safely be left to look after its own interests (though this of course can only apply to a relatively free and competitive economy).

The second consequence of the disappearance of aristocracy would be the domination of public opinion. This is true both at the level of general ideas and of daily political action. Perhaps the former is the more important. Indeed the very heart of Tocqueville's per-

ception of the dangers inherent in a democracy lies in the passages
in which he points out how a citizen of a democracy, although feeling himself fully the equal of any other citizen, is overwhelmed by
the sense of his own insignificance and weakness when he surveys
the whole body of his fellows:

> The public has therefore among a democratic people a singular
> power, of which aristocratic nations could never so much as con-
> ceive an idea; for it does not persuade them to certain opinions,
> but enforces them, and infuses into them the faculties by a sort of
> enormous pressure of the minds of all upon the reason of each.

Tocqueville would find it hard to say today that he knew of no
country in which there was 'so little true independence of mind and
freedom of discussion as in America.' The totalitarian spectre with
its physical and psychological weapons did not yet stalk the earth;
though one thinks that Tocqueville would have understood it had
he lived to see it. But when one thinks of what constraints do exist
in America, and in particular of the readiness with which they are
on the whole accepted, one is brought face to face with some of the
fundamental phenomena that Tocqueville observed. How could
a great university like that of California accept, until rescued by the
courts, the imposition of the 'oath', or the public be willing to see
the humiliation of this repository of its cultural tradition?

'There is,' writes Tocqueville (it is 1840 not 1940), 'no country
in Europe so subdued by any single authority as not to contain
citizens who are ready to protect the man who raises his voice in the
cause of truth from the consequences of his hardihood. If he is
unfortunate enough to live under an absolute government, the people
are upon his side; if he inhabits a free country, he may find a shelter
behind the authority of the throne, if he require one. The aristocratic
part of society supports him in some countries and the democracy in
others. But in a nation where democratic institutions exist, organized
like those of the United States, there is but one sole authority, one
single element of strength and success, with nothing beyond it.'
To this political omnipotence of the majority was joined the moral
omnipotence implicit in its institutions and fortifying its authority
'for nothing is more characteristic of man than to recognize the
superior sagacity of his oppressor.' This problem of the tyranny of
the majority and of the necessity of constant appeal to its prejudices
remains the great problem of American government. Much attention
has been paid by writers like Laski to another danger that Tocqueville
foresaw, the growth of a new aristocracy of industrialists, harsher

and less responsible than any history had known. But this danger has been met and conquered. The more abiding problems of democracy remain.

I have concentrated on the passages where Tocqueville is at his most sceptical and gloomy, because these are the most remarkable testimonies to his peculiar insight. But one must not forget that he still believed that the Americans could overcome their problems, by the outer restraints of their particular institutions and the inner ones of morality and religion. In a divided world his contrast between the American and the Russian still holds good: 'To attain his object the former relies on personal initiative and gives full scope, without controlling them, to the strength and rationality of individuals. The latter in some sense concentrates in a single man all the power of society. The one has liberty as his principal means of action; the other, servitude.'

II

Is there an Anglo-American Political Tradition?[1]

HISTORIANS who are actively concerned with the problems of their own times tend both to gain and to suffer from this concern. Their attention is likely to be called to aspects of history to which the current situation gives a new and hitherto unseen significance. At the same time, they may well be induced consciously, or more often unconsciously, to distort the features of the past in order to render what appears to be a service to the work in hand. In this respect, of course, they are not alone. Those whose business it is to interpret not the past, but the present itself, are all too likely at a time of international tension to stress, for instance, in their portrayal of an enemy country, characteristics that would be passed over in silence were an ally concerned. Nor has this failing been confined to our own contemporaries. At the time of the Crimean War, a French liberal could be shocked at the fact that the British press, which daily denounced the iniquities of Russian Tsardom, maintained a discreet silence about the loss of liberty that the French had sustained at the hands of Napoleon III:

> I receive an English newspaper that I read every day honestly from one end to the other as might an alderman. On the first page it tries to move me to antipathy to Russia, showing me a people held in darkness and silence, citizens abandoned to the arbitrary will of a single individual, sent without trial into deserts to die there. I begin to feel moved, and then on turning the page, I learn that a government that I have no need to name, also based upon absolute power, is full of moderation, humanity, and honesty, almost of open-heartedness, in one word wholly worthy of praise and respect.[2]

[1] A paper read to the Anglo-American Conference of Historians at the Institute of Historical Research, London, on July, 1949.

[2] Alexis de Tocqueville to Mrs R. M. Phillimore, May 1, 1854. [Alexis de

The kind of error into which the historian is likely to fall is a more subtle one, and less easily detected. In these times above all, when the conflict of ideologies plays so great a part on the world scene, people are all too prone to conceal beneath smooth-sounding phrases vital differences, not so much between rival camps, as within them. Some of these differences are much too deep not to reveal themselves as soon as the pressure of actual warfare is removed. It is clear enough today that much confusion was caused during the war years from the assumption that the word 'democracy' meant the same thing to the Russians as to Englishmen or Americans.[1] It is perhaps less obvious that even as between this country and the United States, there are important differences in political thinking that are bound to affect the relations of the two countries as the area of their co-operation extends. It is of course true that such differences are of another order of magnitude from those dividing both countries from the Soviet Union. In this respect that polarization of political power in the world today does correspond to something fundamental in the realm of ideas. 'Who does not know today that Providence has decreed that the future of the world belongs to two races only — the Slav and the English?'[2] This question, asked by Tocqueville in 1853, may well seem far more plausible now.

It is true that the ideas that we have recently come to call 'Western' are ideas that have more than a merely Anglo-American tradition. 'We are defending' — if I may quote the words used by an eminent English historian to the cadets of a famous American military academy:

'the idea of human freedom in the legal, political and institutional spheres in which it is embodied. If you take the great political declarations which have determined our action in the last two- and a half centuries — since the emergence of an autonomous Western tradition — you will notice this concept of freedom in all of them: the Declaration of Right; the Declaration of Indepen-

---

Tocqueville, *Oeuvres Complètes* (ed. Madame de Tocqueville, Paris, 1855), vii, 329.] Here, as elsewhere in this paper, I have translated the original French of Tocqueville's letters.

[1] This problem received its first serious discussion in this country in E. H. Carr's lecture, *Democracy in International Affairs* (Nottingham, 1945). He expanded his ideas on the subject in his *The Soviet Impact on the Western World* (London, 1946).

[2] Tocqueville to Henry Reeve, March 1853; [*Oeuvres* (ed. Beaumont, Paris, 1861), ii, 201].

dence; the Declaration of the Rights of Man; the Atlantic Charter.'[1] Of Professor Woodward's four documents, one is English, one French, one American, and the last, Anglo-American in composition.[2]

Nevertheless, the element of power may suffice to justify us in confining our attention at present to the English and American aspect of this political tradition, to what has been the institutional embodiment of this common reverence for freedom and for personality in the English-speaking lands. Furthermore, ever since the two countries began to display an interest in each other's institutions, it has been realized that the existence of a common language has often been a barrier in the way of understanding. So too has been the very similarity of their institutions in certain obvious respects. It was noted at the time, both in England and America, that one of Tocqueville's advantages over previous writers lay in the fact that America was in every respect foreign to him.

An Englishman it is said has the advantage of knowing the language better; and this is true but only to a certain extent, as it sometimes leads him into serious mistakes. We speak not of insulated words but rather of sentiments; and there is undoubtedly much in the current language of American society which conveys to an Englishman's mind a very different class of impressions from what the self-same words do to the understanding of a native. . . . There is so very much in the institutions of America which assimilates them to the mother country that an Englishman is extremely apt to overlook essential dissimilarities in the general resemblance; and then on many occasions he may miss those very points of distinction upon which the real merits of the question turn.[3]

This comment by a British reviewer almost precisely echoed an American one:

We could almost think that the resemblance which exists between the two countries prevents a more accurate perception of

[1] E. L. Woodward, 'The Heritage of Western Civilization', *International Affairs* (April 1949), xxv, 140.

[2] For American accounts of the drafting of the Atlantic Charter, see Sumner Welles, *Where Are We Heading?* (London, 1947), pp. 1-14; R. E. Sherwood, *The White House Papers of Harry Hopkins* (London, 1948-9), i, Chap xvi.

[3] *Quarterly Review*, September 1836, lvii, 134-6. Professor G. W. Pierson is clearly in error in attributing this review to J. G. Lockhart. Sir John Murray, the present editor, has been good enough to inform me that in all probability the author was Basil Hall.

the state of things, in points where the resemblance ceases and the peculiarities and novelties commence.[1]

Before proceeding to explore the main distinctions between the political preconceptions of the two people, it is worth while noting that there is a school of thought that makes light of them. This has been particularly evident in the many discussions recently of plans for reforming the existing federal government of the United States. The need for some change in American political institutions to meet the external and internal demands of the present age is widely admitted. Indeed part of the need arises from the difficulty of distinguishing today between those spheres of governmental activity that seemed so far apart in the days of the Founding Fathers. As the authoritative 'Hoover Report' puts it,

the traditional line of demarcation between domestic and foreign problems has completely disappeared, and the governmental organization must be shaped to formulate and execute national policies which have both domestic and foreign aspects.[2]

It is therefore assumed that some institutional change is all that is requisite, either by amendment of the constitution or by creating new conventions within its framework. A writer with both academic and practical experience of the problem has written:

The cause of this conflict between Congress and the Executive is not human; it is institutional. The American people are as politically mature as any. Some nations cannot govern themselves under a regime of individual liberty, no matter what form of government is written into their basic laws. But the people of this country have the flair, the educational standards, and the traditions to make representative self-rule a success even under present conditions. The trouble is that we are working under — that is, within the limits of — a structure which makes the task of governing unnecessarily difficult.[3]

These criticisms of a structure that makes the effective formulation of long-range policies and the co-ordination of separate branches of governmental activity very difficult, have such a weight of in-

---

[1] *North American Review*, July 1836. This review is ascribed by Professor Pierson to Edward Everett. See his invaluable survey of the literature dealing with Tocqueville in his *Tocqueville and Beaumont in America* (New York, 1938), pp. 789-93; 825-33.

[2] *Report of the Commission on the Organization of the Executive Branch of the Government* (Hoover Commission), 1949, appendix H, p. 1.

[3] Thomas K. Finletter, *Can Representative Government do the Job?* (New York, 1945), p. 9.

formed American opinion behind them, that the non-American student may well accept them without question. What these critics seem to overlook, is the significance of their failure hitherto to secure the support necessary to put into force one or other of the many schemes suggested as remedies, in the way that the Founding Fathers, for instance, secured the necessary support for remedying the weaknesses they alleged to exist in the Articles of Confederation.[1]

But the American advocates of reform tend to argue that popular opposition would only be evoked by proposals for fundamental change, such as the direct adoption of a parliamentary system on the British model in place of the presidential system. 'The fact is' we are told

'that the popular election of the President is now the keystone of the American system and has been such for nearly a century and a half. The people will not agree to give it up. Nor will they adopt any foreign form of government. . . .'[2]

What the reformers refrain from doing is to go further and to ask where in fact this clinging to the existing state of things does not reflect a deep-seated attachment to general ideas about politics that leave little room for the centralized responsibility and initiative that they hope to achieve.

Whatever weight may be attached to this argument, it is certainly difficult to resist the more general conclusion that both the British and American political systems have, ever since the Revolution, developed along different lines, or as some might argue, along the same lines, but at very different speeds, so that at whatever point one picks up the story and attempts a comparison, one is struck by differences that arise as much from the inherited attitudes of the past as from the conditions of the moment.

Since the original divergence precedes the large scale immigration of non-British elements into the United States, one can dismiss any attempt to attribute such differences to the dilution of the original stock, despite the importance that Tocqueville attached to this point in his later writings.[3] It is clearly to the new environment that we must still look for the motive factors in the development of ideas, even if these did not operate in the over-simplified manner that has sometimes too readily been taken for granted.

[1] See Merrill Jensen: *The Articles of Confederation* (2nd printing, Madison, 1948) and *The New Nation* (New York, 1950).

[2] Finletter, op. cit., p. 135.

[3] See his letter to Gustave de Beaumont, August 6, 1854 (*Oeuvres*, ii, 267-8).

The common origins of the British and American political systems follow clearly from the close connection between the first American constitutions and the political institutions of the first British Empire: 'Mother country and colonies stemmed from the same institutional ancestry; Magna Carta and the common law, parliamentary rule and local self-government, the Puritan and the Glorious Revolutions.'[1] At the height of the Stubbs-Freeman era in English historiography, American scholars were equally open to its teachings, and saw nothing strange in applying them to their own country:

> the student of history who now attempts to trace through two thousand years of vicissitudes and dangers, the slender thread of political and legal thought, no longer loses it from sight in the confusion of feudalism or the wild lawlessness of the heptarchy, but follows it safely and firmly back until it leads him out upon the wide plains of Northern Germany, and attaches itself at last to the primitive popular assembly, parliament, law-court and army in one, which embraced every free man, rich or poor, and in theory at least allowed equal rights to all.'[2]

Colonial society was compounded—slaves apart—of the same elements as society at home, if in different proportions, and the same may be said of colonial thought. It was the Revolution itself that gave this difference in proportion its real significance and the rapid expansion and democratization of American society in the next two generations that made the gap unbridgeable.

Both the fact and the reasons for it were grasped by intelligent contemporary observers. The Americans, wrote Robert Southey in 1809, have 'a distinct national character and even a national physiognomy.' Not continental European immigration, he argued, but rather the effects of living on the edge of the wilderness, with all that this entailed for manners, laws and religion, should be held responsible.[3] Thus do we have the frontier theory fully fledged over four-score years before its celebrated formulation by Frederick Jackson Turner.[4]

---

[1] A. M. Schlesinger, *Paths to the Present* (New York, 1949), p. 171.

[2] Henry Adams in *Essays in Anglo-Saxon Law* (Boston, 1876), p. 1.

[3] Review of Abiel Holmes, *American Annals* (Boston, 1805) in *Quarterly Review*, November 1809, ii, 319 ff. I owe the identification of the author as Southey to Sir John Murray.

[4] Turner first read his paper, 'The Significance of the Frontier in American History' to the meeting of the American Historical Association of Chicago on July 12, 1893. See *The Early Writings of Frederick Jackson Turner* (compiled by E. E. Edwards, introd. by Fulmer Mood, Madison, 1938), pp. 183 ff.

The marked tendency among British historians of America to concentrate upon the making of the federal constitution, and upon the checks and balances devised by the Founding Fathers and defended in the *Federalist*, has led to some neglect of events in the States, where in the long run at least American conservatives were less successful.[1] By the time that Jackson became president, and Tocqueville visited America, the belief in political democracy, and the identification of political democracy with majority rule, had gained an undisputed hold over the American public mind. In that sense, the conservatives of the Old World were correct in their basic assumptions about the significance of the American Republic, however cloudy the image of that Republic when seen through British or continental spectacles.[2] As another British reviewer put it, 'the American revolution has been by many causes and some accidents, the parent, and lies at the bottom, of all the revolutions which have disturbed and distressed and desolated the European world for the last half-century.'[3]

It was thus in strict accordance with the spirit of the times that Tocqueville used his American experiences, not as material for just one more travel book, but as the foundation of a treatise on democracy: '*L'Amérique n'était que mon cadre, la démocratie le sujet.*'[4] While it is true that the manner of his inquiry helped to make him exaggerate the extent to which the democratic impulse had penetrated into every fibre of American society, and while this bias was enhanced by his self-confessed tendency to attach more importance to general ideas than to institutions,[5] it could hardly be denied that the ideas that were gaining ground were those associated in American minds with the notion of democracy.

Americans themselves were ever ready to expound and extol

[1] On the political theories of the Founding Fathers, see the present writer's introduction to the *Federalist* (Oxford, 1948) and the works there referred to. See also Benjamin F. Wright, 'The *Federalist* on the Nature of Political Man', in *Ethics*, lix, No 2 (Chicago, 1949).

[2] cf. Merle Curti, 'The Reputation of America Overseas (1776-1860)', in *American Quarterly*, i, No 1 (Minneapolis, 1949).

[3] Review of *The Influence of Democracy on Liberty, Property and the Happiness of Society, considered by an American, formerly member of Congress* (London, 1835), in *Quarterly Review* (April 1835), liii, 550. The book was by T. Fisher Ames; the review is ascribed to J. W. Croker.

[4] Tocqueville to John Stuart Mill, November 10, 1836, *Oeuvres*, ii, 66 ff; cf. his letters to Louis de Kergorlay and Eugène Stoffels, ibid., i, 378, 427-8.

[5] Tocqueville to F. de Corcelle, September 17, 1853, *Oeuvres*, ii, 227.

the virtues of their system, often in a highly simplified form. 'Popular power,' declaimed one orator, oblivious of the pitfalls of his terminology, 'is the basis of all our institutions; and the general weal is managed by a simple organization of the sense and reason of the community manifesting its general will.'[1] The historian George Bancroft wrote of his love of 'the principle of popular power that lies at the bottom of our institutions.'[2] And like other Americans, he found that experience in Europe only fortified his democratic beliefs:

My residence in Europe has but quickened and confirmed my love for the rule of the people, and I do not believe that any arrangement of political power short of universal suffrage can give to freedom the security which it needs in planning legislation suited to the advancement of the race.[3]

In the circumstances, Tocqueville's book was bound to be used in the English party conflict, in spite of the fact that, as J. S. Mill pointed out, no political writer had had better grounds for believing he had successfully laboured to avoid such use.[4] It is worth remembering too, that Tocqueville's own opinion was that Henry Reeve's translation had made this use more likely, by 'colouring very vividly what was opposed to democracy' and rather toning down 'what could damage aristocracy'.[5] For the booksellers eager to sell the work, the most useful commendation had been that of Sir Robert Peel:

The Republican institutions that will suit a new country may not for that account suit a country which contains men educated as we are, subject to such laws as we are, holding property by such rights as we do, and having prejudices (you may call them prejudices if you will) that connect us with the ancient monarchy of England.[6]

The enforced leisure of opposition gave Peel an opportunity to

[1] Charles Stewart Davies, 'An Address delivered at the Commemoration at Fryeburg, May 19, 1825', quoted from J. L. Blau (ed.), *The Social Theories of Jacksonian Democracy* (New York, 1947), p. 43.

[2] Letters to W. D. Bliss, September 22, 1948 (M. A. DeWolfe Howe, *Life and Letters of George Bancroft*, ii, 37).

[3] Letter to James Buchanan, March 24, 1848 (ibid., p. 33); Jefferson's sentiments had been much the same over half a century before [cf. the present writer's *Thomas Jefferson and American Democracy* (London, 1948), p. 105].

[4] J. S. Mill, *Dissertations and Discussions* (2nd ed., London, 1867), ii, 3. The quotation comes from a reprint there of Mill's review of *Democracy in America* in the *Edinburgh Review*, October, 1840.

[5] Letter of November 15, 1839 (*Oeuvres Complètes*, vii, 178-9).

[6] Speech at Tamworth, September 4, 1835 (*The Times*, September 5, 1835).

document his beliefs by reading the first volume of Tocqueville. At the banquet in Glasgow that came as a climax to the ceremonies attending his installation as Lord Rector of the University, the ex-Prime Minister delivered himself of another defence of the British system of government earnestly advising his auditors to peruse the work of 'a most able and intelligent native of France'.[1] Peel quoted from and summarized the famous passages in Tocqueville about the tyranny of majority opinion, and the danger to free institutions from the unchecked operation of majority rule, repeating Tocqueville's own quotation from Jefferson, to the effect that the tyranny of the legislature was the one to be feared and would be so for many years to come.[2]

'Now,' he went on, 'if you could change conditions of society with the United States, if that was in your power, read the whole of that book, converse with intelligent Americans, before you decide that republicanism would greatly increase either your freedom or your happiness. There are other blessings in life besides cheap newspapers. I do not depreciate the United States, but look at the moral habits and religious feelings, compare the state of refinement and civilization with which we are connected and for God's sake don't be duped by plausible sophistry to run the hazard of change.'

Peel's strictures did not go unnoticed in America, and not for the first time Edward Everett took up the defence of his country's institutions. Tocqueville, he maintained, gave no facts to justify his indictment on the tyranny of the legislature, and the quotations he used referred to the state legislatures prior to the ratification of the federal constitution.[3]

What Peel was doing in effect was repeating the classic argument against democracy that had been given strength in English minds as a result of their reading of the lessons of the French Revolution. The English reviewer of Fisher Ames praised him for his demonstration of

the impossibility of any such thing as democratical government, which is in his opinion, an absolute contradiction in terms and in

[1] Speech on January 13, 1837 (*The Times*, January 16, 1837).

[2] See *Democracy in America* [tr. Reeve (London, 1875)], i, 266-74. The reference to Jefferson is to his letter to Madison of March 15, 1789, in *Writings* (ed. P. L. Ford), v 80-86. The same set of passages had been emphasized in the notice in the *Quarterly Review* already referred to.

[3] Letter to Peel, March 29, 1837, in C. S. Parker, *Sir Robert Peel*, ii, 333-5. Actually Tocqueville had made it plain that he was referring to the state governments only. (*Democracy in America*, i, 273 n.)

fact. A democratical anarchy, or a democratical prelude to an anarchy he easily conceives—it is a part of his case; but that government—the control of the views and passions of man—the guarantees of property and other personal rights—the safeguard of public liberty—should exist under a democratic influence, is what he cannot imagine; and what, he shows, has never yet occurred in the history of mankind.[1]

In the opinion of such English critics what had preserved America hitherto from the 'excesses of democracy' was its partial inheritance from the British system, and the combination of a great extent of territory with federalism, the latter, a clear echo of the celebrated argument of the *Federalist*. In a compact and centralized country like Britain, the danger would be greater.

But it was not this line of argument that American democrats relied upon:

'M. de Tocqueville's theory,' wrote the historian Jared Sparks, 'can only be true where the majority is an unchangeable body and where it acts exclusively on the minority as distinct from itself—a state of things which can never occur where the elections are frequent and every man has a voice in discovering the legislator.'[2]

This same theory, that majority rule was compatible with liberty and justice whenever the division of the population did not congeal according to class, was at the root of the case made out by a reviewer of Tocqueville (probably Edward Everett) in the *North American Review*.[3] It was, he maintained, the particular merit of American institutions to have departed from all systems based upon inherited power or prescriptive right: 'the natural equality of man is embalmed in an elective system'. For this reason universal suffrage was 'unquestionably the master-principle of American politics'. The only prerequisite to its success was that no great and permanent fortunes should be maintained. American legislation abolishing entails, and primogeniture had worked to this end: 'as transmitted power sought the alliance of transmitted wealth, transmitted political equality demands a healthy circulation of property'.

The same line of reasoning appealed to J. S. Mill:

---

[1] *Quarterly Review* (April 1835), liii, *loc. cit.*

[2] J. Sparks to Major Poussin, February 1, 1841; cf. his letter to Prof William Smyth, October 13, 1841 [H. B. Adams, *Jared Sparks and Alexis de Tocqueville* (Baltimore, 1898), pp. 43-4].

[3] *North American Review* (July 1836), xviii, 178 ff.

It is not easy to surmise any inducements of interest by which in a country like America, the greater number could be led to oppress the smaller. When the majority and the minority are spoken of as conflicting interests, the rich and the poor are generally meant, but where the rich are content with being rich and do not claim as such any political privileges, their interest and that of the poor are generally the same: complete protection to property and freedom in the disposal of it are alike important to both. When indeed, the poor are so poor that they can scarcely be worse off, respect on their part for rights of property which they cannot hope to share is never safely to be calculated upon. But where all have property, either in enjoyment or in reasonable hope, and an appreciable chance of acquiring a large fortune; and where every man's way of life proceeds on the confident assurance that, by superior exertion, he will obtain a superior reward, the importance of inviolability of property is not likely to be lost sight of. It is not affirmed of the Americans that they make laws against the rich, or unduly press upon them in the imposition of taxes. If a labouring class, less happily circumstanced, could prematurely force themselves into influence over our own legislature, there might then be danger, not so much of violations of property, as of undue interference with contracts; unenlightened legislation for the supposed interest of the many; laws founded on mistakes in political economy.[1]

That the rise of the demagogue involved dangers in such a system was undeniable. But for these dangers, the reviewer, like most of his countrymen, then and later, felt that 'the most effective remedy must be sought in universal education'. This belief in the political virtues of education had of course deeply impressed Tocqueville himself.

The effort that is made in this country to spread education is really prodigious. The universal and sincere belief that is here professed in the efficacy of enlightenment seems to me one of the most remarkable features of America; all the more so, I admit, because for me the question does not yet seem entirely settled. But it is so, absolutely, in the minds of Americans whatever their political and religious opinions. The catholic himself, on this point, stretches out his hand to the unitarian and the deist. The result is one of those powerful efforts, at once quiet and irresistible, that nations sometimes make when they march towards some

[1] Mill, op. cit., ii, 36-8.

goal by a common and universal impulse; there never was under the sun people as enlightened as that of the north of the United States. It is stronger for it, more ingenious, more able to rule itself and to stand liberty; that is uncontestable. But whether its morality has gained by it — of that I am not yet very sure.[1]

Since the economic conditions that the upholders of the system postulated seemed remote from the realities of the United States of later decades, it is not unreasonable to ask why, in fact, the logic of majority rule was not followed through by those masses of Americans who scarcely seemed to be participating in a 'healthy circulation of property'. Why in fact did the United States develop neither the theory nor the machinery of the 'welfare state', at a time when societies less democratic in their political theory and inherited institutions, were making gigantic strides in that direction? To find an answer to such questions, it is necessary not merely to take into account the effects of dual federalism and the other limitations upon government expounded by the Supreme Court over a long period, but in addition, another and paradoxical feature of the same Jacksonian democratic creed. And this is the pronounced anti-statism, the enracinated suspicion of all government, including majority-rule that is found side by side with the eulogies of popular power and universal suffrage.

When Bancroft talked, as has been seen, of universal suffrage 'giving to freedom the security which it needs in planning legislation suited to the advancement of the race', he was not preaching collectivist or welfare economics, or the advance of the state into new spheres of activity. The majority of his contemporaries who regarded themselves as democrats were convinced that the 'general will' they talked about, would normally function in a negative fashion, to prevent, above all, the rise of privilege.

'It is under the word *government*,' declared a journal that aspired to be the voice of the new age, 'that subtle danger lurks. Understood as a central consolidated power, managing and directing the various general interests of the society, all government is evil and the parent of evil. . . . Legislation has been the fruitful parent of nine-tenths of all the evils, moral and physical, by which mankind has been afflicted since the creation of the world, and by which human nature has been self-degraded, fettered and oppressed. Government should have as little as possible to do

[1] Tocqueville to Monsieur Bouchitté, New York, October 11, 1831 (*Oeuvres Complètes*, vii, 79-80).

with the general business and interests of the people.' Or finally; 'This is the fundamental principle of the philosophy of democracy, to furnish a system of the administration of justice, and then leave all the business and interests of society to themselves, to free competition and association; in a word, to the *voluntary principle*.'[1]

While recent research has called attention to the role of the urban working-class in the Jacksonian movement, Jacksonian democracy remained throughout essentially a political rather than a social creed. The 'so-called labour movement,' declares a recent student of it, 'was anti-aristocratic rather than anti-capitalistic.'[2] And it was this anti-aristocratic bias that seemed at the time, to mark the United States off from Europe in general and England in particular.

Tocqueville found the English scene much harder to analyse that the American.

'It is much easier,' he wrote, 'to acquire clear and precise notions about the American Union than about Great Britain. In America, all the laws derive in a manner from the same line of thought. The whole of society so to speak is founded upon a single fact; everything springs from a single principle. One could compare America to a forest pierced by a multitude of straight roads all

[1] Introduction to vol i, no 1 of the *United States Magazine and Democratic Review* (October 1837), probably written by John L. O'Sullivan (quoted from Blau, op. cit., pp. 26-8). During the discussion on this paper at the Anglo-American Historical Conference, Mr Frank Thistlethwaite argued that the element of *laisser-faire* in Jacksonian democracy had been overestimated since at the state level control was still held to be permissible where strong social reasons for it existed, and since at this level some of the Jacksonians had a positive economic programme including the state-ownership of utilities. This view is based primarily on two studies, O. Handlin and M. F. Handlin, *Commonwealth: A Study of the Role of Government in the American Economy: Massachusetts, 1774-1861* (New York, 1947) and Louis Hartz, *Economic Policy and Democratic Thought: Pennsylvania 1776-1860* (Harvard UP, 1948) which are reviewed in *Economic History Review*, xviii, 104-6; 2nd Ser, ii, 96-7. But as Professor Hartz himself admits, the total amateurishness of the Jacksonian concept of administration rendered the effectiveness of such doctrines very weak, and by the 1850's anti-statism was gaining everywhere.

[2] J. Dorfman, 'The Jackson Wage-Earner Thesis', *American Historical Review* (January 1949), liv, 305; cf. William A. Sullivan, 'Did Labour support Andrew Jackson?', *Political Science Quarterly* (December 1947), lxii, no 4; E. Pessen, 'Did Labour Support Jackson?: the Boston Story', *ibid.* (June 1949), lxiv, no 2. In spite of such criticisms the work that started this controversy, *The Age of Jackson* (Boston, 1945) by A. M. Schlesinger, jun, remains a very important landmark in American historiography.

converging on the same point. One has only to find the centre, and everything is revealed at a glance. But in England, the paths run criss-cross, and it is only by travelling down each of them that one can build up a picture of the whole.'[1]

But he was clear how important was the aristocratic spirit that seemed to him to have permeated downwards through all strata of society; '*Je ne retrouve en aucun-point notre Amérique*', he wrote to the companion of his former travels.[2] Revisiting England as late as 1857, he found its aristocratic institutions more firmly established than in his youth. 'It is still,' he wrote, 'the only country in the globe than can give an idea of the *ancien régime* in Europe in revised and perfected form.'[3] For American visitors to England the same reflection took the form of irritated comments upon the political 'apathy' of the masses.

'Habits of subservience to the aristocracy,' wrote Bancroft to President Polk, 'are so branded into the national character that the people generally are satisfied with their institutions. They keep down pretty well their envy at our success, their consciousness that we are going forward full of hope while their future is clouded.'[4]

But our concern is not with the social structure of the two countries that was in both cases on the eve of major changes, but with the political habits developed in this period, and passed on to later ones.

The English political system was not based, and never had been based in ordinary times upon the idea of self-government in the literal American sense. The only time at which such a basis had been sought—the period of the seventeenth-century interregnum—had left memories that could only produce an unequivocal distaste for further attempts to apply these ideas in this country. The quarrels between Cromwell and his Parliaments so exactly prefigure in their essentials the endemic struggle between President and Congress under the United States Constitution, as to make it remarkable that the warning they provided should never have been considered by those who drew up a system of co-ordinate authorities with the same single popular sanction.

The English idea of government has recently been defined in

---

[1] Tocqueville to le Comte Molé, August 1835 (*Oeuvres Complètes*, vii, 135).

[2] Letter to Beaumont, London, August 13, 1833 (*Oeuvres*, ii, 25).

[3] Letter to La Comtesse de Pizieux, September 21, 1857 (*Oeuvres*, vii, 461).

[4] Letter of October 20, 1848 (M. A. DeWolfe Howe, op. cit., p. 39).

words difficult to improve upon, by one who brings to the study of politics the advantage of long practical experience: 'Our constitution,' writes Mr Amery, 'is still, at bottom, based upon a continuous parley or conference in Parliament between the Crown, i.e. the Government as the directing and energizing element, and the representatives of the nation whose assent and acquiescence are essential and only to be secured by full discussion.'[1] That is to say that even now, the British Cabinet embodies in its collective capacity, the full majesty of government formerly symbolized by the enthroned monarch. Its dependence upon a parliamentary majority does not alter this fact; because all Parliament, or the electorate, can do is to replace one Cabinet by another that immediately enters into the full inheritance of its predecessor. In the last resort Parliament and people will normally give their confidence to government and the servants of government, knowing the full measure of responsibility that they assume, if they deny it to them.

The Government of Great Britain has thus in the first instance the power that it derives from its long continuance and from the gradual building up of the machinery of the state by the often anonymous servants of medieval and Tudor monarchs, and by the new embryo civil service of Stuart and Hanoverian times. It is therefore natural that when those trained in this tradition acquire responsibilities outside Britain their first instinct should be to make certain of the fundamentals of law and order, by calling upon whatever natural loyalties may exist to a monarch, a tribal system, or a previous constitution. For Americans, on the other hand, the essential appears to be that the forms of popular choice be at once revived or created.

The period between 1830 and 1870 was one of rapid development in British as well as in American politics. But in Britain it took two forms, both of which could be interpreted as progress towards the democratic ideal, but neither of which was then so interpreted. In the first place, there was the extension of the political constituency so as to make it correspond more closely with a social structure modified by the development of industrial capitalism. In the second place, there was the recasting of the machinery of government to meet the new problems that the same phenomenon had created. Under that head comes the whole series of measures, including municipal reform, the development of the Home Office as an instrument for the regulation of some of the worst of recognized social

[1] L. S. Amery, *Thoughts on the Constitution* (Oxford, 1947), p. 10.

abuses, the creation of a reliable civilian police, and finally, in the
two middle decades of the nineteenth century, the major reform
of the civil service. It may be argued that nineteenth-century Britain
had too narrow a concept of the proper sphere of government; it
can hardly be denied that it developed a workable instrument for
use whenever that concept should be widened. It was the existence
of an instrument of this kind that made possible the whole idea of
Fabianism, and on a larger, more fanciful plane, the Wellsian dream
of the 'open conspiracy'.

In America however, natural Fabians such as Henry Adams in
one generation, or Colonel House in another, were foredoomed to
frustration.

> All Boston, all New England, and all respectable New York . . .
> agreed that Washington was no place for a respectable young
> man. All Washington, including Presidents, Cabinet officers,
> Judiciary, Senators, Congressmen and clerks, expressed the same
> opinion and conspired to drive away every young man who
> happened to be there, or tried to approach. Not one young man
> of promise remained in the Government service, all drifted into
> opposition.[1]

This could hardly have been said of the London of the 1870's.

Nor can it well be denied that the root of the matter lies in the
preceding period. For while Great Britain was perfecting the
machinery of government, Jacksonian democrats were exulting in
the capacity of the ordinary citizen to fill in turn all the functions
of government, and incorporating the principle of rotation in office
into the very core of their political creed.

> 'Experience has certainly shown,' declared one of them, 'no
> sufficient reason to question the general aptitude of the people for
> self-government. When we observe the capacity discovered by
> the members of society, extending to all relations and equal to
> all occasions, carried also into the duties of administering its
> authority; and when we observe them indiscriminately executing
> or aiding in all its departments, civil and judicial, as jurors, magis-
> trates, legislators, governors, acting as trustees of all the interests
> of the community for the benefit of the public and as guardians
> of all those rights for which law was designed as security, taken
> continually from all classes and returning to the mass by perpetual
> elective process, can we any longer doubt the efficacy of this great

[1] *Education of Henry Adams* (Boston, 1918), p. 296: cf. Ernest Samuels,
The Young Henry Adams (Harvard UP, 1948), pp. 168-207.

principle which is thus receiving refreshment and vigour from its original fountains.'[1]

The idea of a specialized body of administrators remained deeply suspect as necessarily tainted with privilege. This suspicion has clearly not diminished in force, and can always be relied on to fortify suspicions of governmental action that may spring from very different sources. It has been an equally potent force in the history of American education:

> What has been called the 'Jacksonian tradition' in American thinking, combined with the propaganda of certain educators, has spread the idea that the American child can, if he wants, with the aid of proper education, become anything he desires. . . . By denying the reality of intellectual talent, the 'Jacksonian democrat' can also minimize the significance of professional training.[2]

An intellectual like Henry Adams might be convinced that the system of 1789 had broken down by 1870.[3] He could assert that a few years later 'nothing could surpass the nonsensity of trying to run so complex and so concentrated a machine' as the capitalist society of the USA 'by Southern and Western farmers in grotesque alliance with city day-labourers, as had been tried in 1800 and 1823, and had failed even under simple conditions'.[4] But the experiment was to be tried in some form, at least twice again; for both the New Freedom and the New Deal did not essentially depart from the traditional pattern of American popular revolt.

Indeed those who believed that this was insufficient and that a new kind of government was needed for the new programmes, were likely to be handicapped by the suspicions of genuine democrats as well as those who merely used the traditional language for their own purposes. Thus William Allen White—a democrat, even though of course, politically, a life-long Republican—was willing to believe that the young men of the New Deal, or some of them, genuinely thought it possible to combine their belief in a planned economy with democracy, that is with preserving to the people the right to change their government through the electoral process, but he doubted if

---

[1] Charles Stewart Davies, in Blau, *op. cit.*, p. 45. The same political creed, carried over into the post-Civil War period, inspired Walt Whitman's *Democratic Vistas*. [See his *Complete Poetry and Selected Prose* (ed. Emory Holloway, London, n, d.), pp. 657 ff.]

[2] J. B. Conant, *Education in a Divided World* (Harvard UP, 1948), p. 207.

[3] Adams, *op. cit.*, pp. 280-1.

[4] Ibid., pp. 344-5.

this was possible. He distrusted the power that they would generate 'in any human hands' that were 'around this administration or have been around any other administration' he had ever known.

'I believe,' he wrote, 'politicians in the whole are as honest and effective as businessmen, but I never knew a businessman or a politican I would trust with all the power they are generating around the White House there in Washington. They are so liable to be as wicked, as ruthless, as greedy as those men in Wall Street.' For a small group in Wall Street had had all the power which it was now in the third decade of the twentieth century, planned to give Washington.[1] And many were not prepared to believe, as White was, that politicians were as honest or as effective as businessmen.

And of course the politician here includes the administrator. And in a sense the usage is correct. For under such a system, where effective government is curtailed, the arts of the politician are required if the machine is to work at all.[2] In just the same way, the fact that interest-groupings, including organized labour, work directly through pressure-groups upon Congress, rather than through a tidy system of ideological parties, is not simply an anomaly as Professor Harold Laski and other would-be reformers of the system have argued, but is a direct and necessary consequence of the democratic principle upon which the system rests.[3]

It would be unwarrantably dogmatic to say that this state of affairs is unchangeable; nor is it my purpose to speculate upon whether either the system or its consequences—only some of which have been even hinted at here—are better or worse than their British counterparts. What one finds difficult to accept, is the view that those differences are superficial, or even obviously transient.

Some indeed would argue that, even if these differences once existed, they are ceasing to do so, and that the United States has begun to make rapid advances towards the common goal of the 'welfare state'. They may indeed go so far as to argue that it is the British example that has been decisive in this development. A contemporary French writer, with much of the spirit of Tocqueville,

[1] William Allen White to Allan Nevins, May 24, 1934 [*Selected Letters of William Allen White*, ed. Walter Johnson (New York, 1947), pp. 345-6].

[2] See Robert Sherwood s account of Harry Hopkins's experiences with the wpa in *The White House Papers of Harry Hopkins*, i, 68 ff.

[3] See e.g. Harold Laski, *The American Democracy* (London, 1949), pp. 129-37.

and wider information, has written of the result of the 1948 presidential election in America:

> Were they of a boastful disposition — a vice from which I claim for them a delightful immunity — the British might well take great pride in their position; now for the first time, they might say, since the thirteen colonies cut themselves off from us, their discarded mother has resumed her intellectual empire over the giant offspring which now towers above her.[1]

But if one compares the handling by Congress of President Truman's domestic programme and its direct intervention in questions of administration and administrative personnel, with the smooth carrying into effect, both legislatively and administratively, of the highly controversial programme espoused by the British Labour Government elected in 1945, this conclusion must seem somewhat premature. If the sociologist may see less of a contrast between Britain and the United States today than existed a century ago, the political scientist, from his narrower viewpoint, must still find more significance in the area of disagreement than in the fundamentals wherein the two nations are as one.

---

[1] Bertrand de Jouvenel, *Problems of Socialist England* (tr. J. F. Huntington, London, 1949), p. 215.

12

Benjamin Franklin:
International Statesman

TOMORROW is the two hundred and fiftieth anniversary of the birth at Boston, Massachusetts, of Benjamin Franklin.[1] It has been decided that the celebration of this event should in part take the form of lectures on the various aspects of Franklin's career, to be given under the auspices of each of the many institutions with which he came to be connected. In 1785, Franklin was elected a corresponding member of the Manchester Literary and Philosophical Society, though the destruction of the society's records during the war has made it impossible to trace many particulars as to the circumstances.

However, his connection with the Society was not a purely nominal one. His paper *Meteorological Imaginations and Conjectures* written in Paris in May 1784 to explain the exceptionally cold winter that Northern Europe had suffered was for instance communicated to the Society by the then joint President Dr Thomas Percival and read on December 22, 1784.[2] It is this link with Manchester that explains the appearance of this lecture in your proceedings.

It is not, however, as a meteorologist that we are called upon to consider Franklin tonight. The scope of choice has indeed been vast, since even in the many-sided eighteenth century few men could show as wide a range of interest and achievement. No branch of the sciences escaped his notice, and to many he made important contributions, usually with an eye to their practical application. His long life covered the whole process by which the separate colonies clinging to their seaboard footholds were turned into a united and independent nation already bestriding the mountains and looking to the interior. And Franklin, finally, was important not only for what

[1] A lecture delivered before the Manchester Literary and Philosophical Society on January 16, 1956.

[2] *The Writings of Benjamin Franklin* ed. A. H. Smyth. Vol IX. (NY, 1906) pp. 215-18. The paper printed in Vol II of the Society's *Memoirs*. pp. 357ff.

he did or wrote, but for what he was. If Washington was the father of his country and Jefferson the supreme product of its early genius, Franklin more than either typified for the rest of the world what it hoped and expected an American to be; the simple philosopher of the frontier, ready to turn his hand to any practical task, sought after by society though not seeking it—in his manner and appearance the antithesis of the sophisticated European of the upper classes whom it was fashionable to despise even when one belonged to them. Hence Franklin's vogue in the Paris of the pre-Revolutionary decade when he was in far more than a political sense the envoy of the New World to the Old.

Fortunately, however, I am not asked this evening to comment on all these possible aspects of the Franklin theme; you wish to hear of Franklin neither as a scientist nor as an inventor, neither as a business man nor as an intellectual entrepreneur, not as a social lion—a curious role for one whose taciturnity was often noted—and not, I take it, as an amorist. In all these roles he has found an enthusiastic and credible biographer in Carl Van Doren and if you wish to know what Franklin was like I can only commend you to this work.[1] Franklin's own writings are also easy enough to come by, and the American Philosophical Society is preparing for this anniversary a new edition of them to rank with the great Princeton edition of Jefferson. To do more you must go to Philadelphia and seek out in the rooms of the American Philosophical Society, founded on Franklin's initiative in 1744, the portraits of himself and his contemporaries and the collection of personal relics that help to bring them and their times so vividly to life, once the very different Philadelphia of today is shut out.[2]

What I have been asked to do is to talk about the political aspects of Franklin's career and since even this would take us over half a century of American and Pennsylvanian history, I have limited myself still further and wish to consider one aspect only, and that the nearest to our own interests. I am indeed encouraged to look at Franklin's role in international politics because his contribution to American foreign policy has recently been the subject of a specialized study to which I at once confess myself much indebted.[3]

[1] Carl Van Doren, *Benjamin Franklin.* (NY, Viking Press, 1938)

[2] See the 'Brief History of the American Philosophical Society' by Edwin G. Conklin in *Year Book of the American Philosophical Society 1952.*

[3] Gerald Stourzh, *Benjamin Franklin and American Foreign Policy.* (Chicago University Press, 1954)

But I do so also because the general problem with which Franklin was dealing was one which is in two ways connected with certain preoccupations of our own times. And it would seem proper in the case of Franklin, whose own bent was so essentially a practical one, to deal with some living issue rather than to delve into a purely antiquarian enquiry. In electricity we have outshone Franklin and his contemporaries; the same is not true in the field of international relations.

One of the connections between his time and our own is obvious. Franklin was an active participant in events which first brought about the separation of what became the United States from the British Empire, and then removed the United States from all participation in the political affairs of Europe, though this process was not in fact completed until after Franklin had passed from the scene. In our own lifetime we have of course seen this process reversed. The United States has come back into Europe and has, however reluctantly, accepted the view that under modern conditions such a separation between Europe and America is too dangerous for both. It is true that the reversal has not gone the whole way; the United States—despite Bernard Shaw—has not rejoined the British family. Nor do I subscribe to the thesis so powerfully argued in some quarters that the re-knotting of the Anglo-American tie is what Providence has always had in store for us. Nevertheless there is an increasing number of special links between Great Britain and the United States, and out of this fact there may well spring a renewed concern about the origins of the split and its subsequent completion. The wheel has not come full circle, and if it did it would be Britain that would be the dependency, but it has come far enough of the way round for it to be useful for us to look again at the beginning.

Franklin's early position was that of an imperial expansionist concerned to bring about the union, and subsequent extension of the mainland colonies and arguing that this would be a means of strengthening the Empire as a whole. In rejoicing over the conquest of Canada, he writes: 'I do so not merely as I am a colonist, but as I am a Briton. I have long been of the opinion that the foundations of the future grandeur and stability of the British Empire lie in America; and though like other foundations they are low and little seen, they are nevertheless, broad and strong enough to support the greatest political structure human wisdom ever yet erected.'[1] In 1754 in discussions with Governor Shirley of Massachusetts after the inter-

[1] Letter to Lord Kames, quoted Stourzh. op. cit. p. 81.

colonial meeting at Albany and again in 1766, Franklin toyed with the idea of requesting representation for the colonies in Parliament — that is to say with the notion of a federal empire.[1]

But Franklin's theory of imperial unity was increasingly conditional upon Britain's adoption of policies equally beneficial to the mother-country and the colonies. During his residence in London after 1764 as the agent for Pennsylvania and other colonies he gradually came to the conclusion that the conception of a common interest did not in fact inspire the British Parliament or Ministries. In arguing for the repeal of the Stamp Act before the House of Commons, in February 1766, Franklin claimed, perhaps for prudential reasons, that the colonists objected only to internal taxes,[2] but this position was not a tenable one in view of the evolution of American opinion, though he came to drop it only slowly. By 1770, the argument is not one for strengthening the Empire but for the view that without representation in Parliament, the colonies may not be taxed.[3] As late as 1773 he was certainly still talking in terms of a union, but as events succeeded one another the course of Franklin's thinking followed along the same lines as that of many of his fellow-Americans at home, and when in 1774, Joseph Galloway produced a federal plan as the last hope of conciliation, Franklin indicated his categorical dissent:

'When I consider,' he wrote from London, 'the extreme corruption prevalent among all orders of men in this rotten old state, and the glorious public virtue so predominant in our rising country, I cannot but apprehend more mischief than benefit from a closer union. I fear they will drag us after them in all the plundering wars which their desperate circumstances, injustice and rapacity may prompt them to undertake; and their wide-wasting prodigality and profusion is a gulf that will swallow up every aid we may distress ourselves to afford them.'[4]

In unofficial talks in December 1774 Franklin put forward demands which gave the Americans virtual independence in return

---

[1] V. W. Crane, ed. *Benjamin Franklin's Letters to the Press, 1758-75* (Chapel Hill, NC, 1950), introduction, pp. XXXVII ff.; J. C. Miller, *The Origins of the American Revolution.* (London, 1945) pp. 163-64.

[2] E. C. and H. M. Morgan, *The Stamp Act Crisis.* (Chapel Hill, 1953) p. 276.

[3] See the article in Crane, op. cit. pp. 173-77.

[4] Letter to Joseph Galloway, February 25, 1775, quoted Max Beloff, *The Debate on the American Revolution.* (London, 1949), p. 203.

for guarantees on the British trade monopoly; even the conciliatory element in the Cabinet could not accept them.[1]

Thereafter it is with the role of an independent United States that Franklin's political thinking is concerned.

The other link between Franklin's problems and our own is less immediately apparent but perhaps even more instructive. What Franklin was doing when he went to Paris in 1776, and stayed to negotiate first the French alliance and then the Peace with Britain, was to help frame a foreign policy for a newly enfranchised nation, for a new member of international society. This task is one which many other statesmen have had to undertake in this century of crumbling Empire; it is never an easy one. Suddenly freed from the control of a distant metropolis such a nation is all too likely to neglect the services that the metropolis has rendered and think only of the burdens that it has now shaken off. It is likely, in particular, to underestimate the extent to which in a world of competing States, its own security and perhaps it very existence has depended and still depends on an ability to defend them. It will tend to believe that any past wars in which it may have been involved have been due to the connection with the mother-country, and that for its part it can easily live at peace with the rest of the world against which it has no claims of its own. It will therefore be disinclined to continue into peacetime any burdens in the form of military preparations which membership in an Empire may have imposed upon it, and still more disinclined to compensate by its own efforts for the gap created by the removal of the protecting shield of the imperial power. And similarly in the field of foreign policy the government of such a nation is likely to assert its right to cultivate no particular friendships, but to seek for goodwill on all sides and indeed to expect it; it will denounce particular alliances and spurn adhesion to *blocs*. It may, if its independence is the product of a long revolutionary struggle, have learned to justify such policies in terms of a pacific and universalist ideology. To some extent this has been the story of almost every member of the British Empire to which has subsequently come independence within the Commonwealth or outside it,[2] it was though part of the greatness of Sir John Macdonald that he saw that the British 'alliance' was the only safeguard of Canadian

[1] C. R. Ritcheson, *British Politics and the American Revolution.* (Norman, Oklahoma, 1954) pp. 178-80.

[2] I have dealt with this point with particular reference to Australia in my book *Foreign Policy and the Democratic Process.* (Johns Hopkins Press, 1955)

nationality against the annexationist ambitions of the United States.[1] The most salient contemporary manifestation of such an attitude is to be found in the India of Mr Nehru. But the first example of all, that of the United States, is equally illuminating. And the fact that the United States did not retire into isolation until the conditions for its continued independence had been fulfilled, until the Louisiana purchase had given her the promise of expansion she required, and until Great Britain (no longer feared herself) had placed the shield afforded by her domination of the seas between American and all other European nations, is a testimony to the eventual realism of the Founding Fathers. Their formal precepts on foreign policy — separation from Europe and the rejection of entangling alliances — may have harmed America later on because they were applied to conditions which had changed; future generations of Americans elevated the letter of the commandments above their spirit. The Founding Fathers would not have made the same mistake.

Yet the temptations to make precisely this error were present and powerful. The eighteenth century was a century of wars in which the dynastic and the imperial motifs were curiously and inextricably mixed. European radicals believed that all wars were unnecessary and that the reign of reason would reach the need for and possibility of international harmony. In England they attacked the Hanoverian connection on the ground that it brought England into conflicts which her island position would otherwise have enabled her to avoid. In America the same arguments were used to show that the wars in which the colonists had taken part up to 1763 and for which the British had subsequently asked them to help pay, were not fought for their own benefit but wholly for the mother-country's.[2] Once cut the tie with Britain, and the swords could be beaten into ploughshares, literally and at once. It is not surprising that the classic formulation of the case for this view came not from an American but from the exiled British radical Tom Paine, who had crossed the Atlantic and thrown in his lot with the Americans less than two years before he published in January 1776 the pamphlet *Common Sense* in which he urged them to cast aside all equivocation and proclaim their independence:

[1] See D. Creighton: *John A. Macdonald: The Old Chieftain.* (Toronto, 1955.)

[2] On the connection between American thinking on foreign policy and the theories of European and British radicals see the two articles by F. Gilbert: 'The English background of American isolationism in the Eighteenth Century', *William and Mary Quarterly* 3rd Ser, Vol I, 1944; 'The New Diplomacy of the Eighteenth Century', *World Politics* Vol IV, October 1951.

Any submission to or dependence on Great Britain, tends directly to involve this continent in European wars and quarrels, and sets us at variance with nations, who would otherwise seek our friendship, and against whom we have neither anger nor complaint. . . . Europe is too thickly planted with kingdoms to be long at peace, and whenever a war breaks out between England and any foreign power the trade of America goes to ruin, *because of her connection with Britain.*'[1]

As we have seen a similar plaint had actually figured among Franklin's reasons for desiring to see the imperial connection abandoned. In this argument he had preceded Paine, yet at the time of the wars in America he had hardly viewed them as being fought solely in Britain's interest. Political passion had overwhelmed consistency. But he was not to follow this line of thought to the dangerous length of believing that independence would necessarily be self-sustaining. American experience in the colonial period was bound, if seriously considered, to lead to quite different conclusions.

Franklin's own interest in the remodelling of the imperial structure and in creating common institutions for the colonies had, as we have seen, grown out of his conviction that their interests and Britain's were identical. The Americans were concerned to settle the interior of the Continent from which the French and Spaniards threatened to bar them, and Britain was concerned to see her colonies grown and her colonists multiply. He had taken a full part in the outburst of feeling against the two Catholic Powers and their Indian allies which marked the middle of the century, and had welcomed the destruction of French power in North America which was the result of the Seven Years War or, as Americans called it, 'the French and Indian War'. In 1760 he had written of this war: 'If ever there was a national war this is truly such a one, a war in which the interest of the whole nation is directly and fundamentally concerned.'[2]

It is true that the war was not in all respects conclusive. Beyond the Mississippi, and at New Orleans, the Spanish Empire still thrust its weakening tentacles northwards; the British showed an unexpected and much resented kindness to the Catholic French in Canada, whose acquisition in preference to Guadeloupe Franklin had strongly urged in his pamphlet — and when independence came the acquisi-

---

[1] Quoted from Max Beloff (ed.). *The Debate on the American Revolution.* (London, 1949) p. 250.

[2] *The interests of Great Britain considered with regard to her Colonies and the Acquisition of Canada and Guadeloupe. Writings.* (ed. Smyth.) II. p. 51.

tion of Canada for the United States was to be something of an obsession with Franklin — but the major danger, a French encirclement
linking the mouth of the St Lawrence to the mouth of the Mississippi,
was gone; Americans could now afford to enter into contests over
taxation and over their constitutional rights. In the course of it
they began to emphasize their own role in the victory; it was they
who had been essential to Britain. The prophecy that once the danger
which Canada had presented had been removed the Americans would
cease to feel dependent on Britain, turned out to be all too accurate.
Franklin had denied this argument at the time, by declaring that
on the contrary the presence of another European Power on the
North American continent would give a prospect of aid or asylum
to colonial malcontents. And he clung to the same view at the time
of the Stamp Act crisis.[1] Already in the 1760's Franklin's thought
about the American position is concerned with the international
aspect of their demand for a change in status. This was not perhaps
typical of the colonial mind at the time. The principal fact was that
the quarrels of Europe now seemed remote and that foreign politics
had lost ground in their thinking.[2]

But if America neglected Europe, the reverse was by no means the
case. France and Spain were deeply concerned to upset the decision
of 1763. They were indeed, and in particular France, less directly
interested in imperial expansion for its own sake than Britain. But
it had become an axiom that Britain's overweening power rested
upon her imperial position; as Choiseul, France's foreign minister
until 1770, had written: 'It is possessions in America that will in
future form the balance of power in Europe.' Since a direct reconquest of the French position was out of the question the best hope
appeared to be to detach the American colonies from Britain; at
worst Britain would lose the military and commercial advantages
she drew from their possession, at best they might fall into dependence upon France and Spain. As the French observed the course
of events in America they became more and more convinced that
the break would come, and more and more intent on taking full
advantage of it. Spain, as was shown by her attitude during the
Revolution itself, had certain inhibitions — she rightly feared that

[1] On this see Stourzh. op. cit. pp. 77 and 100.

[2] See Max Savelle, 'Colonial Origins of American Diplomatic Principles'.
Pacific Historical Review, Vol III, 1934; 'The Appearance of an American
Attitude toward External Affairs'. *American Historical Review*, Vol LII, July
1947.

if Britain's colonists could bring off a successful revolt, her own, with greater grievances to move them, would not long be held in dependence. But France had no grounds for such scruples and Vergennes, who became foreign minister in 1774 and held office until 1787, in this followed Choiseul.[1]

Franklin's correspondence shows him fully aware of these French calculations—at first hoping that the British Empire would stand together and frustrate these expectations, later, as the conflict with Britain deepened, studying the use to which the Americans could put them.

The dilemma which Franklin and his contemporaries faced in handling the diplomacy of the American Revolution is therefore clear enough: how to take advantage of the French and Spanish desire to weaken and even destroy the British hold in North America without thereby falling into a new dependence upon Britain's enemies. The first objective was involved in seeking a French alliance, the second in securing peace at such a time and on such terms as would meet fundamental American needs and permit an independent policy in the future.[2] Once again an analogy may clarify the problem. For it was the same problem as three-quarters of a century later faced the Southern statesmen who planned secession from the Union. They too were aware that the United States had enemies abroad and hoped that these enemies would help them against the Union. Indeed at the time when the prospect of such a secession first appeared upon the horizon in 1820, John Quincy Adams, whose father had played a role not inferior to Franklin's in the earlier struggle (and was still alive), was told by Calhoun that if the Union were dissolved the South 'would be from necessity compelled to form an alliance, offensive and defensive, with Great Britain', to which Adams replied: 'that would be returning to the colonial state.' 'Yes, pretty much,' said Calhoun, 'but it would be forced upon them.'[3]

The Southern diplomats were less fortunate than Franklin and John Adams had been. In the 1860's, European rivalries worked

---

[1] Max Savelle: 'The American Balance of Power and European Diplomacy 1713-78' in R. B. Morris (ed.) *The Era of the American Revolution.* (Columbia UP, 1939)

[2] See S. F. Bemis: *The Diplomacy of the American Revolution* (New York, 1935), and V. T. Harlow, *The Founding of the Second British Empire 1763-93.* Vol I. (London, 1952)

[3] *The Diary of John Quincy Adams.* (ed. A. Nevins) (New York, 1929) p. 228.

against any Power's intervening in North America, and Canada was an additional hostage against action by Britain on the South's behalf. But the miscalculation was one of fact not of principle. Whether if the South had secured European allies it could have avoided an era of total dependence is an open question.[1]

Both phases of the earlier story involved Franklin at almost every point. One can do no more than try briefly to indicate the nature of his approach to the problems raised. Franklin returned from England in May 1775, and in November 1775 he became a member of a Committee of the Continental Congress set up 'for the sole purpose of corresponding with our friends in Great Britain, Ireland and other parts of the world'.[2] Being the only member of the Committee with European connections he began a fairly voluminous correspondence to see what help the colonists would be likely to get if they broke away finally from Britain and established their independence. It was clear that France was the principal hope, and it was Franklin who, before his abortive mission to Canada in the spring of 1776, drew up the instructions to the first American agent to be sent to Paris— instructions in which it was made clear that the return that France might expect from her assistance was to be the greater share of American commerce. This was in accordance with the prevailing view of which John Adams was the principal exponent that no military or political alliance should be entered into by the new American States. We have Adams's word for it that at the time Franklin agreed with him on this point and his own statement in a letter written to Arthur Lee from Paris in the following March: 'I have never yet changed the opinion I gave in Congress, that a Virgin State should preserve her Virgin Character, and not go about suitoring for alliances, but wait with decent Dignity for the Applications of others.'[3]

By now, however, as Franklin wrote, he had been overruled: 'perhaps for the best'. The original plan for a treaty with France had offered nothing but commercial advantages in return for military assistance. Some within Congress thought the inducement too slight and by the end of 1776 a decision to go 'suitoring for alliances' had been taken.[4]

[1] See Max Beloff: 'Great Britain and the American Civil War', *History* NS Vol XXXVII, February 1952.

[2] E. C. Burnett, *The Continental Congress*. (New York, 1941) p. 118.

[3] Franklin, *Writings*. (ed. A. H. Smyth.) Vol VII, p. 35.

[4] Stourzh, op. cit. pp. 125-26.

Franklin, who had arrived in France early in December, realized the implications of the search for allies: 'While we are asking Aids,' he wrote, 'it is necessary to gratify the desires, and in some sort comply with the humours of those we apply to.'[1] But in subsequent months he was under fire from some quarters in America for the apathy of his diplomacy. The French, while giving secret aid to the colonists, were not unnaturally doubtful about the wisdom of making a formal pact until the colonists had proved their desire and their capacity to stand on their own feet as an independent nation. They were also held up by their wish to act in concert with Spain.[2] Franklin seems still to have believed that America could free herself by her own efforts and that if not France's own interests would lead her to intervention, and still to have been unwilling to offer France more than commercial incentives: an English intelligence agent reported him in October 1777 as saying: 'He is not deceived by France. He dreaded their seizing the opportunity with too much warmth and by relieving the necessities of America too liberally prevent their Industry, their ingenuity and the discovery of the Resources of a Country intended by Heaven for Independence in its utmost Latitude. He cannot bear the faintest idea of reconciliation short of Independency — and is averse in his Conversations, to the necessity of incurring obligations from France, which may bind America beyond its true Interests.'[3] Franklin had no wish to see his countrymen escape from the embraces of one mercantilist-minded Empire to fall into the lap of another, whose record showed a much stronger devotion to principles of monopoly and centralization; what he did do was use approaches for reconciliation from England to get better offers from France.[4]

Vergennes understood his attitude very well, pointing out after his first interview with Franklin that while the French were being asked 'to give up every claim to recover or conquer any part of North America and of the adjacent islands which formerly belonged to us' they were 'offered nothing more than strict neutrality in case we should be attacked on account of this treaty'.[5] He saw too that

---

[1] *Writings*. loc. cit.

[2] On the course of French policy at this time, see the introduction by John J. May to his *Despatches and Instructions of Conrad Alexandre Gérard 1778-80.* (Baltimore, Johns Hopkins Press, 1939)

[3] Quoted Stourzh. op. cit. pp. 133-34.

[4] See Ritcheson. op. cit. pp. 234-41.

[5] Quoted Stourzh. op. cit. p. 137.

this attitude could be regarded as a principle of foreign policy: 'We are informed,' he wrote in January 1778, 'that there is a numerous party in America which is endeavouring to fix as a basis of the political system of the new States that no engagement be contracted with the European powers. Doctor Franklin himself professes this dogma.'[1] By now however the victory of Saratoga was known; Vergennes, unmoved by merely commercial perspectives and realizing that a treaty meant war, was nevertheless anxious not to miss the chance of a political stroke against Britain, or be victim of a reconciliation between the mother-country and the colonies towards which Britain now seemed to be moving. Franklin told Vergennes's negotiator Gérard that the 'immediate conclusion of a treaty of commerce and alliance would induce the Deputies to close their ears to any proposal which should not have as its basis, complete liberty and independence, both commercial and political.'[2]

Although France renounced any future monopolies with regard to American commerce, it was not possible to avoid political commitments in the treaty of alliance. France and the United States agreed not to conclude peace without each other's consent, but the French renunciation of territorial ambitions was less extensive than the Americans had hoped since it included besides Bermuda only such parts of North America as had been British before 1763. Whereas the Americans had tried to bind the French to help them to conquer Canada, Nova Scotia, Saint John's (i.e. New Brunswick) and Bermuda in return for help in driving the British from the West Indies, which were to go to France, and a half-share in the Newfoundland fisheries, they were now obliged to content themselves with a French guarantee of any conquests they could obtain for themselves. And France had no interest in seeing Canada fall to the United States, believing that the United States would feel more dependent on France if she had British territory contiguous to her own — the old argument that Franklin had tried to dispose of now used in the reverse sense.[3] It meant also that France was not bound as regards the possible acquisition of Louisiana, the 'island' of New Orleans or other North American islands such as Cape Breton or even Newfoundland. The needs of the war in America were too strong for Franklin's original plan of political non-involvement to

[1] Quoted ibid. p. 135.
[2] Ibid. p. 140.
[3] See Stourzh, op. cit. pp. 142-6.

be effective. It remained to be seen what would happen when the war was won.

After the Franco-American treaties of Amity and Commerce and of Alliance of February 1778, the diplomacy of the war was largely concerned with the French attempt to bring in Spain as well and to line up the maritime neutrals against Britain. The United States was only involved in most of this at second-hand, and Vergennes failed to get Spain to include American independence as an agreed war aim. Franklin was not himself involved in these negotiations and refused to entangle himself in unofficial talks with British emissaries, which he believed were only intended to disunite the Americans and separate them from their allies.[1] We can therefore move forward to the point at which the American unwillingness to prolong the war further for the sake of French or Spanish objectives led to the beginning of peace-feelers, yet at no period of his embassy must we imagine him idle. The foreign loans on which the colonial cause so much depended, matters arising out of the exchange of prisoners, the issuing of passports and naval prizes all kept him busy. Further-more he was an active if discreet propagandist — and the atrocities committed by Britain's Indian allies gave him opportunities of the kind a wartime propagandist most relishes. It was indeed on Britain's cruelty that Franklin insisted when putting aside the attempts of those who still hoped for some form of reconciliation. Writing to David Hartley from his house at Passy on September 3, 1778, Franklin said: I wish with you as much for the Restoration of Peace as we both formerly did for the Continuance of it. But it must be a Peace of a different kind. I was fond to a Folly of our British Connections [sic], and it was with infinite Regret that I saw the Necessity you would force us into of breaking it. But the extreme Cruelty with which we have been treated has now extinguished every Thought of returning to it, and has separated us forever. You have thereby lost Limbs that will never grow again.'[2]

Franklin's purpose once peace came in sight after North's resigna-tion was to find out how far the essential American points — inde-pendence and freedom for further territorial expansion — could be gained and the French persuaded to accept them as the foundation for a peace, without endorsing all Spain's pretensions, thus bringing about a peace fundamentally favourable to the United States but without a formal breach of the obligations entered into with regard

[1] Ritcheson. op. cit. 241, 257, 267.
[2] *Writings.* (ed. Smyth) VII, p. 186.

to France.[1] Vergennes was indeed agreeable to parallel negotiation provided the treaties were signed together. Franklin regarded fidelity to France as being important, both for the sake of American prestige and because he thought the United States too weak to balance Britain and France against each other. Nevertheless, the temptation to separate was there, particularly since Britain was now prepared to go a long way in order to dissolve the ties between the Americans and her European enemies. For her now, as for France earlier, the international aspect of the Revolution was uppermost. 'Englishmen in 1782,' writes Professor Harlow, 'found it difficult to believe that Americans had become "foreigners" to the extent of preferring to remain in the Bourbon camp and so running the risk of a new war about extraneous objects such as Gibraltar and the Coromandel coast.'[2] Richard Oswald, the Scottish army contractor and slave merchant who acted as Shelburne's unofficial envoy to Franklin, gave an optimistic picture of Franklin's reaction to such suggestions: 'Upon the whole the Doctor expressed himself in a friendly way towards England and was not without hopes, that if we should settle on this occasion in the way he wished, England would not only have beneficial intercourse with the colonies, but at last it might end in a federal union between them. In the meantime we ought to take care not to force them into the hands of other people.'[3]

But Oswald was either deceived by Franklin's tone or carried away by the optimism which seems to be characteristic of unofficial and amateur envoys. In June 1782 Franklin wrote in a private letter: 'England sees at length the Difficulty of Conquering us, and no longer demands submission but asks for Peace. She would now think herself happy to obtain a Federal Union with us and will endeavour it; but perhaps will be disappointed as it will be the Interest of all Europe to prevent it.'[4] To an English friend he wrote: 'It is now intimated to me from several quarters that Lord Shelburne's plan is to retain the sovereignty for the King, giving us otherwise an independent Parliament, and a government similar to that of late intended for Ireland: the thing is impracticable, and impossible, being inconsistent with the faith we have pledg'd, to say nothing of the General Disposi-

[1] A useful account of the negotiations will be found in: A. B. Darling, *Our Rising Empire*. (Yale University Press, 1940) Chaps I-V.

[2] Harlow. op. cit. p. 239.

[3] Oswald to Shelburne. July 10, 1782, quoted Bemis. op. cit. p. 208fn.

[4] Franklin to Jan Ingenhousz. June 21, 1782. *Writings*. (ed. Smyth) III, p. 315.

tion of our People.'[1] A little earlier he had given his views upon such a 'federal union' in a letter to Robert Livingston, the American Secretary for Foreign Affairs: 'However willing we might have been at the commencement of this contest to have accepted such conditions, be assured we can have no safety in them at present. The King hates us most cordially. If he is once admitted to any degree of power and government among us, however limited, it will soon be extended by corruption, artifice and force until we are reduced to absolute subjection, and that the more easily as by receiving him again for our King we shall draw upon us the contempt of all Europe.'[2]

Professor Harlow suggests that Franklin's use of the words 'at present' is 'possibly significant. At some future time, presumably when George III was dead, the two countries might agree to march together.'[3] But this perhaps underestimates the extent to which by now Franklin's thought ran wholly in the groove of national independence. On the other hand, Franklin had already in April put forward the idea that Britain should freely offer to cede Canada. Such a move, he claimed, would have the effect of winning American sympathies and providing a basis for a profitable Anglo-American commercial relationship in the future. This proposal clears Franklin of the charge of subservience to France made by some of his compatriots but it was as over-optimistic one way as was Shelburne's hope of a 'federal union' in another.

Franklin's ill-health in the latter part of 1782 put the furthering of negotiations into the hands of John Jay who was full of suspicion of France and Spain, and therefore keener on coming to an understanding with Britain as soon as possible. It was Jay who took the vital step of reducing American demands to the bare minimum of a recognition of independence, the Mississippi boundary and a share in the fisheries, and of concluding preliminaries on this basis. This meant not only the abandonment of Canada but an acceptance of its old frontiers as a basis for the subsequent demarcation. Franklin, however, when called upon to explain what had been done, used the fact that the preliminaries still depended on a final Anglo-French agreement as a justification for the agreement both to Vergennes and presumably to himself. In fact, however, the long-sought-for

[1] Franklin to Benjamin Vaughan, July 11, 1782, quoted by Harlow. op. cit. pp. 263-4.

[2] Franklin to Livingston, June 28, 1782, quoted ibid. p. 239.

[3] Harlow. loc. cit.

object had been gained. France could not keep America in leading-strings. Indeed by a secret article about the boundaries of Florida, the Americans were already working to get British co-operation to keep the Mississippi open when France should cede Louisiana to Spain. Since Britain never took West Florida this plan came to nothing but it showed that the Americans were already looking forward to the new situation that the peace would bring about.

Franklin, for his part, did not believe that the United States could yet afford separate action; Britain was still a possible danger and a check to her ambitions was necessary. The attempt in 1783 to bring about a close commercial relationship between Great Britain and an independent United States, an attempt which broke on the rock of the navigation acts, may be regarded as the last echo of the idea of a federal union of any kind between the two countries. With Britain entrenched in Canada and a power among the Indians of the North-West, and with Spain beyond the Mississippi, in Florida and on the 'island' of New Orleans, the vision of a whole continent open to the American pioneer was still unfulfilled. Franklin, as a believer in what a later generation was to know as 'manifest destiny', was bound to regard the function of American diplomacy as being first of all to serve the cause of American expansion. At sea, where America did not intend to enter the race for naval supremacy, Franklin now naturally accepted the view of the Powers of the Armed Neutrality that 'free ships make free goods'. He attempted, without result, to get this principle and the abolition of privateering accepted in the Peace Treaty. Only a paper satisfaction was granted to him, that of seeing his proposals accepted in a Treaty of Amity and Commerce signed by him in 1785; his partner in this piece of idealism was Frederick the Great of Prussia.[1] It is certain however that Franklin, who like Jefferson was an agrarian at heart, attached less importance to maritime diplomacy than to the prospects of continental growth. Equal terms of trade with all nations would be an adequate foundation for peace since all would find their interests served by them; the Americans themselves would be too engrossed in their struggle to bring a continent under cultivation to seek for conquest themselves.

If the Louisiana purchase might seem a justification of such optimism, the War of 1812 proved it to be unfounded. No escape from international politics was possible and Franklin's shrewd refusal to accept a completely utopian version of the behaviour of nation-states was proved correct. So too was his insistence on national

[1] See Stourzh. op. cit. pp. 227-31.

strength as the key to a successful foreign policy. Military exercises and the provision of arms could not safely be neglected by the newly-independent nation. Above all, unity under a single government was indispensable. It was in the service of this unity that Franklin performed his last public service, his participation in the debates of the Federal Convention of 1787; but that is, of course, another story.

13

The American Way in Foreign Policy

IT is not surprising that Mr George Kennan's recent book should have attracted so much attention both in the United States and here.[1] Despite its slenderness, it is a book that deserves careful study and that will, or should, provoke much salutary reflection, and that not only among Mr Kennan's countrymen. But the most remarkable thing about the book is that it should ever have been published and written at all. Here is an author who has been for a quarter of a century an official of the American foreign service, rising to be the director of the Policy Planning Staff set up after the Second World War with the object, he tells us, of 'looking at problems from the standpoint of the totality of American national interest, as distinct from a portion of it'. Does our Foreign Office have such a department or even feel the need for it, or is foreign policy still the same hand-to-mouth improvization that one would gather to be the case from certain recent incidents in Britain's relations with foreign countries? Is the need of such long term and all-round study appreciated? Would we have men of Mr Kennan's calibre to manage such a department if one were to be set up?

But that is not the end of it. Here then is a high official who first, under a transparent cloak of anonymity, prints in a public journal, the admirable *Foreign Affairs*, an exposition of the principles that ought to govern United States policy in relation to the most fundamental of its problems, the handling of Soviet Russia. (It is printed as an appendix to the present volume.) That was in the summer of 1947. More recently Mr Kennan was given a long period of 'study-leave', which he spent in part at the Institute for Advanced Study at Princeton. Under Professor Edward Meade Earle this has become one of the major centres in the world for the scholarly study of recent history and international relations. During this period Mr Kennan was free

[1] *American Diplomacy 1900-1950* by George F. Kennan. Secker & Warburg. 12s. 6d.

to write and lecture on the very matters with which as an official he had been concerned; and the bulk of this book is made up of six lectures given at the University of Chicago, while another *Foreign Affairs* article of no less interest than its predecessor also figures in the appendix. Finally, on Mr Kennan's return to duty, he was nominated as Ambassador to the Soviet Union.

The implications of this personal history are of great interest. It is apparently assumed by those responsible for American foreign policy that there ought to be a continual contact between themselves and the informed section of public opinion, particularly in the universities. They believe rightly that the practitioners have something to teach the historians and theorists, and they are not too self-satisfied to believe that they in their turn may actually have something to learn from the non-official expert. This is clear not only from the rather special case of Mr Kennan but from the whole attitude of the State Department to its contacts with scholars outside, and to the publication of documents. No doubt the formidable and indeed exaggerated proportions that the problem of security has recently assumed in the American public mind may make these contacts a little more restrained than previously, but it is still substantially true that the general principle is that of freedom of information and publicity of discussion. In Britain, as in European countries generally, the general assumption is that of secrecy; and documents are published as a sort of act of grace on the part of the State. Some responsibility for enlightening the public mind has, it is true, been assumed of late by the Foreign Office, but even so it is hardly thinkable that an active member of the British diplomatic service, with the peak of his career still in front of him, would be allowed to discuss major issues of policy or problems of the interpretation of foreign countries' actions in the way that Mr Kennan has felt free to do. And there is certainly little sign that the reverse of the process has taken place to any notable extent at all. Indeed it is hard to see how it could. For if information is jealously guarded by officialdom the opinions of the perforce ignorant outsider is hardly worth having.

It will of course be argued that all this springs in part from the necessity of making up for the admitted weaknesses of the American system of government itself where foreign policy is concerned. Mr Kennan himself says:

> I firmly believe that we could make much more effective use of the principle of professionalism in the conduct of foreign policy: that we could, if we wished, develop a corps of professional officers

superior to anything that exists or ever has existed in this field; and that, by treating these men with respect and drawing on their insight and experience, we could help ourselves considerably. However, I am quite prepared to recognize that this runs counter to strong prejudices and preconceptions in sections of our public mind, particularly in Congress and the Press, and that for this reason we are probably condemned to continue relying almost exclusively on what we might call 'diplomacy by dilettantism'.

But it is not only the failure of the American people to strengthen the professional arm of its diplomacy that gives a greater role to the amateur. It is also the general American belief that foreign policy, like all other aspects of national policy, should fundamentally be governed by public opinion, despite the fact that, as Mr Kennan suspects,

what purports to be public opinion in most countries that consider themselves to have popular government is often not really the consensus of the feelings of the mass of the people at all but rather the expression of the interests of special highly vocal minorities — politicians, commentators, and publicity seekers of all sorts: people who live by their ability to call attention to themselves and die, like fish out of water, if they are compelled to remain silent.

One might add that not only diplomacy but war itself, in American eyes, is an activity that should legitimately be governed by public opinion. On this point there is an illuminating episode in Mr Chester Wilmot's recent book. He is discussing the plan put forward by Montgomery after the break through in Normandy, by which Patton's offensive should be halted and all the weight of the Allied might put behind the northern thrust towards the Ruhr.

Eisenhower's first reaction [Mr Wilmot tells us], was that even if it was militarily desirable (which he did not admit), it was politically impossible to stop Patton in full cry. 'The American public,' said Eisenhower, 'would never stand for it; and public opinion wins war.' To which Montgomery replied, 'Victories win wars. Give people victory and they won't care who won it.'[1]

But in the case of foreign policy it is not only the general domination of public opinion, but the particular form which it takes of the political domination of Congress, that provides the core of the American problem. Congress can make the conduct of foreign policy difficult, indeed almost impossible, as in the recent 'loyalty' investigations, but it cannot itself conduct it, any more than any other

[1] See Chester Wilmot, The Struggle for Europe (Collins), p. 468.

assembly, nor under the system of the separation of powers can it insist on its being conducted by persons in whom it has confidence. In a somewhat guarded manner Mr Kennan admits that, like some other devoted servants of the United States—Mr Thomas Finletter for instance—he would prefer something like a Cabinet system for America:

> I find it hard to see how we can live up to our responsibilities as a great power unless we are able to resolve, in a manner better than we have done recently, the great challenges to the soundness of government policy and to the claim of an administration to speak for the mass of the people in foreign affairs.

But Mr Kennan once again does not believe that the American public would accept such a remedy: 'the chances of change in the direction I have indicated are so slight that we must dismiss the possibility as one that might have any particular relevance to our present problems.'

In defending the British Foreign Office attitude one might, then, say that Mr Kennan in America is doing no more than keeping the public mind in tune with the basic direction of government thinking in the way that a British Foreign Secretary responsible to Parliament is compelled to do through his speeches to the House and in the country. One is bound to add that this defence sounds more convincing with a Palmerston or an Eden at the Foreign Office than, say with an Ernest Bevin. Mr Kennan's concern is after all with his own country. And it is impressive to note that, despite the passages already quoted, Mr Kennan cannot bring himself to repudiate the fundamental American credo: *vox populi, vox dei*.

> I would like to emphasize that I do not consider public reaction to foreign policy questions to be erratic and undependable over the long term; but I think the record indicates that in the short term our public opinion, or what passes for our public opinion in the thinking of official Washington, can easily be led astray into areas of emotionalism and subjectivity which make it a poor and inadequate guide for national action.

And again:

> the system under which we are going to have to continue to conduct foreign policy is, I hope and pray, the system of democracy.

In other words, Mr Kennan pins his faith on the ability of the American democracy to become sufficiently well educated in the matter of foreign policy, to cease to behave like a democracy at all and to accept standards of behaviour more comprehensible in those countries of the Old World which still exhibit a certain resistance to the onward march of democracy. For, as he says in the last lecture, reviewing his argument as a whole: 'If this is true, where are we? It seems to me that we are right back in the realm of the forgotten art of diplomacy from which we have spent fifty years trying to escape.'

This argument, which is treated historically by means of a review of American foreign policy in five significant contexts: the war with Spain, the affair of the 'Open Door' in China, relations with Japan, and the two World Wars, amounts in fact to a repudiation of the assumptions that American statesmen have held, or have been held to, in dealing with these and other issues, and a demonstration of what these erroneous assumptions have been. Some of them certainly are peculiarly American and arise directly out of such things as the long previous period of isolation, the overwhelming sense of security—only recently and partially diminished—the reluctance of recent immigrants or their children to get entangled once more in the weary wars of Europe and their belief that this reluctance could be directly translated into policy regardless of the policies of others; and the historic 'anti-colonial' or 'anti-imperialist' prejudice that has made Americans—especially latterly—dig away at the foundations of other empires (and, as Mr Chester Wilmot has again reminded us, particularly of the British Empire) without worrying what was to take their place, and certainly without being willing to take that place themselves: the last perhaps wisely. For in his chapter on the Spanish-American War of 1898 and its consequences Mr Kennan points out that this part of the story moves him to wonder whether America's 'most signal political failures as a nation have not lain in our attempts to establish a political bond of obligations between the main body of our people and other peoples or groups to whom, whether because we wished it so or because there was no other practical solution, we were not in a position to concede the full status of citizenship,' and whether this does not imply a permanent warning for the American nation itself.

In the combination of this insistence on high moral principles, such as anti-imperialism, with a refusal to accept responsibilities for the results of applying them, Mr Kennan sees the root of the tragic paradox of American Far Eastern foreign policy, which more than anything else has provoked the still continuing 'great debate' on the country's foreign policy as a whole:

It is an ironic fact that today our past objectives in Asia are ostensibly in large measure achieved. The Western Powers have lost the last of their special positions in China. The Japanese are finally out of China proper and out of Manchuria and Korea as well. The effects of their expulsion from these areas have been precisely what wise and realistic people warned us all along they would be. Today we have fallen heir to the problems and responsibilities the Japanese had faced and borne in the Korean-Manchurian area for nearly half a century, and there is a certain perverse justice in the pain we are suffering from a burden which, when it was borne by others, we held in such low esteem.

But in more general terms these weaknesses in the attitude of his countrymen in the past which Mr Kennan is at pains to analyse and define would seem to be characteristic not of Americans merely but of all democratic peoples. It is only that American institutions give them greater play and that hitherto American invulnerability has made them less dangerous.

The most important feature of the democratic attitude towards foreign policy is a failure to understand the factor of power, and the consequent belief in the practical value of verbal indication of what is desirable. Mr Kennan's example of this is the 'Open Door' notes about China, which American opinion wrongly interpreted as having been effective. But it is not American diplomatic history only that gives examples, within the last few years, of the over-valuation of mere statements of a point of view without the willingness to follow it up in action, or of the trust put in paper pledges where these conflict with the obvious interests or ambitions of the governments that have signed them.

This tendency to achieve objectives in foreign policy 'by inducing other governments to sign up professions of high moral and legal principle' is linked by Mr Kennan with 'the pronounced American tendency to transplant legal concepts from the domestic to the international field'. And this again is not limited to America. The belief that by creating a set of rules, and institutions to see they are observed, one has solved political conflicts and eliminated the menace of war—what might once have been called the 'League of Nations Union' attitude to foreign policy—is widely held in democratic societies. It is an attitude that can lead to cynicism where the expected action is not taken, or may on the contrary lead to an extension, in the name of 'maintaining international law', of a conflict that might otherwise have been regulated by the ordinary methods of diplomacy.

In the American case it arises largely, as Mr Kennan shows, from an unwillingness to admit that there may be genuine conflicts of national interests which must be faced and resolved by methods having nothing to do with those of the law courts. Japan's population problem and need of raw materials provides him with a good example. It was the unwillingness of American opinion, and of Wilson in its wake, to consider such conflicts in themselves, and the origins of the war which rose out of them, that was the secret of America's ineffectiveness in the process of peace-making in 1919. Because the Americans adopted towards the war in Europe an attitude suggesting that they, and they alone, were above considerations of self-interest and were fighting upon some nobler plane and for some higher ideal, they were incapable of formulating their war aims in a realistic fashion. America had excellent reasons for entering the war, but they were not the reasons that could comfortably be avowed in a nation which denied that it was concerned with the balance of power. Perhaps through longer experience of international complications this attitude is slightly less obvious in Britain. But the whole post-1919 complex was at least in part attributable to a British reluctance to accept the reality and the validity of the desire for security felt by France and her allies. A British author seeking to emulate Mr Kennan would have to look no further than the notorious writings of the late Lord Keynes for examples of a refusal to face the political facts of life that it would be hard to better from any American source.

But in the light of our present predicament—and it is interesting to note Mr Kennan's borrowing of this useful key-word from another Princeton figure, Professor Herbert Butterfield, with whose approach to foreign policy he has much in common—it is not these dangers of over-optimism that are the most worrying. The massive 'peacetime' rearmament which Western opinion has accepted suggests that there has been a change in this respect. What Mr Kennan is concerned with is the paradox inherent certainly in the American, and probably in the general democratic, attitude towards the use of force, towards war itself.

For an absolute monarch it is, or was, normal to go to war for purely material ends, the conquest of some desirable province. For a democracy such an inducement will hardly suffice; it may not even be moved by considerations of national advantage in a broader sense, or the Americans would hardly have awaited Pearl Harbour before going to war against the Axis. They require some moral reason, some overwhelming conviction of the need to chastise evil-doing and to restore what is regarded as the natural state of affairs that the evil-doer has upset. Democracy fights to punish, and once it has decided to do so there are no limits to which it will not go.

'Day before yesterday, let us say,' remarks Mr Kennan, 'the issues at stake between ourselves and another power were not worth the life of a single American boy. Today nothing else counts at all; our cause is holy; the cost is no consideration: violence must know no limitations short of unconditional surrender.'

Not only do democratic wars mean 'unconditional surrender' and the probability, in consequence, that new forms of unbalance will be set up, but war is relied upon to perform tasks of which it is altogether incapable. 'It is essential to recognize,' says Mr Kennan, 'that the maiming and killing of men and the destruction of human shelters and other installations, however necessary it may be for other reasons, cannot in itself make any positive contribution to any democratic purpose.' This does not mean that all wars are 'un-necessary' or 'unjust'; for they may be the only alternative to even worse situations. But they can only perform negative functions. We may say, looking at the past, that successful war prevented Europe from falling under the yoke of the Kaiser or the even worse yoke of Hitler; it has not, so far as we can tell, made good peaceful Western liberals of the Germans.

But Mr Kennan is concerned not with the past, as in our example, but with the future, with what his country is going to do about the Soviet Union. Just as he first achieved public fame with his article expounding the theory of containment, so now he is forced to argue that Americans must get used to the practice of containment, and to its many frustrations and irritations, and not believe that there is a short way round. This reflection is only implicit in the Chicago lectures; it is made explicit in the second *Foreign Affairs* article, 'America and the Russian Future'. It should hardly be necessary to add that Mr Kennan is under no illusions about the Soviet regime, its tyranny at home, the brooding menace it presents abroad. Just as Mr Kennan's cousin, in a once celebrated book, *Siberia and the Exile System*, exposed the evils of Tsarist Russia, so Mr Kennan himself is profoundly aware of the manifold wickedness of its successor. But he is also aware that we cannot expect any future and more congenial Russia to approximate in every respect to the kind of society we ourselves most admire, or the whole Soviet experience to be obliterated from Russian history. There are minimum conditions that a Russian regime must satisfy before it can become a full partner in a working international system; it is no good looking beyond them.

Above all, we must not imagine that even these minimum conditions can be achieved by external pressure; not by atom bombs certainly, and not even by 'political warfare'. 'It is a shallow view of the workings of history,' writes Mr Kennan, 'which looks to such things as foreign propaganda and agitation to bring about fundamental changes in the lives of a great nation.' Our diplomacy must continue to have as its purpose the realistic one of producing situations of such strength that the challenge of war will not come from the side of the Kremlin. But, whether we succeed or fail in averting war, we must understand the limitations upon what can positively be done. It is our own societies that provide the real scope for constructive action; sooner or later, in its own time and in its own way, the Russian people will rejoin the common caravan of humanity. Or is such an expression of faith merely another democratic illusion? We cannot know. Either way, Mr Kennan has wise counsel to offer; it would be foolish to neglect it.

14

The Predicament of American Foreign Policy

TO ask a citizen of the United Kingdom to interpret in the spring of 1957 the foreign policy of the United States to a Canadian audience is to confer a compliment but to take a risk. I can only justify the Editor's confidence by being perfectly frank in this article while admitting at the same time that any attempt at applying an historical perspective to a present predicament is necessarily a subjective one and that I am conscious that others of my compatriots equally or better qualified to treat this subject might handle it in a very different fashion.[1]

If I place the duty to be frank as the first condition for writing on this subject it is not because I want to seize the occasion to envenom current controversies but because all our instincts, in Britain no less than in Canada, are in the other direction. So conscious have we become of the importance of the North Atlantic alliance that it is easy to fall back after any crisis in its affairs upon the well-tried stock of 'Pilgrim Dinner' platitudes of the 'hands-across-the-sea' variety. Even at a scholarly level it is possible to write the history of Anglo-American relations from a teleological point of view as if an indissoluble North Atlantic partnership were the necessary and permanent outcome of the whole long development since the American Revolution.[2] Indeed this is the normal attitude of most of those British scholars and intellectuals—and their number is growing—who make the United States their special subject of study. And their instinctive sympathy with the American point of view and their consequent tendency to equate that point of view with Britain's own best interests may make them good interpreters of

[1] See my article, 'Suez and the British Conscience', *Commentary*, New York (April 1957).

[2] See, e.g., H. C. Allen, *Great Britain and the United States* (London: Odhams, 1954).

the United States to Britain, but certainly makes them dangerous when they act as interpreters of the British scene to Americans or Canadians.

It must be stated quite clearly that the actions of President Eisenhower and Secretary of State John Foster Dulles over the past year have gone far to undo the good in the sphere of Anglo-American relations that was done by President Roosevelt and perhaps still more by President Truman. Whatever gestures may be made, Englishmen will not easily forget that the self-styled champions of the world against Communism made common cause with the Russians against us at the United Nations, or the fact that it was almost certainly the threats against us that made us call off the Suez operation, or the indifference to our national needs and those of our French allies that these actions showed.

As far as the future is concerned all this may be more important for British than for American policy. Britain's decision to continue trying to be a 'nuclear Power', which could be criticized on many grounds, is substantially a vote of no-confidence in the automatic working of the North Atlantic alliance, a refusal to believe that British and American interests are so identical that a total merger of forces is possible. It is not a nostalgia for our position as a World Power that moves us, but rather a feeling that it is not possible to take it for granted that the British and American view of the nature and direction of a major threat will always and necessarily coincide. And yet as the Bermuda agreement has shown, we are in fact assuming that normally the North Atlantic alliance will operate and that in vital respects we can accept dependence.

For such sentiments, and the drawing of such consequences from them, need not of course prove permanent. Indeed a view of the future based upon the inevitability of Anglo-American divergencies would be no more justified historically than one based upon the idea, already criticized, that they must inevitably find themselves in ever increasing agreement. On the contrary, the proper way to regard the history of foreign policy is as a series of choices, each of which is no doubt conditioned to some extent by the choices that have been made in the past, but is nonetheless a free choice within the limits that the country's particular situation imposes. All that need be said to link these preliminary remarks with the main topic of this essay is that the United States appears to be facing some new problems in the development of its foreign policy, and that it appears at the time of writing (April 1957) to be trying to solve them in ways inimical to British interests, and indeed to the interests of the Western world as Britain sees them. What then are these problems and how if at all do they relate to the American past?

In the first place it is important to realize that the present situation is quite novel and one which it would have been difficult even to foresee not so long ago. Lecturing in Paris on this subject in March, I pointed out how easy it was to forget in the stress of present emotion the very diverse stages through which our relations with the Americans had passed: 'We should remember,' I said — I am now translating — 'the very different kinds of criticism that American policy incurred in the first three years of the Eisenhower-Dulles régime. At that time what we reproached the Americans with was being too rigid with regard to Communism. It was we who were afraid of being dragged by them into a war in the Far East, or even — given the Republican platform of 1952 — into a war in Europe. It was at that time we, the Europeans, who warned them against the temptation to consider all policies and all countries simply in reference to the struggle against Communism, and to neglect the opinion of those countries like India who did not wish to declare themselves upon one side or the other. It was we again who wondered whether the Americans would have the good sense to be ready to spend their money in order to give support in Asia to non-Communist governments even when they did not wish to declare themselves anti-Communist.'[1] Lest it should be thought that I exempted myself from such criticism, I might add that in an essay written in the summer of 1956 and recently published, I had made the same point, that it was easier for American Congressmen and the American public to appreciate the need for military assistance for their partners in pacts like SEATO, than the need for economic aid to 'countries like India which expressed disapproval of many United States policies, and arrogantly claimed to be the exponents of a more correct and morally superior outlook on world affairs.'[2]

The decision of the United States not after all to assist with the Assouan High Dam — the one that precipitated the Suez crisis — seemed well in line with such an assessment of American policy. Nor of course has it simply been superseded by a new one. Indeed Far Eastern policy, and for that matter European policy, have been

[1] From 'La politique Américaine vue de l'Europe', a lecture delivered at the Institut des Sciences Politiques, Paris, March 13, 1957.

[2] From my essay, 'American Foreign Policy and World Power', in H. C. Allen and C. P. Hill, eds., British Essays in American History (London: Arnold, 1957).

little affected so far by the subsequent shift in American thinking. And even in the Middle East itself, the decision to join the military committee of the Baghdad Pact indicated that something of the old methods was being carried over into the new period. On the other hand, the events in Hungary amply demonstrated that any idea of 'liberation' as the object of American policy towards Communism was an illusion — that in a nuclear age, the West would not risk war to help rescue a captive people from Communist bondage, and that the great mistake had been to let propaganda give currency to any such idea.

The foreign policy of the United States as revealed after Nasser's seizure of Suez was thus not composed of solutions to a single predicament. On the contrary, as far as most of the world was concerned, Americans seemed conscious of no predicament at all. The policy inherent in the 'Truman doctrine', in NATO, and in the intervention in Korea — the policy rightly known as 'containment' — remained in force. A clear attempt to extend by force the area of Communist control in those zones covered by security pacts would be met with forcible resistance. The predicament arose over other areas, immediately and most forcibly in the Middle East, but with a possible extension ultimately to other doubtful and 'uncommitted' parts of the globe.

The simplest way towards defining the predicament that the United States faces in regard to those areas is to ask why it was not possible for the United States Government simply to extend to them those policies which it had adopted elsewhere. In trying to answer this question, there is the obvious difficulty that must arise when one tries to assess, without full knowledge of the facts, the contemporary policy of a foreign government. In this case the obvious problem is the extent to which the policy represents not some general shift in American attitudes but a narrowly personal choice on the part of the President himself, Mr Dulles, and some of their more intimate advisers. We do know that some aspects of the policy have come in for hot criticism from leading figures in the preceding administration and from other quarters and that in revising the original version of the Eisenhower doctrine, Congress for the first time showed some independence of the Presidential wishes.[1]

We can nevertheless say that whatever the weight to be attached to personal factors in this case — and one should never forget that

[1] The revisions were principally directed towards strengthening Congressional control over the action to be taken.

the American system of government is the most dangerously per-
sonalized one among all the major democracies—they cannot be
held to be the dominant element. President Eisenhower may have
been highly incensed at the 'deceit' practised upon him by the
British and French Governments—though there is good reason to
believe that not all American governmental circles were equally
ignorant of these governments' intentions—but this cannot by itself
explain subsequent policy. For the basic line was obvious from the
time that Mr Dulles made it clear that the Suez Canal Users' Association was not a means of bringing any real pressure upon Egypt;
this decision was thus a cause not a consequence of the Anglo-
French intervention.

The American policy that has developed over the past year is then
a policy that has, as one might expect, its roots deep in American
attitudes and opinion. The personalities of Mr Dulles and of President Eisenhower have been responsible perhaps for giving a rather
different emphasis to its two most striking aspects. It is Mr Dulles
who seems to have been the most determined to try to secure
America's desires in the Middle East by seeking Arab friendship,
and President Eisenhower who seems to have been the more determined to make the United Nations the foundation of American
policy here and elsewhere. For it was, after all, Mr Dulles himself
who was so reluctant to allow the nationalization of the Canal
to be referred directly to the United Nations when it was first
proclaimed.

In giving a statement of what this American policy is, it is perhaps likely that the outside observer will be more precise than is
possible for its official defenders who have to be on their guard,
especially in view of the divergencies of opinion within the United
States itself. But up to the time of writing there has been a fair
degree of consistency in action if not always in speech. Where
purely military considerations have still been dominant, as in relations with Saudi Arabia, political considerations have, as one
might expect, been overruled. It is salutary to remember that in
1911, the United States denounced its 1832 treaty with Russia because that country had refused to honour the passports issued to
American Jews, following in this action on a resolution of the
House of Representatives which includes the statement that the
United States Government will not be 'a party to any treaty which
discriminates, or which by one of the parties thereto is so construed
as to discriminate between American citizens on the ground of race

or religion'.[1] In 1957, on the other hand, the United States accepted as part of the price for continued use of the Dhahran air-base a provision that no American serviceman of the Jewish faith would be allowed to form part of its garrison. A right upheld against the Tsar of all the Russians was waived for the sake of an Arab slave-trading potentate to whom the Mayor of New York rightly refused a civic welcome.

But even where the more political aspects of the policy are concerned, the American willingness to neglect the problem of Israel's security and maritime rights for the sake of securing Arab friendship is noteworthy, and not simply because American political pressure had so much to do with the actual creation of the Israeli state. It is important because it bears out one's general impression that with the United States' emergence on the main theatre of world politics as a principal actor, and not simply an occasional auxiliary, considerations of internal policy are bound to exercise less weight than previously. Mr Dulles has effectively exploded the myth that American Middle Eastern policy must always be determined by the 'Jewish vote'.[2]

Nevertheless, it is a part of the American predicament that this policy probably cannot be carried to its logical conclusion, which would mean acceding to the often-voiced demands of the Arab States for the total destruction of Israel. It is hard to see how this consummation, which American public opinion at large could hardly swallow, could be permitted by any American administration. And for this reason, it is possible to say that the solution to the local aspect of the predicament has not in fact been found.

But the desire to be associated with the Arab States while simultaneously avoiding the issue of the annihilation of Israel is only the most acute form that the American dilemma takes. For even among the Arab States themselves there is, despite the appeal for some intellectuals of pan-Arabism or pan-Islam, a wide diversity of interests which but for the existence of common enemies in Israel and 'Western Imperialism', of which Israel is regarded as the agent, would probably by now have erupted into overt hostilities. The American attempt to make light of these and to act on the assump-

[1] House Joint Resolution no. 166, 62nd Congress, 2nd Session. Cf. C. Adler and A. M. Margalith, *With Firmness in the Right* (New York: American Jewish Committee, 1946), 278 ff.

[2] I made the same point in a lecture given at Johns Hopkins University in November 1954. See my book, *Foreign Policy and the Democratic Process* (Baltimore: Johns Hopkins Press; London: OPU, 1955), 80-1.

tion that they all have common ground in their objections to Soviet Communism—a remote and uncomprehended threat—is almost certainly foredoomed to failure.

The Middle Eastern predicament thus illustrates from one angle the most important and persistent of America's inheritances from a simpler past, the tendency to overlook the real constituents of a situation and to impose upon it instead a pattern predicated on the assumption that the world is populated entirely by Americans, or would-be Americans. The main trouble about Mr Dulles's Middle East it that it does not exist. In the Middle East, this attitude in fact leads to a policy which in other circumstances has been styled the policy of 'appeasement'; and it is perhaps no accident that the modern statesman whom Mr Dulles most nearly recalls to a European observer is Mr Neville Chamberlain, whose own policy towards Hitler—equally pacific and honourable in its purposes— was also vitiated by the fact that he was dealing with a quite imaginary Germany. But such impatience with the facts need not involve appeasement; it may on the contrary involve extreme rigidity. Thus the policy of non-recognition of Communist China would only make sense if there were a reasonable prospect that Chiang Kai-shek, with or without foreign aid, was in the near future going to make an end of the Chinese Communist régime. It can only be justified by another refusal to face the facts—since non-recognition as a sign of moral disapprobation has been proved over and over again to be a diplomatic error of the first order.[1]

There is ample evidence now available—and it will I hope one day be fully explored—of President Roosevelt's strong and often uninformed bias against European empires and the British Empire in particular and of his use of the wartime alliance to try to bring pressure on the British Government to hasten its liquidation.[2]

The present state of affairs in South-East Asia, in particular the chaos in Indonesia, gives adequate warning of the consequences of premature grants of independence; while the relative stability of the Indian sub-continent is clearly due not so much to any greater natural unity, but to the inheritance from generations of British rule of a steel framework of civil and military organization available for the new leaders of its countries to work with. But the lessons of

[1] Cf. ibid., 45-6.

[2] For a discussion of the relation of this sentiment to Anglo-American financial and commercial negotiations during and after the Second World War, see Richard N. Gardner, *Sterling-Dollar Diplomacy* (Oxford, 1956).

this have not so far been applied by the United States in the Middle East, though America's scarcely veiled political responsibilities in South Korea and Southern Vietnam suggest that the inhibitions against political intervention in the affairs of other countries can be weakened where the necessities of the anti-Communist struggle demand it. Nevertheless the Eisenhower doctrine with its self-denying ordinance restricting intervention to where the local government actually demands it, is not an acceptance of responsibilities but a refusal of them. What Europeans have cause to complain of is that in an area vital to their security and prosperity, the United States will neither let them exercise their strength nor use its own.

With the anti-colonial element in this line of approach is linked the other principal stand to which I have alluded. The European student of American policy-making cannot but be struck by the great difficulty which Americans seem to find in considering military and political problems as part of a single whole. This again is understandable in the light of the nineteenth century abeyance of foreign policy, although it would hardly have seemed realistic to the Founding Fathers who took care to make the nation's executive head also its commander-in-chief.

There are, however, two other important strands in American thinking on foreign policy to which recent American action in the Middle East gives a useful clue. In the first place, there is in Mr Dulles's obvious belief that he can win the Arabs (and others) into the anti-Communist camp provided he can steer clear of involvement with British and French policy, an important vestige of one of the most enduring of American attitudes—anti-colonialism. The fact that the American belief that 'manifest destiny' would one day bring Canada under the stars and stripes has waned in the present century, may lead Canadians to forget too easily the persistent hostility of many Americans to empires in general and to the British Empire in particular. Americans have consistently tended to over-estimate the positive values of self-government and under-estimate those of government as such, and to be unaware of the real difficulty in many areas of the world of finding a form of government that does not rest overtly or covertly upon exterior power. If the ability to achieve self-government and prosper under it had been as wide-spread as American democratic theory assumes, there would have been fewer empires. Europeans, seeing how often in post-war years European power and influence have been more or less succeeded by

American power and influence, not unnaturally tend to give credence to the view, so often espoused by Communist and Communist-inspired propaganda, that American anti-colonialism is merely a cover for America's own form of imperialism, that its true device is: 'Ote-toi que je m'y mette.' But such cynicism though tempting is unrealistic. It is far truer to say that until very recently the problem of authority itself has played so small a role in American thought, that the problem of what would happen when the European empires were removed in Asia and Africa has hardly impinged upon the American consciousness.

What happened when both foreign policy and defence considerations became more important was that the President retained control of the former while accepting in the case of the latter the advice of his military representatives. A corollary of this development was the growth of a tradition among American military men that the political consequences of their actions were no part of their business. In the Second World War they voiced consistent suspicion that their British allies took a different view and were too prone to allow long-range political objectives, other than total victory, to distort their strategical arguments. When it was suggested at a late stage in the war that the Americans should make an effort to liberate Prague before the Russians got there, General Marshall commented: 'Personally, and aside from all logistic, tactical or strategical implications, I should be loath to hazard American lives for purely political purposes.'[1] A British commander would have found it hard to see for what except political purposes it is right to hazard lives in war at all; and would hardly allow war aims to be limited to imposing 'unconditional surrender' upon the immediate enemy. Europeans know — as Americans are learning — that power politics and all that this implies are the necessary consequence of living in separate political societies and that war does not enable one to contract out of this condition.

It is true that the post-war development of American Government, particularly the growing role assigned to the National Security Council, suggests that the gap between military and civilian thinking is now better recognized and that attempts are being made to bridge it; but the legacy of the past is strong and it is certainly true that in the Middle Eastern affair no clear relation between political and military ends or means has yet emerged.

[1] *History of the Second World War: Grand Strategy*, vol. VI, by John Ehrman (HMSO, 1956), 161.

It is nevertheless evident that although it is over the Middle East that American policy has shown its principal divergence from that of its main European allies, it is the different attitudes towards the United Nations that look like causing most trouble in the future; and it is indeed the one point of difference that the British Prime Minister insisted upon when giving his own account of the Bermuda conference.

Just as anti-colonialism is simply the carrying too far of an idea which has much to commend it in itself, so too the American insistence upon the subordination of national policy to the United Nations is the product of a generous and far-sighted impulse – the only trouble is that it may once again be too far-sighted and too negligent of more immediate aspects of the international situation. Thoughtful Americans were bound to feel, once the Second World War came upon them, that they might after all have done better to heed Woodrow Wilson's warning, and to take part in the first attempt to organize world affairs on the basis of collective security. The creation of an effective world organization was thus an important American war-aim; and the shape which the United Nations Organization ultimately took owed more to the United States than to any other Power.

The principal demand made by the United States was that the new organization should be universal, making no concessions to regionalism; its political demands were thus in harmony with its contemporary economic attitudes, which were expressly hostile to all forms of economic co-operation limited to specific groups of countries such as the British system of Imperial preference and the sterling area. On the other hand, it was realized at the time that responsibility could not be divorced from power; and the so-called veto in the Security Council reflected the contemporary hope and belief that the victorious Great Powers who formed the core of permanent members of that body would stay united.

Rightly fearful of a return to isolationism, successive American administrations have failed to make it clear to the American public how far the United Nations has departed from its original shape and purpose. Its history has indeed been one of a series of paradoxes in which each American move has produced results the contrary of what was intended. The unanimity of the permanent members proved an unattainable fiction from the beginning and was relentlessly used by the Soviet Union to make up for the fact of its own minority position. Against the wise warnings of Sir Winston

Churchill, President Roosevelt insisted upon China being one of the original permanent members of the Security Council, expecting no doubt that its Government would accept the American lead. Instead, Chiang Kai-shek was swept away by the Communists, and the United States, by denying to the Chinese Communist Government its undoubted right to China's seat in the United Nations, made the first major breach in its own principle of universality.

But the greatest paradox was yet to come. Because of the fact that Russia was temporarily absent from the Security Council at the time of the Korean aggression, the 'collective security' provisions of the Charter were able to work in favour of the United States and its allies and a new enthusiasm for the institution itself was generated. Realizing that this state of affairs could only be temporary, the American Government then set itself to try to get round the Soviet veto by inflating in the 'Uniting for Peace' resolution the role of the General Assembly to which the makers of the United Nations had rightly refused to grant major political responsibilities. The United States seems to have taken the view that it could rely upon the 'free world' being able to outvote the 'Soviet bloc'. But this also was proved to be an illusion with the rapid increase in the non-Western membership of the United Nations. The balance of voting power is now in the hands of the so-called 'uncommitted' nations — that is to say countries which are not themselves pro-Communist (and may even in some cases be quite strongly anti-Communist) but which regard the main issue in world politics as being that of 'Western imperialism' and not that of Communism or Communist aggression. The very different conduct of these countries over the alleged Israeli 'aggression' against Egypt as compared with that towards the undoubted Soviet aggression against Hungary was significant enough.

The predicament of United States policy has now been made clear here also. Either the United States in trying to clear itself from the taint of 'colonialism' must, as in the Suez affair, part from its natural allies and associates in the West, or it must accept the fact that since it will be unable to get majorities for its policies in the United Nations, reliance upon that body condemns it to a permanent state of inaction. The gallant attempt of Canada to give some effectiveness to the United Nations has only proved its incapacity.

Once again, one has the feeling that a reading of America's own unique historical experience into a quite different contemporary situation is largely responsible for the illusions that American statesmen entertain. They tend to think of Asian anti-imperialism as a simple reaction to the fact of foreign rule. But as recent events have shown, it can be as virulent among countries which are not (and have not been for some time) so subordinated. It is not the desire to be sovereign but the desire to equal the material achievements of the West that provides the main driving-force behind these movements — and it is the belief that Russia has a technique for catching-up with the West in a brief space of time that gives Soviet Communism its major appeal in these countries. America cannot therefore escape from enmity by not having colonies of her own or by dissociating herself from other people's colonies. The real division is between the rich and the poor — and how can America avoid being classed with the rich?

Even her generous programmes of foreign aid — the whole 'Point Four' concept — perhaps do more to emphasize America's wealth than they do to relieve Asia's poverty. Why should American 'experts' be popular when the humblest of them may be living on a standard above that of a local cabinet minister or high official?

What brings prosperity and progress to a country is neither technique nor even a good endowment from nature, but a social system that enables that technique and those resources to be exploited. Social and legal institutions, even the heritage of religious and philosophic attitudes, may account for more in purely material terms than material circumstances themselves. Whether foreign assistance of an economic or technical nature is of value or not will depend on the social and political structure of the receiving country more than on the intentions of the givers. The brilliant success of 'Marshall Aid' in Europe has provided a totally misleading analogy for considering policy in Asia. Western Europe was a society equipped with the means for economic development but one that had suffered a temporary set-back. American aid helped it to get over that set-back without recourse to the more barbarous Soviet methods of economic development and the consequent subordination of its needs to the demands of the more primitive economy of the Soviet Union itself. But aid on a similar scale given to 'under-developed countries' without any political controls could easily seep away in a morass of inefficiency and corruption.

Reflections of this kind which come naturally to any European student of the contemporary scene, are obviously 'un-American' in the most literal sense of the word. Yet until Americans have grasped their implications it is all too likely that they will be confronted by the most severe of all their predicaments: the frustration of their most generous impulses to share their own achievements and conquests with suffering humanity at large.

The fact that the United States seems to be confronted at the present time with a series of interlocking problems to which the term predicament can well be applied, means no more than that its great position of strength does not render it immune from the common fortune of states and empires. If it seems occasionally to hesitate and confound the expectations of its friends, we should remember that in moments of supreme crisis in the Western world it has hitherto always intervened before it was too late, and with decisive effect. Certainly we in Britain cannot forget what American aid and comfort have meant in the past. Given the general attitude of the United States to the rest of the world half a century ago, the wonder may indeed be not that it has made so many mistakes, but that so far it has made so few, and no irretrievable ones. And from its own people's point of view, what other country has come through two world wars as a belligerent with its own territory untouched and its own prosperity and vitality enhanced?

And in accounting for such errors as we believe we see, two more things must be taken into consideration. In the first place there has in the last few decades been an acceleration of the historical process of a kind particularly likely to disturb a people that not only relies upon historical example for guidance, but that has also inherited from the past a system of government whose conventions were elaborated under vastly different circumstances. It has had to learn too many lessons and those too quickly.

In the second place we must remember that so far we have been talking only about predicaments peculiar to the United States. There is also, overshadowing all aspects of foreign policy, the greater predicament that the United States shares with all the world. No generation before this one has had in its hands the power of life and death over the whole of civilization and perhaps over humanity itself. This very fact is itself enough to explain why an historical explanation of national policies is inadequate. All Great Powers in the past have had the possibility of waging a major war as the implicit sanction of their policies; with this virtually removed, the difficulty of making policy is surely intensified. And if this were not enough, this perilous gift has been given to mankind just at the moment when the civilized world is more deeply divided than at any previous period in history. It is not that American and Russian interests are more strenuously in conflict than has been the case with other pairs of warring empires in the past; it is that their ideological antipathy makes negotiation between them scarcely possible because of an almost total inability to communicate. For this inability to communicate, the United States is only to the smallest extent responsible. It is the Russians who, by subordinating the realities of politics to the demands of Marxist dogma and national self-assertiveness, have made it so difficult to have a genuine exchange of views even on issues where the common interest is glaringly obvious. Meetings at the 'summit'—a favourite American formula—have revealed their inadequacy.

Nevertheless, whoever may be responsible, the 'bomb' and all that it entails remain, and the United States has to face in the first instance its responsibility for a weapon it was the first to use. In the clear American awareness of this predicament, in America's obvious devotion to peace—even at times to peace at any price—in its refusal to be stampeded into accepting its enemy's lineaments, those of a 'garrison-state', lies the best hope of all of us.

15

Anti-Colonialism in American Foreign Policy

THE foreign policy of the United States in the last few years has obviously been affected by the belief that it is possible to acquire the support in the struggle against Communism of newly independent states in Asia and Africa, or of peoples likely soon to be independent, provided always that the United States takes care to dissociate herself from her partners in the Western alliance who are still committed to maintaining imperial positions overseas, or who are tainted in the minds of their previous subjects by what the latter now regard as a record of domination or exploitation. The Suez affair showed that the United States was prepared to go so far in this direction as actively to range herself against her principal Western allies—Britain and France—on an issue which found the latter in conflict with most of these new nations.

In so far as this American position is a deliberate corollary of the general attitude adopted by the United States toward the problems of foreign policy now confronting her, it is understandable enough. Having first insisted, in the flush of enthusiasm over the Korean intervention, upon inflating the role of the General Assembly of the United Nations, and having then made the subordination of her policies to the decisions of that body a proclaimed principle of action, the United States was bound to take account of the increasing numerical weight of the Afro-Asian bloc within it. And even when acting outside the United Nations, as in the case of the 'Eisenhower Doctrine', it was understandable that once the winning over of 'neutralist sympathies' was deemed essential, care should be taken to give to the countries in question a view of the United States which it was felt would tally with their prejudices. It was the same kind of calculation that led to the United States' acquiescing in Saudi Arabia's demands for the exclusion from the Dhahran airbase of American servicemen of the Jewish faith, even though it has been a rigid principle of American foreign policy in the past that foreign countries should not be allowed to make discriminations between different categories of American citizens which are unknown to American law itself.

Nations must be their own judge of what *Realpolitik* demands and it is not for foreigners to lecture them on the subject. But of course this 'anti-colonial' emphasis in current policy is more than an application of *Realpolitik*: it is presented and accepted as a natural extension of fundamental American principles; and it ante-dates not only the most recent phase in the cold war, but the cold war itself. Even the non-American historian is therefore entitled to examine this claim and to suggest some of its consequences.

It is platitudinous to remark that a struggle for independence from foreign rule is the key event in the United States' own history, as American citizens are taught it, and that in consequence a sym-pathy with other peoples struggling for freedom is natural to them. The simple fact that the former Indian national movement took the name of 'Congress' was a powerful factor in winning American support for its aims. But it would be a mistake to imagine that from the days of George Washington to those of John Foster Dulles, American support for subject peoples has followed an unswerving line. There is the old story of the British lecturer in America in the 1920's or 1930's who got tired of the repeated interjection from his audiences: 'What about the Indians?' and shot back: 'Which Indians does the questioner refer to—those whom his ancestors massacred and dispossessed, or those whom we are peacefully leading toward self-government?' And behind this rather bitter quip lies an im-portant clue to the whole question.

For if Americans have certainly attributed great significance to struggles for political independence, they have been equally moved by the romance of settlement. Next to the heroes of the Revolu-tionary War and the makers of the new nation, and only just next to them, come the heroes of frontier settlement. Davy Crockett treads hard on the heels of Thomas Jefferson. And indeed, the settle-ment of new lands—whether in America or Siberia—is one of the great epic themes of modern history. But this continental settle-ment has in both cases been carried on largely at the expense of scattered and primitive peoples whom the conquerors have not turned into colonial subjects, but swept aside, on the whole, un-concernedly—at least until very recently. The strict logic of self-determination would have required that the Red Indians be per-

203

mitted to keep the North American continent the largely empty and uncultivated wilderness, suited to their own primitive state, that it was when Jamestown was founded. But no Americans have seriously pushed logic so far; Manifest Destiny may have had its victims, but the less said about them the better. Americans have not therefore been opposed to the principle of the expansion of the white Western nations by colonies of settlement; they have only been concerned to see that these colonies should in time achieve their political emancipation from their mother-countries.

Consider for instance, the American attitude toward Zionism. It has from the beginning been marked by a sympathy arising from the New World's traditional commitment to the positive values of pioneering settlement, rather than by solicitude for the rights of the native Arab population. Despite the fact that ultimately — as many of the wisest Zionists have always seen (and Weizmann's own autobiograph is eloquent on the point) — Israel's main political problem is that of her relations to her Arab milieu, American support for the Jewish National Home and subsequently for the State of Israel was never accompanied by any positive policy on Arab-Jewish relations. It was not that the Americans could not agree on the solution to the problem presented by a multi-racial Palestine, it was that they largely ignored the existence of the problem altogether, except for a limited number of Arab-oriented specialists who went to the other extreme and regarded the Jews purely as colonialist interlopers. For most Americans, the Arabs were, like the Red Indians, not a part of the story. And more recently the adoption by the Eisenhower administration of a pro-Arab point of view has simply meant passing from one oversimplified version of the circumstances to another, under the dictates of considerations extraneous to the problem itself — with the result that Israel remains as vulnerable as ever and that the Arab refugees continue to vegetate in penurious and dangerous idleness.

The Palestine case is one reminder, if the most vivid one, of the fact that apart from North America, Siberia, and Australia, the settlement of relatively empty vastnesses by white immigrants has been an exceptional, and not a normal, development and that an ideology drawn from such experiences is likely to prove irrelevant over much of the rest of the world.

Most of today's colonial and ex-colonial territories fall into one of three categories which 'anti-colonialist' theory does not always sufficiently distinguish. There are, first, the colonies of settlement where the indigenous population was not swept aside but brought into some kind of relation with the immigrant groups, but where the latter, being a minority, insisted upon institutions designed to safeguard their own supremacy. South Africa, parts of Central and East Africa, as well as Algeria fall into this category. This kind of settlement represents the most acute problem of all for the colonial powers. If they accept the colony's demand for autonomy, it will lead almost inevitably, at first, to the rule of the white minority— as in South Africa. Since the white minority will be trying to keep a position of privilege—justified on material or cultural grounds— that runs counter to the predominant trends of world sentiment, it is likely to end up by espousing a rigidly racist ideology. The South African Dutch—whom the great majority of Americans sympathized with during the Boer War—have developed independently most of the apologias for racial oppression and Negro servitude which were familiar in the American South in the ante-bellum period. There is no Calhounian extravagance that Strydom would not be prepared to repeat. Yet the example of the American South would seem in indicate that mere criticism from outside is unlikely to contribute much to the resolution of one of the most difficult of all political problems—that of the 'plural society'.

If on the other hand the mother country does what England tried to do to some extent, if not for the same reasons, in the American colonies before the Revolution—to protect the indigenous inhabitants against the pressure of the settlers—it can only do so by checking the full progress of the colony toward autonomy: that is, by denying to its sons abroad the political liberties they would enjoy at home. The American anti-colonialist has thus either to advocate self-government and allow the more powerful (generally minority) groups in the colony to establish their rule, or to deny self-government in the interests of the majority. The only way out is to suggest that universal suffrage should accompany the grant of self-government—which means asking the imperial government to face the odium of an experiment on the lines of the post-Civil War Reconstruction in the United States. Is this really possible? Would Americans accept it for themselves? Nothing in their record suggests that they would.

Secondly, there are the territories which became part of European empires not for purposes of settlement, but because the process of economic expansion necessitated political control as well, in order to give commerce and industry the protection which the

indigenous authorities were unable to supply. This kind of imperialism is symptomatic of the social weaknesses of the conquered
rather than of the special greed of the conquerors. Such forms of
empire are the most vulnerable under modern conditions but present
the easiest problem in some ways. The imperial government needs
only to withdraw and leave the field clear for local independence.
That is what has happened in the case of the British in India, the
French in Indo-China, and the Dutch in Indonesia. It is happening
at this moment in West Africa and Malaya, where the British are
abdicating their control.

But the relative success achieved in countries like India should
not blind us to the real difficulties in the way of the simple withdrawal of the colonial authority. Under present conditions, the
newly enfranchised state must be able to set up the full apparatus
of modern government. But for this it needs an adequately trained
elite; and the existence of this depends in turn, at least in part, upon
the previous duration of imperial rule. Thus to hasten the process
may make it impossible of achievement, except at the price of self-
government turning out to mean either native tyranny or native
anarchy. The fact that the United States can offer one good example
in the Philippines of how this operation can be brought off does not
prove that circumstances are everywhere as favourable. Furthermore, the lack of racial and social homogeneity obtaining in many
of the countries concerned may not be due to settlement by immigrants from the ex-imperial power, but to other movements of
peoples either before or during the period of imperial rule. American
political thinking offers no solution to the problems of government
which this situation poses and which an independent Malaya with
its Chinese and Indians will now have to face. And there is also the
complication caused by the existence of Communist pressure which
the indigenous régimes may be unable to resist without external
aid. From the American point of view, there is all the difference in
the world between the kind of assistance the United States is giving
to South Korea or Southern Vietnam and the colonial rule exercised
by the old imperial powers; but for the Asian peoples themselves,
the differences may be less obvious. The suspicion with which the
Eisenhower Doctrine has been greeted cannot be set down wholly
to the efficacy of Soviet propaganda.

Finally, there are places on the map, acquired as strategic bases
or commercial *entrepôts* for the furtherance of the imperial
country's own commerce, but usually to the benefit of everyone, in

which great cities may have sprung up, as in the case of Hong Kong or Singapore, where nothing at all existed previously. President Roosevelt's pressure on the British Government in wartime to 'retrocede' Hong Kong to China took account neither of the fact that, apart from the rock on which it stands, Hong Kong was not and never had been Chinese, nor of the probable preference of its inhabitants, nor of the services to trade it could render as part of the British maritime empire but only very doubtfully under the kind of régimes that China had so far shown itself capable of developing.

These distinctions between forms of colonial rule may seem banal; but the record of American anti-colonialism, especially under Franklin Roosevelt, suggests that they cannot be stated too often or too simply. For the American pressure was not solely exercised against this or that aspect of British imperial rule, but against the whole concept of special ties existing between Britain and overseas countries, even when, as in the case of the then self-governing dominions, they were almost wholly economic. The sentimental anti-colonialism of a Roosevelt (upon the limitations of whose knowledge in the field a rather alarming light is cast by Mrs Roosevelt's memoirs) was reinforced by the more doctrinaire conceptions of Cordell Hull.

On matters such as India's progress toward self-government, the difference between Britain and the United States was one of timing only; but on the development of a Commonwealth of Nations whose members would be at different stages on the road to ultimate independence and would would be linked by economic and other arrangements entered into for mutual benefit, the disagreement involved matters of principle. For the Americans, the future of the world lay in its division into a number of entirely separate political units connected by the universalist machinery of the United Nations and its associated organizations, but without any special groupings. The effect of this on the commercial and financial negotiations of the war and post-war periods has been traced in Richard N. Gardner's remarkable work, *Sterling-Dollar Diplomacy*; but its political repercussions are also of importance and are not yet exhausted.

It is a curious testimony to the extent to which unanalysed prejudices swayed American thinking that it should have been possible for the United States before and during the war to ignore the fact that all the forms of colonialism described above were practised or envisaged by the Russians without exciting at that time anything like the same measure of American reprobation.

Indeed, it was possible for Roosevelt to imagine that he could secure a measure of understanding with Stalin, on the basis of a common anti-colonialism, which he could not hope for with Churchill. Russia had, as we have seen, her colonies of 'pure settlement' in Siberia; but in Central Asia she had acquired a whole empire based on various kinds of settlement but all of it enjoying less autonomy than all but the most backward of Crown colonies. The purely formal incorporation of these vast areas into the Soviet Union's quasi-federal system seemed sufficient to cleanse her of the taint of imperialism despite the fact that her empire was subject to economic planning of a wholly centralized kind, and despite the fact that an alien culture and ideology was forcibly imposed upon its component peoples. It was only when Russia showed signs, in her claims against China, of wanting to go over to strategic imperialism as well — to make a Russian Hong Kong and Singapore out of Port Arthur and Dairen — that American suspicions were finally aroused. One need not press the point against Roosevelt too far; similar illusions were held in some quarters in Britain. But the whole story provides an apt illustration of the inherent confusion of American thought on the anti-colonialist side.

Britain was not, in fact, the chief sufferer from American anti-colonial pressure, since on the whole she was able at the end of the war to resume her programme for the peaceful development of the Commonwealth. It is rather in American policy toward Indo-China and Indonesia that we should have to look for the practical consequences of the anti-colonialism of the period.

The United States would seem unconsciously to have adopted the Lennist classification of the non-white world into colonial and semi-colonial countries — the latter being those dominated by foreign capital though preserving the forms of political autonomy. Toward the latter countries, Americans have shown a wholehearted and unequivocal sympathy, provided they were non-Communist. It has been assumed that such countries, if furnished a certain amount of external aid, could develop direct from the more primitive forms of political organization inherited from their own past into states on the Western model, with no intervening period of foreign tutelage. The same assumption has more recently coloured United States attitudes toward the Middle East, and is indeed at the very heart of the Eisenhower Doctrine.

This American attitude rests, of course, on two unverified and improbable assumptions; first, that Asian and African countries are capable of passing by themselves from one stage of political and administrative development to another without falling into chaos or under some despotism denying full play to the country's human and material resources; and second, that in no circumstances can self-determination lead to the adoption of a Communist system and hence to dependence upon the established Communist powers. Neither of these assumptions is any truer of semi-colonial than of ex-colonial countries. American anti-colonialism assumes that a capacity for creating an ordered and peaceful society is within the grasp of any people no matter what its stage of economic and social development, instead of accepting the far more compelling evidence that goes to show that the free institutions of the Western world are the sophisticated products of a series of historical developments of a unique kind. Nor does the order of priorities in the development of political and social institutions that commends itself to Americans or Western Europeans necessarily appeal to people living under very different conditions.

Again one is unjust if one suggests that no Americans can see beyond the preconceptions induced by their own good fortune. Indeed, the best statement of the intellectual and moral problems involved is probably David Potter's, in his book *People of Plenty*, significantly subtitled 'Economic Abundance and the American Character'. What other peoples admire and envy in America is not her democratic order but her material abundance; and it has yet to be proved to them that the former has contributed to the latter. Until they have been shown the connection they may very well be inclined to feel—and without the persuasion of Russian or Chinese bayonets—that Communism can lead them direct to the abundance. And where colonialism has been given no chance (or has not taken its chance) to produce an elite differently minded, this is a quite likely event.

But one finds the final confusion of illusion and reality in the support given by the United States to the United Nations—not in the grave affairs of foreign policy to which we have alluded at the beginning of this essay, but on colonial questions in the Trusteeship Council or the Fourth Committee of the General Assembly. Sir Alan Burns, for ten years the permanent British representative on these bodies, has shown in his book, *In Defence of Colonies*, the futility of expecting useful criticism of the work of an administering power to come either from countries serving the political ends of the Soviet bloc, or from countries committed to anti-colonialism but without real experience of the problems posed by the government of backward peoples. There is something fantastic about talking of the beneficent effects of 'world public opinion' when what is meant is speeches highly critical of the British, French, or Australian record by the representative of some 'banana republic' that has scarcely made a start toward solving its own problems of poverty and illiteracy. But for the anti-colonialist, the peoples of the 'banana republics' are free, and those under the protection of a 'colonial' power enslaved.

I do not mean to give the impression that there is a ready-made, tested doctrine of beneficent and active imperial rule to oppose to American anti-colonialism. On the contrary, there are fundamental differences in outlook among the remaining imperial powers and within their own people, and their views have undergone more than one change. It should be easy for Britain to understand the American attitude because she too passed through an important phase of anti-colonialism in the first half of the nineteenth century. The arguments then used appeal principally to British self-interest. Experience had proved that trade was as profitable with countries which were not politically controlled as with colonies; and the latter involved burdens in the shape of the costs of administration and defence which thrifty middle-class radicals saw no need to shoulder, particularly since the jobs so created normally fell to the aristocracy and gentry. Where continued control seemed unavoidable, as in India, the position of the metropolitan country should, they thought, be used in order to promote Europeanization, since only civilized countries — by which was meant countries like nineteenth century Western Europe — could ever usefully rule themselves.

By the late nineteenth century, a more positive conception of empire had developed and one that has yet perhaps to find its historian. In part, it undoubtedly reflected a rethinking of commercial policy in the light of increased competition, growing protectionism, and a fiercer struggle for markets. But in part, too, it involved an ideology of paternal service to the less fortunate peoples. And gradually the two have merged in the present century into a notion of an evolving, and perhaps even expanding, commonwealth of free peoples. Yet the radical anti-colonial tradition has never vanished altogether and anti-colonialist preaching from outside continues to be sympathetically received within Britain.

The great American argument on the subject, at the turn of the century when the question of expansion outside the areas of continental settlement first had to be faced, was thus conducted in terms that were not so remote after all from British experience. The expansionism of the 1840's had not presented the issue in this way because the inhabitants of the conquered Mexican territory and of Oregon could be assimilated into the American system without raising any question as to the preservation or modification of the United States' cultural homogeneity upon which its institutions have always implicity rested. The island possessions of Spain raised different questions, as Howard K. Beale has recently reminded us in his important book, *Theodore Roosevelt and the Rise of America to World Power*.

Quotation illustrates the sentiments of the time better than analysis: 'The tendency of modern times is towards consolidation. . . . Small states are of the past and have no future. . . . The great nations are rapidly absorbing for their future expansion and their present defence all the waste places of the earth. It is a movement which makes for civilization and the advancement of the race.' Not the English imperialist Joseph Chamberlain but the American Henry Cabot Lodge. . . .

Indeed, the British example was sometimes explicit avowed. Thus Senator Albert J. Beveridge:

American factories are making more than the American people can use; American soil is producing more than they consume. Fate has written our policy for us; the trade of the world must and shall be ours. And we will get it as our mother has told us how. We will establish trading posts throughout the world as distributing posts for our American products. We will cover the ocean with our merchant marine. We will build a navy to the measure of our greatness. Great colonies governing themselves, flying our flag and trading with us, will grow about our posts of trade. Our institutions will follow our flag on the wings of commerce. And America: American order, American civilization and the American flag, will plant themselves on shores hitherto bloody and benighted, but by those agencies of God henceforth to be made beautiful.

The counter-arguments were not, however, principally concerned with the effect of territorial acquisition upon the indigenous populations. It was far more a question of whether such action was in accordance with the spirit of America's republican institutions. Thus Carl Schurz who, half a century later, could still talk the language of 1848 and 1861:

I believe that this Republic . . . can endure so long as it remains true to the principles upon which it was founded, but that it will morally decay if it abandons them. I believe this democracy, the government of, by, and for the people, is not fitted for a colonial policy which means conquest by force, or as President McKinley called it, 'criminal aggression' and arbitrary rule over subject populations. I believe that, if it attempts such a policy on a large scale, its inevitable degeneracy will hurt the progress of civilization more than it can possibly further that progress by planting its flag upon foreign soil on which its fundamental principles of government cannot live.

And again on another occasion, Schurz tried to prove that colonial acquisitions would not only involve America in the burden of defending them and help to provide the occasions for new wars, but would also fail to reap the expected benefit of gratitude for the favours American rule might confer — and this to an American was clearly an extremely important consideration, as it still is:

We may flatter ourselves that, as conquerors, we are animated with purposes much more unselfish, and we may wonder why not only in the Philippines, but even among the people of Puerto Rico and of Cuba, our benevolent intentions should meet with so much sullen disfavour. The reason is simple. We bring to those populations the intended benefits in the shape of foreign rule: and of all inflictions foreign rule is to them the most odious, as under similar circumstances it would be to us.

The conclusion of the argument was stated by William Jennings Bryan when, in his speech accepting the Democratic nomination in 1900, he argued against the retention of the Philippines:

Whether the Spanish war shall be known in history as a war for liberty or as a war of conquest, whether the principles of self-government shall be strengthened or abandoned; whether this nation shall remain a homogeneous republic or become a hetero-geneous empire — these questions must be answered by the American people — when they speak, and not until then, will destiny be revealed.

The upshot was paradoxical. The United States, having acquired the embryo of an empire, then set to work getting rid of it; so that the Schurzes and the Bryans now appear to have triumphed. It is worth noting that what exceptions there have been to the American retreat from empire have been justified not on economic but on military grounds — not on any grounds connected with the territories themselves, but simply because these territories have been thought necessary to the defence of the continental United States. The acquisitions in the Pacific made at the end of the Second World War were exclusively of this kind.

The Marxist analysis of imperialism, which has had an impact well outside Marxist circles, was based on the assumption that a developing capitalism would need foreign markets to absorb its surpluses, and that its struggle to obtain such markets or outlets for investment would drive it along the imperialist road. Recent developments in the economic policies of capitalist countries, influenced by Keynesian economic thought, have taken some of the force from this argument. But if these earlier economic arguments, adduced to suggest the inevitability of all capitalist states, including the United States, adopting imperialist policies, are no longer persuasive, serious economic issues remain that cannot so lightly be dismissed.

An important characteristic of all advanced economies today is their increasing dependence upon a regular and guaranteed supply of raw materials and sources of energy—oil and uranium—from areas abroad. To this the American economy has hitherto presented something of an exception, because of the great variety of its own continental endowments. But there is reason to believe that this is ceasing to be the case. It is unlikely, then, that the United States will always be able to rely on purely commercial transactions for acquiring some of the materials she vitally needs. This is partly so because there may be régimes which, for political reasons, will want to deny them to her or use their control of them for political blackmail. America's fear of Communist expansion is justified on this ground alone, quite apart from ideological considerations.

But it is also the case that not every country in the world is able to mount unaided the economic effort necessary to exploit its own economic resources, and that the social transformation necessary to enable it to do so may crack its traditional structure of authority. The United States will then learn—and may in the Middle East and elsewhere already be learning—the hard truth that great nations cannot necessarily choose whether they will be 'colonialist' or not. The important thing is that Americans should come to understand the difference between doing the 'colonial' job properly and doing it badly—and certainly they will not learn this lesson by indiscriminately abusing those countries which are already confronted with responsibilities of this kind, and by accepting at face value the propaganda of every Asian and African nationalist movement.

The problem of the world today is not so much its ideological as its material divisions; the United States belongs with the rich and not with the poor, and can get nowhere with an ideology proper to the latter group of countries. Since it will not accept demotion into the ranks of the poor, it has to spend part of its substance on elevating them into the ranks of the rich before it is overwhelmed in a flood of envy and hate. Its destiny, then, is no different from that of other Western nations—the occasional self-righteousness of its leaders to the contrary notwithstanding.

16

Theodore Roosevelt and the British Empire[1]

IT is appropriate that we should pay tribute to the memory of a great President of the United States who was also a Doctor of this University. It is further appropriate that this tribute should be paid at Rhodes House, for one of the engagements that Roosevelt fulfilled when he visited Oxford on June 7, 1910, to receive his honorary degree from the Chancellor, Lord Curzon, was to take lunch with the American Club. In the course of his speech to the Club, Roosevelt said that he noticed that his audience was largely composed of Rhodes Scholars, and that he wished to take the opportunity of expressing on behalf of the American people 'their very deep sense of obligation for what Mr Rhodes did and for what those who were carrying out his bequest were doing in bringing to this ancient University Americans as they had brought Canadians and Australians'.[2] It is true that we now know that Roosevelt's enthusiasm for Oxford was a little less than he made it out to be at the time, since he wrote in a private letter: 'In Oxford I of course enjoyed visiting four or five of the colleges. The whole life was charming with an old-world flavour very attractive to me as an onlooker —I cannot understand any American failing to find it attractive as an onlooker, and on the other hand I cannot understand any American caring to be educated there rather than at one of his own universities.'[3]

The visit generally was a great public success, with crowds flocking to see the ex-President fresh from his hunting exploits in Africa and his triumphal progress round the courts of Europe. The degree ceremony in the Sheldonian was also attended by an en-

[1] Lecture delivered at Rhodes House, Oxford, May 23, 1958, at the request of the Theodore Roosevelt Centennial Commission of New York.

[2] *The Times*, June 8, 1910.

[3] E. E. Morison, *The Letters of Theodore Roosevelt*, Vol 7, p. 406.

thusiastic and good-humoured multitude. It was observed that the behaviour of the undergraduate members was excellent but that the same could not be said for the massed MA's in the arena. The *Oxford Magazine* noted: 'To applaud learned jests is well: but to laugh whenever the Chancellor speaks Latin is to impair the dignity of academic functions.'[1] After receiving the degree, Roosevelt delivered his Romanes lecture on 'Biological Analogies in History'.[2] Roosevelt had given a great deal of thought to the preparation of this lecture, which dealt in an elaborate and detailed manner with the analogies that can be drawn between the rise and fall of animal species and the rise and fall of nations and empires. One of his naturalist friends had, indeed, been obliged to suggest that he omitted some of the more definite comparisons on the ground that they might affect the national susceptibilities of some of the countries involved. The lecture, thus weighted down with rather primitive Darwinism, is not, I think, one of Roosevelt's best efforts, and it is not surprising that the then Archbishop of York, Dr Lang, should have commented to Roosevelt's friend: 'In the way of grading which we have at Oxford we agreed to mark the lecture Beta Minus but the lecturer Alpha Plus. While we feel that the lecture was not a very great contribution to science, we were sure that the lecturer was a very great man.'[3]

Nevertheless, at certain moments in this performance, Roosevelt touched upon a topic which came very close to his own interests as a statesman and historian, and a topic which has seemed to me to be the most suitable one for us to explore today. He dealt, that is to say, with a comparison between the civilizing roles of the Roman and the British Empires and with his own deep belief in what was later to be called the doctrine of trusteeship. As befitted the academic audience he was addressing, Roosevelt spoke in relatively abstract and general terms. He had not always done so during his visit to England, and as was noted 'there was some pleasant and kindly irony in the Latin part of the proceedings referring to the occasions when Mr Roosevelt has advised and exhorted this country.'[4]

The principal exhortation of this kind had been the address given by Roosevelt at the Guildhall, London, on May 31st.[5] In addition

[1] *The Oxford Magazine*, June 9, 1910.
[2] Theodore Roosevelt, *Biological Analogies in History*, Clarendon Press, 1910.
[3] Henry F. Pringle, *Theodore Roosevelt*, Jonathan Cape, 1932, p. 520.
[4] *The Oxford Magazine*, June 9, 1910.
[5] *The Times*, June 1, 1910.

to giving once more his well-known views on the importance of firm and just government in overseas dependencies, in the course of which he made the famous and much quoted remark that 'of all the broken reeds, sentimentality is the most broken reed on which righteousness can rest', he described the effect upon him of his recent visit to Kenya, Uganda, the Sudan and Egypt:

'I grew heartily to respect the men whom I there met, settlers and military and civil officials; and it seems to me that the best service I can render them and you is to tell you how I was impressed by some of the things I saw. Your men in Africa are doing a great work for your Empire, and they are also doing a great work for civilization.

'The great fact in world history, during the last century, has been the spread of civilization over the world's waste spaces. The work is still going on and the soldiers, the settlers, and the civil officials who are actually doing it are, as a whole, entitled to the heartiest respect and the fullest support from their brothers who remain at home.'

In Kenya he found that the British settlers reminded him of those pioneers of the American west whose history he had written: Uganda, unsuitable for white settlement, offered a great opportunity for helping in the development of the local population; with regard to British rule in the Sudan, he condemned the 'sentimentalists' who objected to 'the spread of civilization at the expense of savagery. I do not,' he declared, 'believe that in the whole world there is to be found any nook of territory which has shown such astonishing progress from the most hideous misery to well-being and prosperity as the Sudan has shown during the last twelve years while it has been under British rule. I feel about you in the Sudan just as I felt about us in Panama.' From Roosevelt there could be no higher praise.

These compliments might have been accepted with equanimity; what caused trouble was the nature of Roosevelt's reference to Egyptian affairs; in that country growing nationalist agitation had recently led to the murder of the Prime Minister, Boutros Pasha, and the Liberal Government was under fire for having assisted the progress of the agitation by too rapid a concession of democratic institutions and too weak an attitude in face of disorder. Roosevelt showed himself to be on the side of the critics:

'You have given Egypt,' he said, 'the best Government it has had for at least two thousand years'; and then, raising his eyebrows, he explained: 'Why I put in 2,000 years is because I happen not to know the details of the Ptolemaic Government.' But this Government could be jeopardized by weakness: 'Weakness, timidity and sentimentality,' he declared, 'may cause even more far-reaching harm than violence and injustice.' Keeping public order was Britain's justification for being in Egypt at all, and in the passage that created the most excitement he added: 'You are in Egypt for several purposes, and among them one of the greatest is the benefit of the Egyptian people. You saved them from ruin by coming in, and at the present moment, if they are not governed from outside they will again sink into a welter of chaos. Some nation must govern Egypt. I hope and believe that it is your duty to be that nation.'

Roosevelt's comments were frequently referred to in the debate on Egyptian administration in the House of Commons on June 13, 1910.[1] For the Opposition, Mr J. L. Baird declared that Roosevelt's remarks were perfectly justified and had been received both in Egypt and in Britain with 'the utmost relief, because it is felt that only a man in the position of Mr Roosevelt would carry enough weight' with the Government 'to induce them to reconsider and to some extent modify their policy.' This was certainly a remarkable testimony to the importance attached to someone who was a private citizen of a foreign country and one for whom American constitutional convention held out little hope of a political future.

On the other side, the radical J. M. Robertson declared that Roosevelt's remarks were widely regarded as an insult to Britain. Where, he asked, would the doctrine laid down by Mr Roosevelt lead to? 'Mr Roosevelt belongs to a country where three Presidents have been assassinated over half a century. What, I wonder, will Mr Roosevelt say, and what will his friends here say, if it be suggested on his own line or argument that these assassinations, or that any one of them, proves that the government then in power in America had been misgoverning, or not maintaining order, or that Mr Roosevelt's friends were doing too much?' On the whole, however, Roosevelt's supporters in the debate outnumbered his critics; and they included Balfour, Henry Chaplin, a future High Commissioner in G. A. (later Lord) Lloyd and Edward Wood, now Lord Halifax and Chancellor of this University, who in the course of answering Robertson's attack on Roosevelt and his reference to the murders of American Presidents, emphasized the point that colonial government itself depended upon consent and not on force and that there-

[1] 17 H.C. Deb. 5s. Col. 1103-1160.

fore it was essential to maintain its prestige. 'If that is true,' he said in words that could have been spoken by Roosevelt himself, 'if that is true, as I think it is, surely the argument that under all conditions and at all times all men are equal is one of the most flimsy and most academic that could possibly be brought forward. It is no more true to say that all men are equal at all times than to say that all men have red hair or false teeth. And while we on our side most emphatically disclaim any attempt permanently to hold down black races, we do at the same time insist that if our position in those countries is to be maintained it can only be, as it is at the present moment, by maintaining the position and fulfilling the functions of a superior race.'

In the course of his speech another Conservative, Mr Gretton, declared that he could not believe that Roosevelt had made his speech without communicating its substance to the Foreign Office beforehand, and giving the Government an opportunity to object to anything they found embarrassing; if so, the Foreign Minister should tell the House. Grey, when he came to speak, indicated that Roosevelt had indeed communicated to him his observations on the British territories through which he had travelled and that no suggestion had been made that their exposition in public would be disagreeable to the Government. Grey had listened to the Guildhall speech with the greatest enjoyment and he thought that everyone would have felt that it was, 'taken as a whole, the greatest compliment to the work of one country in the world ever paid by the citizen of another'.

Grey's statement may be thought rather curious in view of the fact that on Egypt, Roosevelt's views had provided so much ammunition to the Government's critics. But the Roosevelt papers provide at least a clue to what lay behind it. In the first place, Roosevelt was genuinely critical of what he believed to be the British weakness in handling the situation—a weakness he attributed to the Government and public opinion at home rather than to the men on the spot. In a private letter written a couple of months before the Guildhall speech he said:

'I had a most interesting time in the Sudan and Egypt and I must say I have come away with rather a contempt for the English attitude in Egypt. I don't believe that it is any worse than we would take, if at this time we had what the *Evening Post* desires, a mixture of mugwumps, ultra peace-advocates and maudlin hysterical sentimentalists, plus Bryanites to dominate our foreign affairs. But it certainly makes the English look flabby.'[1]

In a long letter written the year after his visit to England, Roosevelt asserted that 'All through Africa, but especially in the Sudan and in Egypt, the British military and civil officers had been pathetically anxious that I should say something for them in London because they felt that the situation in Africa was not understood at home, and that somebody who was not afraid of criticism, and other consequences, ought to speak for them. I felt,' he says, 'a very sincere desire to help them out, to lend a helping hand to Great Britain in its really admirable work in Africa; but I wanted to be sure that I would do good and not harm before I spoke.'[2] He had made such speeches to the Native Officers' Club and at the University of Cairo; the latter had attracted much attention and the congratulations of Sir Eldon Gorst, Cromer's successor in Egypt, and of the Sirdar of the Sudan, Sir Richard Wingate.[3] Roosevelt made wide inquiries in London about the likely reactions to a speech on these lines; among those he spoke to were the King, Lord Cromer and Balfour. But clearly the important person was Grey, whom Roosevelt called on in company with the American Ambassador. Roosevelt, who had not then met Grey, did not wish to risk any subsequent difference of memory about what had passed. He was, however, reassured:

'Grey,' he wrote, 'is one of the finest fellows I ever met, and now I should unhesitatingly see him and talk with him on any subject knowing that I could trust his memory absolutely. I found that Grey was not merely acquiescent in my delivering the speech, but very anxious that I should deliver it. Asquith and Morley would, I knew, and as Grey showed that he knew, disapprove, but this was evidently in Grey's mind merely another reason why I should make it. He was obviously very uneasy at the course his Party was taking about Egypt. He was in the unpleasant position of finding his Party associates tending as a whole to refuse to allow him to do what was necessary; and he wanted his hand forced. I told him that I should never tell anyone that I had seen him, and that he could absolutely disavow responsibility for all that I said, but he answered at once that if any debate arose upon it in the House of Commons he would state that he had seen me and talked the matter over, and that he

[1] Letter to Henry White, April 2, 1910, *Letters of Theodore Roosevelt*, Vol VII, p. 65.

[2] Letter to David Grey, October 5, 1911, ibid., Vol VII, pp. 402-3.

[3] Letter to Sir George Trevelyan, October 1, 1911, ibid., Vol VII, pp. 350-4.

not only approved of what I intended to say but believed that I was rendering a real service to Great Britain by saying it and that was strengthening his hands.'[1]

Grey's own later account is less dramatic. He merely stated that having heard Roosevelt read the manuscript of his speech, he felt that 'it would have been a poor and paltry thing to say that we appreciated the praise but resented the criticism; to ask him to let the tribute stand but to leave out the advice. I had therefore,' wrote Grey, 'no hesitation in deciding that the speech as a whole was so valuable to us that I would ask for no alteration and accept it as it was.'[2] According to Lord Charnwood, Roosevelt was reluctant to speak and only 'yielded to the strong persuasion of some of the very foremost English statesmen'.[3]

Roosevelt himself also added, to indicate the degree to which the speech was intended as a contribution to the British controversy over imperial policy, the fact that it was gone over word for word by Arthur Lee (later Lord Lee of Fareham), who had been British military attaché in Cuba at the time of the Spanish-American war and an honorary member of Roosevelt's 'Rough Riders', and Cecil Spring-Rice, then on leave from his post as Minister to Sweden, whose presence in London at the time of his visit had been urged by Roosevelt in a letter in the previous October: 'You *must* be in London next May. I have any amount of things to talk over with you, especially as regards what I have seen in your African colonies. I greatly like and admire your officials, and your settlers seem to me in all essentials just like our westerners. It is difficult for me to remember that I am not a fellow-countryman of theirs; and they certainly act as if they thought I was an especial friend and champion, who sympathized with and believed in them.'[4] Roosevelt's own vision of himself in all this, as champion of the British overseas, whose work was being underestimated and whose safety was being jeopardized by the ignorance and negligence of their own countrymen, is clear enough: in attacking the 'Little Englanders' Roosevelt was attacking what he believed to be the British counterparts of the anti-expansionists against whom he and his friends had

[1] Letter to David Grey, October 5, 1911, *Letters of Theodore Roosevelt*, Vol VII, pp. 402-3.

[2] Lord Grey, *Twenty-five Years* (London, 1925), Vol II, pp. 89-90.

[3] Lord Charnwood, *Theodore Roosevelt* (London, 1923), p. 185.

[4] S. Gwynn ed. *The Letters and Friendships of Sir Cecil Spring-Rice* (London, 1929), Vol II, p. 141.

fought in the 1890's. But since our concern is with Roosevelt and not with Grey, I shall not go on to inquire how far Roosevelt may have exaggerated Grey's positive enthusiasm for his activities — retrospective exaggeration was a well-known Rooseveltian failing — nor to raise the question of the constitutional propriety of the Foreign Secretary using an American ex-President to strengthen his own hands against his Prime Minister and colleagues. Incidentally, according to one source, Asquith actually knew what Roosevelt was going to say.[1] For our present purpose it is more relevant to inquire what attitudes and opinions of Roosevelt had put him into a position in which he could be cast for an active role in the British debate over the future of imperial rule and make possible the claim that the sending of Kitchener to Egypt in 1911 was a direct result of the speech.[2]

Throughout Roosevelt's career there was a marked ambivalence in his attitude towards Britain. On the one hand, the group of nationalists with whom he was associated and whose ideas played so large a part in his own thinking, shared in many ways the traditional suspicion of Britain and her purposes in international politics. And in Roosevelt this suspicion was fortified by his deep dislike for what he thought to be the aristocratic and effete elements in British society and more especially for those Americans — literary expatriates in particular — who seemed to be attracted by them.[3] And this is, of course, the background to the remarks we have already noted about Americans who wished to be educated at Oxford.

For the other and more positive aspect of Roosevelt's attitudes towards Britain and the British Empire, a clue is again provided in Oxford. More than a year before Roosevelt's visit, on March 8, 1909, a lecture was delivered at the School of Geography under the rather striking title: 'Theodore Roosevelt: Dynamic Geographer'. The speaker was one F. B. Vrooman, an American-born geographer and explorer, now domiciled in Canada and a member of what must have been a remarkable family, one of his brothers being Walter Vrooman, the founder of Ruskin College: 'Theodore Roosevelt,' said the lecturer, 'is a new kind of geographer. There are static geographers and dynamic geographers. Mr Roosevelt is a dynamic

---

[1] L. F. Abbott, *Impressions of Theodore Roosevelt* (New York, 1920), p. 157.

[2] Ibid., p. 161. He calls this section of his book 'How Roosevelt helped to save Egypt'.

[3] See e.g. Howard K. Beale, *Theodore Roosevelt and the Rise of America to World Power* (Baltimore, 1956), pp. 81-3.

geographer. One studies and describes that geography which man helps to make; the other helps to make that geography which other men describe.'[1] Mr Vrooman seems to have been thinking mainly of Roosevelt's activities in the field of conservation; a subject about which he felt strongly. He was to write on another occasion: 'We have been boasting of our inexhaustible resources until there is only one inexhaustible resource left—the complacency of the American people.'[2] But Mr Vrooman was well aware that Roosevelt's 'dynamic geography' was not confined to America's frontiers; trusteeship in the Philippines and the building of the trans-isthmian canal stood as evidence to the contrary, and did not stand alone. 'Just now,' Mr Vrooman told his Oxford audience, 'Mr Roosevelt is to try a new geographical role. He is becoming an explorer in Africa before he is to become your distinguished guest at this University. . . . It is also said that he is going lion-hunting. So far his special animosity has been the bear'—the old Victorian image for Russia had not exhausted its utility. 'He has hitherto shown no special grudge against the lion, especially of the British variety. But if he does not make some new and striking contributions to geographical dynamics in Africa before he returns this way, those who know him will miss their guess.'[3]

Whatever precisely may have been the significance that Mr Vrooman attached to the phrase 'dynamic geography', it is clear enough that Roosevelt himself, like Henry Adams and Mahan, among his associates, took what might be called a dynamic view of world geography, and thought about international relations in terms of what a later period would style 'geopolitics'. He saw the world as developing towards a situation in which political sovereignty would rest with a relatively small number of great and expanding powers, and in which world peace would depend upon harmonizing their relationships. This development was an inevitable consequence of the spread of the white race and its civilization. Although under no illusions as to the cruelties and injustices attendant upon this process, Roosevelt never wavered from his belief that this process was ultimately a beneficial one. In his book the *Winning of the West*, Roosevelt had justified the expulsion of the Red Indians and declared that it was indeed 'a warped, perverse and silly morality

[1] F. B. Vrooman, *Theodore Roosevelt: Dynamic Geographer* (Oxford, 1909), p. 9.
[2] F. B. Vrooman, *The New Politics* (New York, 1911), p. 284.
[3] *Theodore Roosevelt: Dynamic Geographer*, p. 10.

which would forbid the course of a conquest that has turned whole continents into the seats of mighty and flourishing civilizations'. And at this time already — 1896 — he accepted the analogy of what had happened in North America with the history of white settlement elsewhere: 'The most ultimately righteous of all wars is a war with savages, though it is apt to be also the most terrible and inhuman. The rude, fierce settler who drives the savage from the land lays all civilized mankind under debt to him. American and Indian, Boer and Zulu, Cossack and Tartar, New Zealander and Maori — in each case the victor, horrible though many of his deeds are, has laid deep the foundations for the future greatness of a mighty people.'[1]

Similarly, where the question was not one of settlement but of the rule over peoples who lacked or seemed to lack for the time being the capacity to rule themselves and to make the best use of the resources at their disposal, Roosevelt was, as we have seen, convinced that foreign rule — provided it was conducted with a proper concern for the welfare of the ruled — was not only tolerable but even desirable. Nor did he distinguish between such rule when exercised by Americans, as in the Philippines, and the empires of the British and other European peoples. In 1899 he talked of the difficulties the United States was facing in Cuba and the Philippines, and of the danger of a series of disasters 'at the very beginning of our colonial policy'.[2] He believed that it was a good thing for the world and for the peoples concerned 'that France should be in Algeria, England in the Soudan and Russia in Turkestan'.[3] He used arguments in regard to the dangers of premature self-government for unready peoples that have found repeated expression in the course of British imperial history. It is natural that British statesmen such as Joseph Chamberlain rejoiced in the new realism forced upon the Americans by their own responsibilities in the colonial field. But the particular contribution of Roosevelt to the theory of imperialism was undoubtedly his insistence that the imperial powers were not trustees for themselves only, but for the civilized world as a whole, which had therefore the right to judge of their execution of their trust. This was the justification of the Guildhall speech: 'Mankind as a whole,' he said, 'has benefited by the noteworthy success that has attended the French occupation of Algeria and

[1] Beale, op. cit., pp. 160-1.
[2] Ibid., p. 65.
[3] Ibid., p. 72.

Tunis, just as mankind as a whole had benefited by what England had done in India'. And this meant that there ought to be agreement between all the civilized countries engaged in subduing the wilderness.

But this sense of the solidarity of the great imperial powers ran across the possibility that some of them would fail to accord what Roosevelt regarded as America's proper share; so that it might be inevitable that America should find herself in opposition to one or more of them. His feelings about the British Empire fluctuated according to the extent to which his American nationalism overrode his enthusiasm for empire-building and for empire-builders.

Importance must be attached to the fact that Britain from the 1890's was on the whole the Power most favourably inclined towards the evidence of a new American interest in expansion and naval power. In this respect, the Spanish-American war made it possible to dramatize the new-found friendship.[1] But this did not mean that Americans in general or Roosevelt in particular were likely to give way on what they regarded as vital issues and Roosevelt's firmness, not to say truculence, on the Canadian boundary issue is a case in point; since one can imagine him flattered rather than amused by the petition of the gold-miners of Porcupine in the disputed territory, which ran in part:

'We firmly believe that the young man that tackled the Lions in their den among the N.Y. police commissioners, who throttled vice and immorality, also corruption in high places while Governor of the Empire State, and faced clouds of lead and steel in a Southern clime, will be equal to this task, and we leave our interests with you, Mr President, believing our interests are the Nations' interests and you, by God's help, will guard them sacredly.'[2]

The nation's interests were certainly safe in Roosevelt's hands. Once agreement had been reached over outstanding issues in the western hemisphere, and once Britain had accepted American domination of the Caribbean and the monopoly of the United States in the projected isthmian canal, the annexation of Canada which had been a part of the expansionist programme of the 1890's ceased to be seriously considered.[3]

[1] See on this, Charles S. Campbell, Jr, *Anglo-American Understanding 1898-1903* (Baltimore, Johns Hopkins Press, 1957).
[2] Ibid., pp. 243-4.
[3] Cf. Beale, op. cit., p. 147.

The development of more friendly relations between the United States and Britain was further complicated by the effects of the Boer War.[1] President McKinley's administration was determined not to allow friction arising out of the war to affect the understanding that had grown up in the course of the Spanish war, and American imperialists like John Hay certainly felt a direct sense of sympathy for Britain. More important still was the effect of Britain's early reverses, which seemed to endanger the balance of world power in a manner directly detrimental to American interests. Despite considerable support for the Boer cause in Congress, the American Government steered clear of the attempts made by the continental Powers, and in particular Russia and Germany, to get America to take the lead in imposing a joint mediation upon the belligerents. In the early stages of the war Roosevelt himself was decidedly favourable to Britain. 'I have a great sympathy for the Boers and a great liking for them,' he wrote, 'but I think they are battling on the wrong side in the fight of civilization and will have to go under.[2] Or again, as he put it to Spring-Rice: 'I have been absorbed in the Boer War. The Boers are belated Cromwellians, with many fine traits. They deeply and earnestly believe in their cause, and they attract the sympathy which always goes to the small nation, even though the physical obstacles in the way may be such as to put the two contestants far more nearly on a par than at first sight seems to be the case. But it would be for the advantage of mankind to have English spoken south of the Zambesi just as in New York, and as I told one of my fellow-knickerbockers the other day, as we let the Uitlanders of old in here I do not see why the same rule is not good enough in the Transvaal.'[3]

A year later Roosevelt was apparently convinced that if necessary America should intervene rather than risk the British Empire being shattered by a coalition of European Powers.[4] At the same time, he was affected by the change of view which the Boer victories had brought about, as he observed, among many of his fellow citizens. Sympathy, he noted, was bound to be widespread for 'two little republics struggling for their freedom'.[5] On the other hand, the

[1] See John H. Ferguson, *American Diplomacy and the Boer War* (Philadelphia, 1939).
[2] Letter to Hermann Speck von Sternberg, November 27, 1899, *Letters*, Vol II, p. 1098.
[3] Letter to Spring-Rice, December 2, 1899, Gwynn, op. cit., Vol I, pp. 305-6.
[4] Ferguson, op. cit., pp. 208-9.
[5] Letter to Arthur Hamilton Lee, March 18, 1901, *Letters*, Vol III, p. 20.

failures of Britain, who was bound to win in the end anyway, had had the desired effect of making Americans less afflicted with anglomania and thus made friendly political relations with Britain easier.[1] As the war went on, his gloom about it increased:

'It certainly does seem to me that England is on the downgrade. The English-speaking race shares with the Slav the future; although the German, too, will play a great part in the present century. But while the future of North America and of Australia under the dominion of the people who speak English is very great, and while I hope English will grow to be the tongue of those who will undoubtedly some day form a practically independent commonwealth south of the Zambesi, and believe that England may yet accomplish a great deal in Africa, I do not see how she can fail to lose ground relatively to Russia in Asia, and she is so spread out that I think it will be very difficult to make a real and permanently imperial federation.'[2]

Roosevelt did not subsequently alter his views on becoming President and we need not perhaps give too much attention to the sympathetic reception he gave the unofficial Boer envoys in March 1902.[3] His fundamental attitude was based on the analogy with the United States; although self-government in some form would come to the whole of Southern Africa, it would be the British strain that would be the dominant one. As with most others on both sides in the struggle, the future of the actual majority of the population — the Africans — was ignored.

As he wrote in January 1900: 'There will come peace and the Afrikander will grow up like the Australian, the Canadian and the American. Here our people of different race origin do get fused very soon. . . . In two generations you cannot tell the average man of German or Scandinavian descent from the average man who is descended from those who came over on the Mayflower.'[4]

And on the same day he wrote to Spring-Rice in very much the same terms:

'I earnestly hope that when the war is over and South Africa south of the Zambesi under one flag (as it would have been in 1890 if Mr Gladstone had not possessed that weak sentimentality which in a statesman produces more harm than vice), then the

[1] Letter to George von Lengerke Meyer, April 12, 1901, ibid., p. 52.
[2] Letter to G. F. Becker, July 8, 1901, ibid., p. 112.
[3] Ferguson, op. cit., pp. 218-21.
[4] Letter to John St. Leo Stracey, January 27, 1900, *Letters*, Vol II, p. 1145.

process of amalgamation will turn the country into an English-speaking commonwealth like Australia; where the descendants of the Englishman and the Dutchman will live together side by side, gradually growing indistinguishable from one another until they become fused exactly as they have become in the United States.'[1]

It is not possible to overestimate the contribution of Roosevelt's ideas about what the history of the English-speaking peoples had in common to his view that their wider interests were identical. And although this outlook was to some extent overshadowed in Roosevelt's later years by his curiously equivocal attitude on the outbreak of war in 1914, it was certainly the dominant one during his second Presidential term and the years immediately after it. But, like other American Presidents, he had to reckon with constitutional and political facts that made it impossible to translate this conviction into a foreign policy. And were we able to go into Roosevelt's activities in regard to the Far East, we should be able to see the limitation that this placed upon him and the inability therefore of Britain to recede from the Japanese alliance as her main reliance there.

We are concerned, however, not with the facts of diplomacy but with the ideas that underlie them, and it remains for us to see how those of Roosevelt look now in retrospect. In doing so, we must remember that these ideas were not dogmas and that Roosevelt preserved a capacity for seeing what the practical limitations of his own policies might be. By 1907 he was arguing that although a long period of firm and wise government from outside might be the best thing for the Philippines, the temper of the American people was such as to make it unlikely that they would be willing to provide for it. The Filipinos' capacity for self-government could not be placed on the low level of that of the Egyptian *fellahin*, who required the firm rule of a Cromer. On the other hand, the British system was not everywhere admirable, and the Americans in the Philippines had done better than Britain in Malaya. 'We,' wrote Roosevelt with more than a touch of self-righteousness, 'are content to accept a deficit rather than to get a revenue from opium and drink and licentiousness or to destroy the natives by bringing in Chinese.'[2] But on the whole, his conviction that imperial rule could be a positive good remained unshaken.

Again, Roosevelt did not believe that mere exhortation without a

---

[1] Letter to Cecil Spring-Rice, January 27, 1900, *Letters*, Vol II, p. 1146.
[2] Letter to Silas McBee, August 27, 1907, ibid., Vol V, p. 775.

willingness to take responsibilities in action was either useful or honourable. And here, there is one of the major things that distinguishes him from his successors.[1]

We have indeed come a long way today from Roosevelt and his belief in the virtues that sustain empire. The modern American historian is more likely to feel sympathetic to Franklin Roosevelt's undisguised desire to see the liquidation of the British Empire and to the strong suspicion of imperial rule that underlay the whole approach to foreign affairs of the New Deal President and his closest advisers.[2] The most recent of the students of the earlier Roosevelt's policies can see only a failure where his most important objectives were concerned; 1914 proved the vanity of his attempts to keep the peace in Europe, and in China the balancing of Japan and Russia was very far from creating that commercial equality for all nations that had been the aim of his policy there. Despite the fact that America had followed his advice and built up great armaments, within thirty years after his death she was living 'in dread of destruction of her cities in an atomic war'. But it is particularly the alignment with Britain that the historian deplores: 'He thought,' writes Professor Howard Beale of Roosevelt, 'he had prepared the way for a century of the "English-speaking" man, and yet by the middle of that century Britain had lost much of her empire and was struggling desperately for survival. By joining forces with British imperialism, he imagined he was assuring the orderly government of colonial areas that domination of the "civilized" imperial powers would create. By the mid-century, nationalism among colonial people had led to uprisings all the world over of a sort that military might and superior master races could not prevent or quell. America's tying herself to British imperialism had left her holding the bag and paying the price of liquidating, everywhere outside the Western Hemisphere, the imperialism that Roosevelt helped to create. America was left fighting a costly rearguard retreat in defence not only of British, but of Dutch and French Empires in opposition to the aspirations for freedom that America would once have befriended. Instead of helping Britain maintain the balance of power in the *world* as Britain had more than once done on the Continent of Europe, the United States found itself the only remaining

[1] See, for instance, his letters to Sir George Trevelyan, May 13, 1905, *Letters*, Vol IV, pp. 1173-1176.

[2] See e.g. F. R. Dulles and G. E. Ridinger, 'The Anti-Colonial Policies of Franklin D. Roosevelt', *Political Science Quarterly*, March 1955.

nation with power to stand up on one side of a balance that was precarious.'[1]

It is perhaps surprising to find both a belief that American policy in recent years has so largely concerned itself with support for European imperialisms and the certainty that events have already proved the case for an alternative policy of supporting claims to self-determination whatever the capacities or the representative nature of those who make them. Professor Beale suggests that one miscalculation of Roosevelt and his friends had been that while fore-seeing Russia's rise, they had failed to take into account the rapidity of Britain's decline: 'they had still believed Britain's pre-eminence would last out the twentieth century'. This argument at least seems untenable. In the first place, Roosevelt was, as we have seen, very conscious at least from the time of the Boer War that Britain could not retain the place in world affairs that she had seemed to occupy in the last decades of the nineteenth century. It was this that had helped to remove some of his earlier suspicions of Britain as a rival to the United States itself and had caused him to adopt instead Admiral Mahan's convictions about the utility of the British Empire for America's own world purposes. In the second place, one could point out that in writing in this way, Professor Beale shows himself less realistic than Roosevelt as to the consequence of Russia's rise to world power.

Roosevelt's concern with Russia was based on a perception of long-term trends, not her immediate military might which, as he pointed out in 1901, was everywhere exaggerated and had been exaggerated ever since Poltava'.[2] For the present she was not so organized as 'to be able to exert anything like her full strength in offensive movement'.[3] For the time being it was Germany that was the most formidable rival of the English-speaking peoples; but in the long run 'the steady ethnic growth of Russia in Asia as opposed to Britain's purely administrative and political growth does make the Asian problem look serious'.[4]

Three years earlier he had written on the same theme a passage which sounds strangely prophetic:

'Indeed Russia is a problem very appalling. All other nations of European blood, if they develop at all, seem inclined to develop

[1] Beale, op. cit., pp. 417-8.
[2] Letter to G. F. Becker, July 8, 1901, Letters, Vol III, p. 112.
[3] Letter to Speck von Sternberg, July 12, 1901, Letters, Vol III, p. 117.
[4] Letter to Cecil Spring-Rice, August 11, 1899, ibid., Vol II, p. 1052.

on much the same lines; but Russia seems bound to develop in her own way and on lines that run directly counter to what we are accustomed to consider as progress. If she ever does take possession of Northern China and drill the Northern Chinese to serve as her Army, she will indeed be a formidable power. . . . The strength of the great Russian state in Siberia is portentious [sic]; but it is stranger still nowadays to see the rulers of the nation deliberately keeping it under a despotism, deliberately setting their faces against any increase of the share of the people in government'.[1]

For Roosevelt it was not thinkable that any people could permanently be kept under the yoke of a despotism; all peoples were bound to travel the same way, some faster some slower. 'The Russian,' he wrote, 'started far behind, yet he has travelled that path very much farther and faster since the days of Ivan the Terrible than our people have travelled it since the days of Elizabeth.' For this reason, 'if Russia chooses to develop purely on her own line and to resist the growth of liberalism, then she may put off the day of reckoning; but she cannot ultimately avert it, and instead of having occasionally to go through with what Kansas has gone through with the populists' — note the wonderfully parochial simile — 'she will sometime experience a red terror which will make the French revolution pale'.[2] Now although the Soviet Union of the mid-twentieth century (the product of the Red Terror that Roosevelt forecast) is different in many respects from the Tsarist Empire whose overland expansion gave him so much concern, it has not renounced its belief that force remains a powerful ingredient in the relations between peoples and in the maintenance and overthrow of political societies. The test for the political emancipation of previously subject peoples has not (at least since the Second World War) been solely the one that arose for consideration in Roosevelt's time, whether or not they were capable of establishing an ordered society, but whether or not their emancipation from Western rule would amount to accepting the subjugation of their national lives and purposes to those of the world Communist movement as defined by the Russians.

It is idle and indeed impertinent to speculate on what view Roosevelt might have held of such contemporary issues had he lived to celebrate his own centenary. Men live in their own times and

---

[1] Letter to Cecil Spring-Rice, August 5, 1896, ibid., Vol I, p. 553.
Letter to Cecil Spring-Rice, August 13, 1897, ibid., Vol I, p. 647.

their thought is bounded by their own field of observation. But it is by no means certain that all those things that Roosevelt held to be virtues are now to be rejected as evil. Two world wars, to say nothing of our present dilemmas, have given us views on the futilities and iniquities of war which men of an earlier generation could not have been expected to share. We are more conscious than they were of the danger that the idea of the trusteeship of the more advanced for the less advanced peoples may degenerate into the quite different belief (not held by Roosevelt) that one race is inherently and permanently better than another and has a right to treat its alleged inferiors as means towards its own ends, and not as ends in themselves. On the other hand, we may be less awake than was Roosevelt to the necessity for preserving and appreciating those qualities which enable men to rule fearlessly and without regard for popular clamour for the sake of those whose welfare they have at heart and who put their trust in them. The 'retreat from Empire' may have been inevitable: it may have been inspired in the case of many who took part in it by the highest and most disinterested of motives: but it would need a bold man to say that lassitude and a selfish desire to be rid of difficult and costly problems have played no part in it. It is easy to caricature the strenuous virtues that Roosevelt admired so much; but it is easy for the caricaturists themselves to incur the charge of preferring softness and ease for their own sakes. It is perhaps a pity, but it is a fact, that the admirers of the strenuous are nowadays mainly found in the ranks of our deadliest adversaries.

For these reasons, I find it difficult to lay the blame for our present dangers upon the line that American policy took under Theodore Roosevelt; and would feel obliged to attach at least as much weight to the very different set of values that inspired some of his successors. And however old-fashioned the words now sound, I would like to remind you, in remembering Theodore Roosevelt, of the words with which Lord Curzon greeted him on that summer's day in Oxford nearly fifty years ago: 'They greeted him,' said the Chancellor, 'not merely as a great ruler of men, the most conspicuous figure in America's history since Abraham Lincoln, not simply as a sincere and outspoken friend of this country, though from his utterances they knew that he was, but also as a student of many forms of knowledge; a writer of books, fearless preacher of a robust and manly faith, a relentless foe of conventions and shams, and, above all things, in all that he said and did, he was as Browning said of Clive "pre-eminently a man".'

INDEX

THE END